northwest
BOUNTY

northwest BOUNTY

SCHUYLER INGLE & SHARON KRAMIS

A COOKBOOK Celebrating

the EXTRAORDINARY FOODS of

the PACIFIC NORTHWEST

Foreword by Barbara Kafka

SASQUATCH
BOOKS
SEATTLE

For my parents, John and Joyce Ingle.

—S. I.

A special thank you to my father, who taught me to love to eat,
to my mother, who taught me to love to cook,
and to my wonderful husband, family, and friends.

—S. K.

Printed in the United States of America
Distributed in Canada by Raincoast Books, Ltd.
03 02 01 00 99   5 4 3 2 1

Northwest Bounty was first published in 1988 by Simon and Schuster.

Cover design: Karen Schober
Cover photograph: Michael Skott
Interior design: Kate Basart
Copy editor: Rebecca Pepper

Ingle, Schuyler.
    Northwest bounty / text by Schuyler Ingle and recipes by Sharon Kramis; foreword by Barbara Kafka.
        p.   cm.
        Includes index
        ISBN 1-57061-225-0
        1. Cookery, American—Pacific Northwest style.   I. Kramis, Sharon.   II. Title.
    TX715.2.P32I54   1999
    641.59795—dc21   99-15347

SASQUATCH BOOKS
615 Second Avenue
Seattle, Washington 98104
(206) 467-4300
www.SasquatchBooks.com
books@SasquatchBooks.com

Contents

Acknowledgments

I am very fortunate to spend my summers on Hammersley Inlet in the South Puget Sound region, an hour and a half from Seattle and twenty minutes from Olympia, our state capital. My front yard is literally acres and acres of clams. We can gather five pounds in fifteen minutes. We have four heirloom apple trees, one Bartlett pear tree, and a garden filled with herbs, lettuces, tomatoes, sugar snap peas, and bushes of raspberries, blueberries, and boysenberries. And of course, our fence line hangs heavy with wild blackberries in late August. Truly Northwest bounty!

I would like to express my appreciation to the following: Anthony's Restaurant, for sharing the freshest Northwest seafood available; the Puget Soundkeeper Alliance, for their commitment to clean water programs; my co-author Schuyler Ingle; Marion Cunningham, my favorite cooking friend, who always shares new happenings in the food world; and Sasquatch Books for showcasing our *Northwest Bounty* again. And a special thank you to our Northwest farmers and fishermen, who provide the bounty.

—S.K.

Ten years gives a guy a little time to consider who his influences really might be. So I want to thank the following people: Riz Rollins; Barbara Donette, Pappy, and P-Patch Sue; Tom Douglas, Shelley Lance, and Steven Steinbock; Scott Carsberg; Katherine Lewis and Stephen Lospalluto; Carol Field; Alice Waters and Paul Bertolli; Nancy Jenkins; Rebecca Staffel; Marguerite and Gary Margason; Mitch Karton; Bob and Jan Gross; Robert Friedman; Keri Shaw; Victor and Marcia Lieberman; Andrea Jarvela; Adam Somers; Mark Musick; Barbara Kafka; Fred Carlo; Park Kerr; Adam Block; Colleen Byrum; Elizabeth Jenkins; Bob Kramer; Stephen McCarthy; Barbara Figueroa; Niloufer Ichaporia; Sally and Roger Jackson; Peter Lewis; Ruth Reichl and Laurie Ochoa; John and Linda McMillin; Charles Krafft; Glenn Paulson; Sally Schneider; Harry Yoshimura; David Shepard; Susan Vanderbeek; Maria Concordia, Rosa Parilla, and Flor Fernandez for teaching me that angels speak with Latin accents; my children—Farrell, Ian, and Alexandra—for keeping me amazed and unfailingly proud; and my wife, Joyce Thompson, who with grace and unending support helped me see this project through to completion. We are two writers sharing a single office, two writers with few writerly secrets. And yet, Joyce let me stare out the window and call it the creative process when we both knew I was daydreaming. My best work is better because of her. I'm a happy man. My life is good.

—S. I.

FOREWORD: Local Bounty

One of the most important phenomena of recent years in fine American cooking has been the appreciation and use of fresh, local ingredients—the wild as well as the cultivated—in their appropriate season and, when possible, organic. One of the leaders in bringing these ingredients to our attention has been and is Schuyler Ingle. The flavor and texture of such ingredients determine how they should be cooked and seasoned. It is in this domain that Sharon Kramis comes to the forefront, developing recipes that star the foods and focus on flavor.

Both Schuyler and Sharon live in and around Seattle, Washington. They are natives of the Pacific Northwest, as familiar with the east side of the Cascade Mountains as they are with the west side. Their world is bounded by rivers, lakes, Puget Sound, and the Pacific Coast, by mountains and forests, by farmland and desert. They know and respect their regional food and share that appreciation with us in *Northwest Bounty*. Those of us who do not live in the Pacific Northwest may have to do a bit of searching for some ingredients, or make a few substitutions, but there is enough in these pages to please cooks and eaters from all over.

The fact-filled and evocative descriptions, rich with information, are worth the price of admission. For an information junkie such as myself, *Northwest Bounty* is invaluable. Schuyler Ingle writes so well, introduces us to such a fascinating cast of characters—farmers, fishermen, and other gatherers and producers of fine foods—and tells us so evocatively of the products that I feel that I am being taken into a whole new world of pleasure.

This is a world with seasons where oysters firm with the cold weather. It is a world with sex—just read Schuyler on how oysters spawn. It is a world where the foods and the people have histories and passions.

There is Karin Temple, college teacher of French, German, and world literature, who delights in the hard work of raising pigs and growing her kitchen garden. Connie Hattfield is another ecologically attuned producer—in her case, of Oregon Country Beef. Her customers are willing to pay more for better-tasting and leaner meat, and she listens.

Schuyler and Sharon's Pacific Northwest, with its mushroom hunters, bakers, and organic gardeners, strongly reminds me of my own Eden in Vermont. These are places that nourish the passionate eaters and lovers of good food and the good earth. No one should miss this book. We should cherish it as we cherish our suppliers and our gardens.

—*Barbara Kafka*

Introduction

In the ten years since the first edition of *Northwest Bounty* was published, real bread has come to the Pacific Northwest. The Gwenyth Caldwell of the first edition, a sheep breeder and new widow, remarried (she goes by Bassetti now), moved back to Seattle, and, with Leslie Mackie's help, opened Grand Central Bakery in Pioneer Square and started producing hard-crusted loaves of delicious bread. Leslie went on to open Macrina Bakery in Belltown. Portland saw the same light at about the same time and good bread is as readily available there as anywhere. It's hard to believe that ten years ago if you wanted good bread you had to open Carol Field's *The Italian Baker* and bake the bread yourself.

The same is true of a lot of fruit and produce. It is now possible to find good-quality fruit and produce in supermarkets as well as in farmer's markets. And I'm not talking about out-of-season asparagus flown in from New Zealand. It's hard to find a market these days that doesn't at least attempt to put up a display of organic fruit and vegetables. Ten years ago Pacific Northwest organizations such as Tilth, and Pacific Northwest organic farming institutions such as Mark Musick, were howling in the wilderness to a bunch of true believers. Who among us today doesn't look guiltily at the organic broccoli when we buy its cheaper, chemical cousin?

So times have changed, and in many ways for the better.

But some things just don't change at all. As interesting as the ever-growing restaurant scene in the Pacific Northwest might be, the real food of the region still happens at home. There's still no regional cuisine in the Pacific Northwest the way there is in New Orleans or Santa Fe. But there is a style, a way with food not hounded by tradition. Everybody but the Indians arrived in the Pacific Northwest too recently for regional traditions of any great meaning to have taken hold. So European-based cuisine gets jumbled up with Asian ingredients and cooking techniques. It all depends on who's in the kitchen, and who did the shopping.

The recipes Sharon Kramis has accumulated and developed for this book reflect the style of the Pacific Northwest. They are straightforward, simple, and flavorful, and they will be as relevant in fifty years as they are today.

I would like to think that the last ten years have seen a growing awareness of how food penetrates every facet of life, from politics to diet fads. I have tried to reflect this notion in my essays. To grow the best oysters, you need clean water. With luck, anyone drawn into oyster culture by my essay in this book will take a very personal interest in clean water issues close to home. How we treat domesticated farm animals, a subject I raise in the chapter about meat, says a lot about how we treat the land and each other. The essay on food gardening raises the question of hunger, both physical and emotional. The importance of an individual's hand in the kitchen, his or her attitude about the labor of making a meal, resonates in the essay about my Aunt Lilian.

It is all too easy to think the sum total of the Pacific Northwest is the rainy weather in Seattle, that all we eat in this corner of the country is Pacific salmon. There are too many of us moving in too many different directions for those superficial stereotypes to hold.

The cowboy moving cattle from winter to summer range in central Oregon; the Croatian fisherman heading north out of Puget Sound for Alaskan fishing grounds; the Scandinavian loggers; the Italian miners; the Basque shepherds; the Scots wheat farmers; the Dutch orchardists; the Tarheel millworkers; the Asian truck farmers; the Ethiopian restaurateurs; and the young viticulturalists newly arrived on land that has seen farms come and go and forests rise and fall—and the people who have been here forever, the Indians of the coast, of the rivers, of the interior plains, the ones who embrace modern logging and sawmill and aquaculture technology, and the ones who retain the old ways, who each year celebrate the coming of First Salmon, First Berry, First Nut, First Root, and First Deer. All of these are the Pacific Northwest.

Oregon, Washington, Idaho, British Columbia. Mountains, rivers, rain forests, islands, deserts, prairies. Cattle, sheep, apples, wheat, oysters, salmon, potatoes, wild mushrooms. Rain that lasts forever, and sun that burns late into the night. The Pacific Northwest is all of these, too.

The real trick is trying to put a taste of all that between two covers.

SHELLFISH

A Renaissance of Oysters:
THE EDIBLE OCEAN ON SHAVED ICE

As soon as summer has scooted away like a duck flapping furiously across the water, there are no more workable low tides in daylight hours in the south end of Washington State's Puget Sound. That's where Taylor Shellfish Farm is headquartered and where the majority of the company's oyster and clam beds can be found—and their mussel racks as well, for that matter.

Taylor is probably the world's largest shellfish producer at this stage in the game; it is certainly out there on the cutting edge of shellfish production technology. At low tide this subtidal zone isn't a lot to look at: a sloping beach of crumbled sidewalk that on closer inspection turns out to be hundreds of thousands of oysters lying about in big, ragged clumps like something spit up by an earlier geologic era. These oysters are headed for the shucking shed and a second life in a jar.

Then there are acres and acres of bulging black pillowcases. These are the oysters grown one by one, as singles, and they are headed for beds of ice and white tablecloths somewhere in America. It is these oysters that have oyster lovers longing for the change of season, when the water gets clear and cold and the oysters harden up and pack on their distinct sweetness. The days shorten and the nights get longer. A certain crisp snap gets into the air. More and more wet weather descends on the Pacific Northwest with each passing day, and the daylight sky takes on a mother-of-pearl hue. It's oyster weather. You can feel it on your skin. If your flavor memory is intact, you can taste it in your mouth.

Harvest crews will soon be working the low tides by Coleman lantern light. In the months when oysters are at their best, the lowest tides come at night. The harvest crews empty of their harvestable single oysters the acres and acres of heavy rubber-mesh bags laid out on the beach below the tideline. It wasn't always so. Twenty years ago outfits like Taylor concentrated on the meat business: shucked oysters in the jar. The half-shell business was something imported from the East Coast. But all that changed when visionaries, marine biologists, and oyster-loving gourmands all found themselves bobbing around in the same boat. It didn't come easy.

People thought Bill Webb was a little cuckoo twenty years ago when he packed it in as a biology teacher and "retired" from California to the backwaters of Westcott Bay on Washington State's San Juan Island to tinker with this idea he had about aquaculture. He wanted to "farm" on water, to control and raise crops in a wild environment. Bill and his wife, Doree, had the right chunk of waterfront property with a long dock stretching out into Westcott Bay. The trick would be coming up with the right "crop."

Lots of people had been talking about aquaculture back then in the 1970s, and a lot of people had tried one thing or another and failed. Webb had been preceded at Westcott Bay, for example, by an underfunded marine biologist struggling with clams and oysters and a divorce. Of aquaculture in general, investors had become wary. "I maintain aquaculture had such a bad reputation among the money people back then," Webb says in a voice permanently fixed in enthusiasm mode, "because there had been so many screwballs involved in it."

There was a time when more than one passing acquaintance would have suggested, sub rosa, that Bill Webb could count himself among the bigger screwballs. (They wouldn't say that today of a man who, at 76, has retired yet again and been able to sell a highly successful shellfish farm to his key employees and partners.) What the man wanted to do back there in the Howling in the Wilderness Time, after all, was grow oysters specifically for the half-shell oyster market. Half shell: as in slurping down freshly shucked raw oysters off the half shell.

This was a time when the finest restaurants in Seattle, a town that skated on a sterling seafood reputation more delusion than reality, served "oysters on the half shell" by plopping oyster meats removed from the quart jar onto shells that had been run through the dishwasher on countless occasions. We're talking the mid-1970s here. Bill's trouble would begin and end, his wiseacre detractors would tell you, the day he discovered that the only market for half-shell oysters existed between his ears. Bill Webb's cackle, in this case, is the last laugh. "We probably have the finest European flat oyster in the world here at Westcott Seafarms," Webb says. "Hands down."

There are those who say oysters are brain food. And if Bill Webb imagined a half-shell oyster market where none existed before simply from a diet rich in oysters, then brain food it is. The proof is on the shell before you. Today, oysters are big and getting bigger. Oyster bars are springing up all over, particularly in areas of the nation where oysters have always been part of the landscape. And it's hard these days to hold on to your status as a white tablecloth restaurant if there aren't at least several oyster selections on the menu during oyster season. In parts of the country not normally associated with oyster culture—Southern California, for example—oysters are being consumed in Diamond Jim quantities. Westcott Bay oysters, be they Pacifics or Westcott Bay Flats, are shipped as far as New York and Hong Kong from the waters of San Juan Island. Bill Webb knew all along that, given enough time and a fantastic oyster, the world would come around to his way of seeing things.

This isn't the first time around for America and the oyster. They were always an important part of the diet of anyone living anywhere near the oyster grounds of the Eastern seaboard—rich or poor. Oyster houses, oyster bars, oyster saloons, and oyster cellars grew in proportion to the population and the popularity of the bivalve. And as railroads spread out across the country, the oyster followed. By the turn of the century, oyster-eating establishments in all of the grand cities sometimes rivaled the best restaurants as places to be seen (and sometimes not seen), places to cut deals, places to rub shoulders. The classic San Francisco tomato ketchup cocktail sauce served with oysters and shrimp alike may well have done its initial duty by masking the off taste of oysters that had traveled across the country and were, as a result, a little road weary upon arrival. There were West Coast oysters too: the tiny Olympia (*Ostrea lurida*), found from Puget Sound to San Francisco Bay. But by the turn of the century, popularity and pollution had all but wiped them out.

The same double-barreled threat descended on the eastern oyster (*Crassostrea virginica*). They were overharvested and, as the population and industry boomed, pollution followed right behind. But the real decline came in the 1920s. It was common practice then to harvest oysters and keep them in holding bays for shipping. Pollute the water with the right mix of raw sewage and you get typhoid traceable to oysters. Which is what happened. Major epidemics occurred in Chicago, Philadelphia, and New York. Hundreds died, and thousands got sick. It was coast to coast headlines shouting out the health risks of eating oysters, and the public responded. Oyster houses died overnight. The Chicago Health Department prohibited the consumption of oysters. It was a $25 fine if you were caught.

Combine all this with Prohibition—because the conviviality that goes along with good wine or ale is central to enjoying oysters—and you are hearing a death knell. The oyster as darling of America ceased to exist in all but a few places: the Grand Central Oyster Bar in New York, the Union Oyster House in Boston, the Cape Cod Room in the Drake Hotel in Chicago, Swan's Oyster Depot in San Francisco. And, of course, the South in general, from rural oyster shacks to fresh-shucked oyster bars in New Orleans. And in Europe. The taste for oysters never let up in Europe, but had to be rediscovered and reported back to us by the Hemingways and Fitzgeralds, the M.F.K. Fishers and Julia Childs of the world. And by Henry Miller. It seems to me he had a thing or two to say about oysters.

So along comes Bill Webb with his quirky ideas about aquaculture. He had considered importing young lobsters from Maine and growing them in pens. But you have to feed lobsters the same way you have to feed penned salmon. And then there's the problem of disease. If one salmon in a pen gets sick, they all get sick. No. What Webb wanted was something as hassle-free as possible, something that would feed itself, drawing nutrition from the plankton-rich waters of Westcott Bay. The oyster was a natural. But there was a catch. And solving the catch—something that was going on in a bunch of different places at the same time—is what broke open the whole venture.

"Oyster hatcheries changed everything," Seattle food consultant Jon Rowley explains. Rowley's no marine biologist, mind you, but few men have salivated quite so excessively at the mere memory of an oyster moment in their lives. Some men recall in the clearest detail passionate kisses that have occurred at different times in their lives. And Rowley's like that. But he also remembers the oysters and the sharp wash of a crisp white wine across his palate that preceded either the kiss or the subsequent adventure. "Oysters are always a beginning," Rowley says, "a prelude to a life-enhancing experience about to happen."

At the time Bill Webb was working out his half-shell oyster production in the early 1980s, Rowley was teaching Seattle restaurants the basics of fresh fish. The exquisite basics. And he always had a pitch and passion for oysters, too. Because in gastronomic terms, oysters simply have to be there. The tradition is too old, the culture too complex, the product and the experience too wonderful to be overlooked or avoided. Yet the problems of oysters seemed all but insurmountable. Because other than imported *Crassostrea virginica* oysters from the East or South, local half-shell production simply didn't exist.

"There's a reason for that," Rowley explains. "In the 1920s, when the Olympia oyster was all but wiped out, an oyster from Japan was brought in in hopes that it could revive production—*Crassostrea gigas,* the Pacific oyster." Every year, oyster growers imported cases of *gigas* shells from Japan, then spread the shells on their beds. Minute oysters were attached to each shell, and they would grow out in the course of a couple of years into big clumps of oysters that would then be hauled by the truckload to shucking sheds where the clumps were hammered apart and the meats removed from the shells and then put up in jars, or steamed and tinned for export.

And in Japan each year, oystermen would suspend oyster shells in oyster waters, and when the water reached the right temperature and the level of nutrients became intense enough, one male oyster somewhere would spurt his glory into the water and start the female oysters broadcasting their eggs by the multimillions. Sperm meets egg, okay? And what you get is an oyster larva swimming around minding its own business. But about two weeks into the life cycle, this overwhelming urge kicks in, and the larva wants to make a permanent attachment. It wants to set. Enter the suspended shell, called cultch. So the larva attaches to the cultch in clumps, the cultch gets shipped to the Pacific Northwest and spread on oyster beds, and a couple of years later you have truckloads of oysters. What you don't have is a *single* oyster, an unattached oyster. There is no elegant way to open and serve a clump of oysters.

Manila clams piggybacked their way into Pacific Northwest waters from Japan with the *gigas* oysters. And so too did some pests. But by and large, it was one of the great intercontinental food transplants of history. By the 1940s, there were enough Pacific oysters living in Pacific Northwest waters that oystermen could take their cultch to one of two local bays when the temperature was just right and capture the spat, as the free-floating oyster larvae are called. Pity, of course, the poor native Olympia oyster, *Ostrea lurida*, whose natural habitat was pretty much smothered in an excess of Pacific oysters. Fortunately, in some areas of South Puget Sound, Olympia oysters survived. And Olympias have benefited from the same grand environmental advances as all the other oysters, not the least of which is the Clean Water Act.

After World War II, the Kumamoto oyster (*Crassostrea sikamea*) was imported from Japan in an attempt to replace the small Olympia. The Kumo, as you will find it called in oyster bars, is small, less than 2 inches long, with a deep, uniform cup. The Olympia shell is about the size of a 50-cent piece but is much flatter. Where the Olympia has a sharp, coppery taste that follows on the heels of its sweet, briny kiss, the Kumo can be sweeter and nuttier, and mild. An easy oyster in other words—a good place to begin where oyster complexities aren't rife. But the oystermen hated it for being small and difficult to handle—it was too expensive to open for the shucked meat trade. So the imports were left on the oyster beds of the Pacific Northwest to grow or die as they pleased. They were discovered again later, when the tides of oyster technology and taste had changed.

Similarly, the eastern oyster, *Crassostrea virginica,* king of the half-shell trade, was brought in. But Pacific Northwest water never gets warm enough for this oyster to spawn. And when oyster disease and pest problems became apparent in eastern oyster beds, it was banned altogether from Pacific Northwest water.

"Natural spawning was always unpredictable among the imported oysters," Jon Rowley explains. "But the biologists figured out what it took to artificially stimulate oysters to release their eggs. The age of the hatchery and the nursery was upon us, asking to be exploited, and Bill Webb was right there with the vision and the facilities."

If you raise at a certain rate for a certain time the temperature of the water in which oysters live, increasing the nutrients they adore, they will spawn. It's that simple. It's that complex. Everything has to be just right to produce viable oyster larvae, and the hatcheries are as devoted to growing very specific strains of algae to feed the larvae as they are to the oysters in question. It's all part and parcel.

But in the case of the Pacific oyster, the old clumper, here's what's so delicious: At the moment the millions upon millions of larvae swimming around in the tanks want to set on something, gluing themselves permanently into place on their road to becoming true oysters, the hatchery technician introduces to the water oyster shell ground finer than sand, so that each particle floating in the tank is no bigger than the point of a pin. There's only room for one occupant in such a situation, hence the single oyster fit for the half-shell trade. Such single oyster production gave Bill Webb the technological turbocharge he needed to grow the kinds of oysters he had in mind in waters that had never before seen the like. And then, oysters in hand, he had to go to town and convince restaurants that they wanted to buy his product at three times what they were paying for East Coast and Gulf Coast oysters.

"When he started out," Jon Rowley recalls, "Bill Webb was likely the only guy in the Pacific Northwest growing oysters exclusively for the half-shell trade. 'Gourmet' was a big word in all the Westcott Seafarms literature back then, but Bill had the vision. He was growing his oysters for the M.F.K. Fishers of America who hadn't forgotten. He drove his product to town, he knocked on doors, and he preached the gospel. He spent as much time marketing as he did working with his oysters. Bill used a system of suspended lantern nets to grow his oysters. Randy Shuman, who came along after him, but out on the coast at Willapa Bay, was the first to use the French rack and bag method of growing single oysters. You see both methods today, as well as some others. A lot has changed. But Bill Webb's a true pioneer."

Webb settled on two primary oysters to grow in Westcott Bay, the Pacific oyster and the European flat oyster (*Ostrea edulis*), which had been introduced to East Coast waters in the late 1940s but had never been grown before on the West Coast. The European flats—which go by traditional names in France such as Belon and Marenne, in Holland as Zelande, in Belgium as Ostende, in Ireland as Galway Bay, and in England as Whitstable, Colchester, and Pyefleet—take three years to mature. This is probably why, of the two thousand dozen oysters Westcott Seafarms ships each week, only six hundred dozen are flats, and the waiting list for them is long. Bill Webb started out with one thousand lantern nets hanging in phytoplankton-rich water. Today, Westcott Seafarms works four thousand lantern nets on twenty-seven acres of water.

Bill Webb insists on calling his flat oyster Belon, after the famous *Ostrea edulis* from the Belon River estuary in south Brittany. But this is where the naming of oysters gets tricky, and this is where Jon Rowley gets his back up. All the time Webb was working the water and banging on doors, Rowley was working the restaurant side, drawing on the passion for oysters he had discovered in France, putting together entire oyster programs in restaurants, training the staff in the fine points of presentation, the gastronomy, in the culture, in the two thousand years of nomenclature, the tradition.

"For two thousand years an oyster has gotten its name from the bay it comes from because of distinctive flavor characteristics," Rowley says. "That's a far cry from some snappy, yuppie name that looks good in print. So I work to maintain that conservative tradition on restaurant menus. Webb was taken aback when his Belon showed up on restaurant menus as Westcott Flats. But of all the oysters, *edulis* is most sensitive to its growing location and gives up distinctive taste differences. If everyone growing the flat oyster called it Belon, which is the name of one area where it's grown in France, you would never know the 'where' of an oyster and develop a loyalty to something you like."

Along with the hatchery technology came the trade in oyster seed. Today there are nurseries that grow oysters to a certain size before shipping them to the growers. Michael Watchorn and John Finger of Hog Island Oyster Company in Tomales Bay were to San Francisco's oyster scene much what Bill Webb was to Seattle's: early innovators breaking trail in the new half-shell market. But they buy their flat oyster seed from Westcott Seafarms and "plant" it in Tomales Bay. The water of the two bays isn't going to taste anywhere near the same. What if you prefer the Westcott flat to the Hog Island flat? If they are both called Belon oysters by a distributor or restaurant that doesn't know any better, how can you expect to order what you have come to love and desire? And at $2-plus a pop, you deserve what you desire. Such was Rowley's point all along.

When you attach one of those funny-sounding place names oysters have to a culinary experience that forever changes your life, an experience that opens you right up like a flower to the bee, you tend to go back and order another dozen by that same silly name without even looking at the price tag. You have become part of the oyster renaissance, part of the culture.

In the intervening years, small "farms" have popped up all over the place, up and down the coast, serving a relentlessly increasing trade in half-shell oysters. A lot of these small operators have come and gone; others have paid their bills and made it to the next level. Still others—Taylor Shellfish Farms comes to mind—are testing new waters.

When Bill Webb started his operation, Taylor Shellfish Farms, in the south end of Puget Sound, was already three generations old, going on four. It was a shucked-meat operation. Very traditional. But there was a canny enough mix of old experience and youthful enthusiasm for Taylor to start looking around. And today this one company grows more species of oysters commercially than any other company in the world. They brought in the eastern oyster, *Crassostrea virginica*, after World War II, in a failed attempt at transplanting them. Some of those oysters didn't die. They just didn't breed. So Taylor has been able to condition *virginica* oysters in its hatchery to produce viable seed (the ban on importing stock from the East Coast is still in effect) and bring West Coast *virginica* oysters to market.

Where Bill Webb favored the hanging lantern net technique for growing his oysters,

Taylor uses heavy mesh bags on the beach for theirs. It depends, actually. Every oyster and every location is a little different—the tides, the prevailing winds, all of it calling for a different take on this "new" technology.

Good science and good business, a lot of hard work, and self-trusting visionaries like Bill Webb have paid off. There are today more good oysters in more varieties available to more people in more places than at any time in modern history.

The oyster renaissance in America is upon us.

Shellfish

Oysters

The OLYMPIA OYSTER (*Ostrea lurida*) is the only one native to the Pacific Northwest. The only commercial quantities grow in South Puget Sound. A tiny oyster, the Olympia has a mild flavor followed by a metallic aftertaste.

The PACIFIC OYSTER (*Crassostrea gigas*), a native of Japan, was imported early in the century when the Olympia oyster population declined in the Pacific Northwest. By the 1950s natural reproduction was occurring in some Puget Sound bays, and today the Pacific oyster is as much a native as the Olympia. It is sold under various names, including Quilcene, Hamma Hamma, Canterbury, Willapa Bay, and Shoalwater, and in most instances the names reflect flavor nuances as well as place of origin.

The KUMAMOTO OYSTER (*Crassostrea sikamea*) is a Pacific species. It is smaller, deeper cupped, and slower growing than the more common Pacific oyster, and has a rich, buttery flavor. The Pacific oysters sold by Westcott Seafarms are a hybrid cross of Pacific and Kumamoto.

EUROPEAN FLAT OYSTERS (*Ostrea edulis*) are grown in Pacific Northwest waters and, like those grown in Maine, are commonly marketed with the name Belon.

Mussels

Two kinds of mussels grow in Pacific Northwest waters: the NATIVE MUSSEL, *Mytilus trosulus,* whose season mirrors that of oysters, and *Mytilus galloprovincialis,* a mussel native to the Mediterranean Sea. Look for the MEDITERRANEAN MUSSEL throughout the summer. Both mussels, in their appropriate seasons, are delectable.

Clams

Three common hard-shell littleneck clams are harvested and sold in the Pacific Northwest: the NATIVE LITTLENECK (*Protothaca staminea*), the NATIVE BUTTER CLAM (*Saxidomus giganteous*), and the MANILA CLAM (*Tapes philippanirum*), a littleneck that was introduced to Pacific Northwest waters when Pacific oysters were imported from Japan. The Manila settled into an ecological niche and proved to be a rapid and hardy breeder. Today, Manila clams are the bulk of the Northwest clam industry. Where native littlenecks have dull shells, the Manila sports a shell with beautiful black stripes, like *sumi* brushstrokes. Steaming is the most popular method of cooking either clam. The debate over which is better, sweeter, and more clamlike is never-ending.

The GEODUCK, pronounced "gooey-duck," is a remarkably unattractive bivalve that makes delicious chowder when ground. Sushi bars serve part of this clam as "giant clam," but geoduck it is. The clam commonly weighs several pounds, its long, flaccid siphon much too big for its shell. When you see one at a fish market, give the siphon a gentle poke. It should react, pulling in. If it doesn't, it's dead and should be avoided. The coarse skin that covers the geoduck is easily removed by plunging the clam into boiling water, then into cold water to cool. Like calamari, geoduck can be either cooked in an instant and served as a tender morsel or cooked for hours to tenderize. Commercial harvesting is done by divers who uproot the geoduck from the sand with high-pressure hoses. These clams are next to impossible to dig at low tide because they can burrow deep into the sand at alarming speed.

The RAZOR CLAM is another clam capable of burrowing at high speed. The shell—long, narrow, and thin—is well named. An unsuspecting clam digger can split open a finger reaching too fast for a clam quickly disappearing into the sand. Razor clam digging has become something of a regional sport, attracting tens of thousands of people to beaches in midwinter in the middle of the night at low tide. Some commercial production makes these clams available in fish markets, most of them coming from Alaska. Ground razor clam makes magnificent chowder.

Shrimp

COONSTRIPED SHRIMP. SIDE STRIPE SHRIMP. SPOT PRAWNS (actually a shrimp, not a prawn). The names accurately describe the markings on shrimp found in Hood Canal off Puget Sound, as well as in the waters off southeastern Alaska. They are sweet, meaty morsels. Since they grow in cold water, no deveining is necessary. When fresh Alaska spot prawns appear on the fishmonger's ice, it's time to get excited. These shrimp taste the way shrimp should taste, yet rarely do.

Crayfish

While they don't reach the size of their Louisiana cousins, PACIFIC NORTHWEST CRAYFISH, trapped in lakes and streams, are increasingly available on the retail market. Scandinavians in particular are fond of boiled crayfish, chasing the meat of the freshwater crustaceans with a shot of ice-cold aquavit.

Crabs

DUNGENESS CRAB is certainly what crab in the Pacific Northwest is all about. Popular with the Asian and Anglo communities alike, crab is boiled, steamed, and even barbecued in the Pacific Northwest. The tradition in my family was to sit down to a plate of cold, cracked Dungeness crab that had been boiled, and then to pick out the meat and dip it in different sauces. There are pickers and pilers, and pickers and eaters, and it doesn't take long to find out which is which.

Scallops

PINK SCALLOPS are popular in Pacific Northwest restaurants. Small scallops with a lovely shell, they gape when steamed, giving them the appearance of open-mouthed singers; hence their popular name, "singing scallops."

WEATHERVANE SCALLOPS are big and meaty and sweet. Shellfish enthusiasts who have given up on scallops for their bland flavor might give these a try. The scallop fishery is important both in Oregon and Alaska.

Alaskan abalone

The meat of ALASKAN ABALONE is no bigger than a hockey puck and can be just as tough if overcooked for more than 10 seconds at high heat. While California abalone shells end up as soap dishes, the shell of the Alaskan abalone is barely big enough to double as an ashtray.

Traditional Oyster Stew

Just oysters and milk—so simple, but an oyster lover's delight. I confess to liking lots of buttered saltines with oyster stew, but crusty garlic bread is another great accompaniment. Add a nice salad and you have a satisfying but easy dinner. Small bowls of oyster stew are also lovely as a first course at a more elegant dinner. I like our extra-small Quilcene (Pacific) oysters best for stew, but any fairly small, sweet oyster will do as well.

4 cups whole milk (or half-and-half if you like a richer mixture)

4 tablespoons butter

¼ cup thinly sliced yellow onion

2 dozen small shucked oysters, with their liquid

Salt and pepper

Worcestershire sauce

Additional butter

Paprika

Heat the milk in a saucepan just until steaming. Melt the butter in a separate 3-quart saucepan. Add the onion and cook until soft. Add the oysters and heat until the edges fan open. Pour in the hot milk. Bring to steaming again; remove from the heat and season to taste with salt, pepper, and a dash of Worcestershire. Serve in large, shallow bowls with a lump of butter and a dash of paprika. Oyster stew purists might say to leave out the onions, but I like the sweet flavor they add to the soup.

Makes 4 main-course servings or 6 first-course servings

Baked Oysters with Peppered Bacon

2 cups roughly chopped spinach

2 tablespoons butter

12 oysters on the half shell

½ cup diced peppered or thick-sliced bacon, cooked

Freshly grated Parmesan cheese

French bread croutons

Preheat oven to 375°F. In a skillet, sauté the spinach in the butter. Place the oysters on a baking sheet. Carefully place 1 tablespoon spinach on each oyster in its shell. Sprinkle with bacon and cheese. Bake in the oven just until the cheese melts. Serve with toasted, buttered French bread croutons.

Serves 4

Oyster Sausage

You have not lived until you have gone to the trouble of making and then eating oyster sausage. The trouble isn't all that great, and the sausages are absolutely remarkable. They are meant to be served the day they are prepared. You will need a sausage horn to stuff the sausage into the casing.

2 cups shucked oysters

2 cups fresh bread crumbs

2 eggs, beaten

2 tablespoons finely chopped parsley

Salt and pepper to taste

Dash of ground nutmeg

Hog casing

4 tablespoons butter

Additional finely chopped parsley for garnish

In a saucepan, gently poach the oysters in their own liquor until they plump up and their gills fan out. Drain off the excess liquid and reserve in a bowl. Chop oysters finely with a chef's knife and add to the liquid in the bowl. Stir in the bread crumbs, beaten eggs, parsley, salt, pepper, and nutmeg.

Hand-stuff the mixture into a medium-sized hog casing, holding the sausage horn in one hand while stuffing the mixture in with the fingers of the other hand. It is a soft, squishy endeavor that doesn't look too pleasing. Take care not to overstuff the casing because the egg, when cooked, will make these sausages expand. When finished, make links by squeezing the casing at the desired length and then twisting a couple of times to secure the casing. Poke a number of small holes in each sausage with a small needle. Refrigerate if not cooking immediately.

When ready to cook, place them in a pan with water coming halfway up the sausage. Bring the water to a simmer and cover the pan. Don't let the water boil. Poach gently for 6 to 8 minutes. If the sausages show signs of splitting, prick them with a fork.

To serve, melt the butter, add a good handful of finely chopped parsley, and pour over the sausages.

Makes 1 dozen

Oyster Loaf

For oyster lovers, this is a great sandwich, delicious for an informal supper with friends, along with your favorite beer. When buying oysters in a jar, be sure the liquid surrounding the oysters is clear. If it is cloudy, the oysters are not fresh.

½ head iceberg lettuce

2 tomatoes

½ pound bacon strips, cut in half

½ cup milk

1 egg, beaten

1 cup flour

½ cup cornmeal

1 jar (10 ounces) small fresh oysters, drained

4 tablespoons butter

¼ cup vegetable oil

Salt and pepper to taste

1 long loaf French bread

Tartar Sauce (page 258)

Finely shred the lettuce. Slice the tomatoes. Cook the bacon and drain well.

Mix the milk and egg together in a shallow dish, and combine the flour and cornmeal in a second shallow dish. Dip the oysters in the egg mixture, then roll in the cornmeal-flour mixture.

In a skillet, heat the butter and oil, and then cook the oysters over medium heat until golden. Remove from the pan and drain on paper towels. Season with salt and freshly ground black pepper.

Cut the bread in half lengthwise, and with your fingers pull out some of the inside of the loaf, leaving a hollow. Spread each side with some of the tartar sauce. Place the oysters on the bottom half of the loaf first, then layer the bacon, tomatoes, and lettuce over the oysters, in that order. Place the top half of the loaf on top, and slice into sandwiches.

Serves 4

Heck's Oyster and Hazelnut Stuffing

Oregon hazelnuts and fresh oysters combine to make a moist, delicious dressing. This is enough to stuff a 20-pound turkey. I think it is the best part of the Thanksgiving dinner.

Turkey giblets

1 cup water

1¼ cups hazelnuts

¼ pound plus 2 tablespoons (1¼ sticks) butter

1 large yellow onion, finely chopped

2 stalks celery, finely chopped

½ pound fresh mushrooms, sliced

1 jar (10 ounces) small fresh oysters, drained

1 tablespoon poultry seasoning

1 teaspoon dried thyme

2 tablespoons fresh sage, chopped

2 teaspoons kosher salt

½ teaspoon freshly ground black pepper

10 cups diced bread cubes (day-old white bread)

2 to 3 cups chicken stock

Preheat the oven to 275°F. Simmer the giblets in the water over low heat until tender, about 1 hour, and reserve the cooking liquid. Finely chop the giblets.

Spread the shelled hazelnuts in a shallow pan and roast in the oven for 25 minutes. Remove and let cool. Remove skins by rubbing the hazelnuts with a cloth towel. Coarsely chop.

Melt 4 tablespoons of the butter in a large skillet and sauté the onion and celery until soft. Add the mushrooms, and continue cooking for 2 minutes. Remove from heat. Chop the oysters.

Combine the sautéed vegetables, chopped oysters, poultry seasoning, thyme, sage, salt, and pepper in a large bowl and mix well. Melt the remaining 6 tablespoons of butter and add to the bowl. Mix in the bread cubes, and add enough chicken stock to make the stuffing moist but not soggy. Stuff the dressing into turkey just before roasting. If you have any left over, put it in a buttered casserole, cover, and bake for about 1 hour.

Makes enough for a 20-pound turkey

Scalloped Oysters

This is an easy Friday-night supper in the wintertime, when the fresh shucked oysters that come in a jar are firm and flavorful.

6 tablespoons butter

2 cups coarsely crushed soda crackers (more if needed to cover oysters)

1 jar (10 ounces) oysters, drained

½ cup cooked diced bacon

¾ cup half-and-half

Preheat the oven to 375°F. Melt the butter in a small pan. Spread half of the cracker crumbs in the bottom of a 1½-quart casserole. Top with the oysters. Sprinkle with the bacon. Cover with the remaining cracker crumbs. Add the half-and-half. Drizzle with the melted butter.

Bake for 30 to 35 minutes.

Serves 2

Grilled Oysters in Herb-Butter Sauce

We love gathering oysters and cooking them on an outdoor grill. They steam just a bit and the shells open, revealing a nice, plump cooked oyster.

½ cup melted butter

2 tablespoons lemon juice

½ teaspoon black pepper

1 tablespoon chopped parsley

Dash of Tabasco sauce

3 dozen fresh oysters in the shell

Prepare your charcoal grill and let the coals reach a medium heat. Mix together the melted butter, lemon juice, pepper, parsley, and Tabasco sauce, and keep warm.

Place the oysters on the grill, 4 or 5 at a time. With a heavy oven mitt, remove the oysters to a serving platter as they open, being careful not to spill the nectar. Spoon a little of the melted butter sauce over each oyster.

Makes 6 appetizer servings

How to Catch and Cook Dungeness Crab

In the Northwest many people who go boating in the San Juan Islands have the opportunity to catch fresh Dungeness crab. Live crabs are also available in some of the fish markets.

How to catch a crab:

32-inch ring trap

Large ice chest filled with ice

Damp burlap sacks

Bait

The bait has to be fresh. Chicken backs, fish heads and scraps, or horse clams work the best, but Dungeness crabs are fussy eaters, so the fresher the bait the better.

Put your baited trap 50 feet down. If you bring up all females, throw them back and move a little shallower or a little deeper. Crabs tend to cluster, and the males are always close by. Be sure to throw back all females and any undersized males. The underbody of "keepers" must measure at least as wide as a dollar bill is long.

Place the crabs in the ice chest on a layer of ice and cover with a damp burlap sack. Don't keep the crabs in water. It is better to wait 8 hours to cook the freshly caught crabs, to allow the membranes joining the legs to the body to firm up; the crab will then hold together when it is cooked. The crab will stay fresh in the ice-filled chest for several days.

How to cook a crab:

16-quart canning kettle

Rock salt

Fresh whole Dungeness crab

Fill the pot two-thirds full and add one closed handful of rock salt per crab to be cooked. Bring the water to a boil. Put the crabs in nose first and return the water to a boil for 15 minutes (turn the heat down slightly so that you have a gently rolling boil). When you remove the crabs from the water, cool them down immediately under slow-running cold tap water—this keeps the meat moist and easy to remove from the shell.

To clean the crab for eating, pull off the large back shell and, under running water, rinse the crab clean. Pull off the featherlike gills attached to the body. Break the body in half. Have on hand nutcrackers to crack the shells for easy eating. The pointed tips of the small legs make good picks for removing the meat.

Crab Bisque

This delicious recipe is from Marianne Zdobysz.

½ pound (2 sticks) unsalted butter

1 whole Dungeness crab

3 Dungeness crab shells

2 carrots, chopped

1 onion, chopped

2 leeks, chopped

3 stalks celery, chopped

2 bay leaves

½ teaspoon whole black peppercorns

2 tablespoons tomato paste

½ cup flour

Water or fish stock to cover

1 tablespoon salt

½ teaspoon cayenne

1 tablespoon brandy

Preheat oven to 500°F. In a large pan with a tight-fitting lid, melt ¼ pound (1 stick) of the butter. Add the crab and crab shells, cover tightly, and sweat over low heat for 10 minutes. Add the carrots, onion, leeks, and celery, and roast in the oven for 30 minutes to 1 hour.

Melt the remaining ¼ pound of butter in a stockpot. Add the roasted crab, shells, vegetables, bay leaves, peppercorns, and tomato paste and sauté for 5 minutes. Add the flour and stir while smashing the crab to release the flavor. Add enough water or fish stock to cover and simmer for 1 hour, skimming frequently.

Strain into a container, then strain again through a fine sieve, discarding the solids. Season with salt, cayenne, and brandy.

Serves 4

Kay Karcher's Crab, Cheese, and Green Pepper Sandwich

If you have more crabmeat than you can use right away, Kay recommends a method for freezing crabmeat: Pack it into a plastic container, add cold water to fill any air spaces, and seal with a tight-fitting lid. Once thawed, she claims, the crabmeat tastes just as fresh as when you caught it.

2 cups crabmeat

2 cups grated cheddar cheese

½ cup diced green pepper

½ cup chopped green onion

Mayonnaise

Worcestershire sauce

Lemon juice

4 English muffins or French rolls, cut in half and toasted

Preheat the broiler. Mix together the crabmeat, cheddar cheese, green pepper, green onion, and just enough mayonnaise to bind the mixture together. Season to taste with Worcestershire sauce and lemon juice. Spread generously on toasted muffins or rolls and place on a baking sheet. Place in broiler, 8 to 10 inches away from the source of heat, and broil until bubbly and golden.

Makes 8 open-face sandwiches

Dungeness Crab Cakes with Tarragon Mayonnaise

These are crunchy on the outside and smooth and creamy on the inside. The sweet flavor of the Dungeness crab is complemented by the tangy mustard. This is a delicious way to use fresh Dungeness crabmeat for a simple but elegant dinner. Serve with shoestring fries and a tangy coleslaw.

4 tablespoons butter

½ cup finely diced yellow onion

¼ cup finely chopped red pepper

1 tablespoon Dijon mustard

¼ cup chopped parsley

½ cup mayonnaise

1 pound Dungeness crabmeat

1 tablespoon lemon juice

¼ teaspoon Tabasco sauce

½ cup soft bread crumbs

2 cups Panko crumbs

Butter and vegetable oil for frying

Tarragon Mayonnaise (recipe follows)

In a large skillet, melt the butter. Add the onion and red pepper and cook over low heat for several minutes. Remove from heat and let cool. Transfer to a glass bowl. Stir in the mustard, parsley, and mayonnaise. Add the crabmeat, lemon juice, Tabasco sauce, and the ½ cup bread crumbs. Chill the mixture for at least 2 hours.

After chilling, shape the crab mixture into 12 small round cakes, 3 inches in diameter and ¾ inch thick. Lightly coat with the Panko crumbs.

In a skillet or griddle over medium heat, heat enough butter and oil to coat the bottom of the pan. Cook the crab cakes for 2 to 3 minutes on each side, until golden brown. If necessary, place on a paper towel–lined baking sheet and keep warm in a low oven until ready to serve.

Serve with Tarragon Mayonnaise.

Makes 12 cakes

Tarragon Mayonnaise

1 egg

¼ teaspoon dry mustard

2 tablespoons tarragon vinegar

1 tablespoon fresh tarragon

1 cup light olive oil

Salt and pepper to taste

Put the egg, mustard, vinegar, and tarragon in a food processor or blender and process briefly. Then, with the machine running on low speed, add the oil in a slow, steady stream until the mixture thickens. Season to taste with salt and pepper.

Grilled Crab and Cheddar Cheese Sandwich

Crab and cheddar cheese is a classic combination. Larry Brown, a good friend and an excellent cook, developed this version of a Northwest favorite.

½ cup mayonnaise

½ cup chili sauce

1 cup Dungeness crabmeat

4 cups grated medium cheddar cheese

¼ cup chopped green onion

¼ cup chopped red bell pepper

¼ cup chopped celery

12 slices Sourdough White Bread (page 206)

½ cup melted butter

In a medium bowl, stir together the mayonnaise, chili sauce, and crabmeat. Add the cheese, onion, pepper, and celery and mix thoroughly.

Divide the filling among 6 slices of the bread and top with the remaining slices. Brush the top of each sandwich with melted butter. Grill, buttered side down, in a skillet, until the cheese melts (cook over low heat so the bread doesn't brown too quickly). Brush the remaining side with melted butter, turn, and continue cooking until both sides are golden.

Makes 6 sandwiches

Avocados Stuffed with Crab Salad

A favorite first course or a simple lunch. The combination, which is by now a classic, really developed farther south along the Pacific Coast. Eventually, the universal availability of avocados brought the dish "home," where the Dungeness reigns.

½ pound Dungeness crabmeat

Juice of ½ lemon

½ cup mayonnaise

1 tablespoon ketchup

4 drops Tabasco sauce

½ cup finely diced celery

½ cup finely chopped green onion

2 large, ripe avocados, halved lengthwise and pitted

Lemon wedges and fresh parsley

Mix together the crabmeat, lemon juice, mayonnaise, ketchup, Tabasco sauce, celery, and green onion. Mound into the avocado halves. Garnish with lemon wedges and fresh parsley.

Serves 4

Marinated Prawns

Chilled marinated prawns, deviled eggs, and chicken sandwiches make a great picnic. This is also a good dish for a first course, served with sliced avocados.

2 pounds medium-sized prawns

¼ cup pickling spices

1 cup vegetable oil

¾ cup white vinegar

½ cup sugar

1 teaspoon salt

1 large white onion, cut in half and sliced

Place the prawns in a saucepan. Cover with water. Add the pickling spices. Cover and simmer very gently for 5 minutes. (If you keep the water just below the boiling point, the prawns won't toughen.) Pour into a colander to drain. Transfer to a bowl and cover with ice to cool quickly. Peel and devein the prawns.

In a small bowl, mix together the oil, vinegar, sugar, and salt. Layer the shrimp and sliced onion in a bowl. Pour in the vinegar mixture and refrigerate for 4 to 6 hours.

Serves 8 to 10

Hood Canal Spot Prawns with Roe

There is a very short season in the summer when these delicious, sweet prawns are available from Hood Canal, near Seattle. You can also find them at the fish markets when they are brought down from Alaska. A great delicacy, these prawns are soft and sweet. The larger size usually all have roe, which is attached to the body and is considered a delicacy. You first eat the roe and then peel and eat the prawn. If you purchase them in the market, they should always have the head off. If any black spots appear on the shell, don't buy them.

12 fresh Alaska spot prawns, with roe, unpeeled

2 cups water

1 teaspoon salt

2 thin slices of fresh ginger

¼ cup melted butter

Place the prawns in a 2-quart saucepan. Add the water, salt, and ginger. Bring to a slow, rolling boil and cook 4 to 5 minutes. Remove and place in a serving dish. Serve while still warm with the melted butter.

Makes 4 appetizer servings

Crayfish

Whether you gather your own crayfish or buy them (they are being farmed in the South and are becoming available in fish markets all over the country), the best and simplest method of cooking is to drop them into a large pot of boiling water with a generous amount of salt added. Cook them just until they turn a nice orange color, and then remove them from the cooking liquid. Serve with homemade mayonnaise as a dipping sauce. For a variation, we like the flavor when they are cooked this way.

¼ cup salt

2 cups red wine

1 white onion, sliced

2 oranges, sliced

1 lemon, sliced

2 tablespoons pickling spices

3 quarts water

4 pounds live crayfish

In a large pot, combine the salt, wine, onion, oranges, lemon, pickling spices, and water. Bring to a boil, and boil hard for several minutes. Plunge as many live crayfish as you can into the pot and cook until their color changes to orange. Remove from the liquid, cool to room temperature, and serve.

Serves 6

How to Clean Littleneck Clams

Use this method to purge the sand from clams that you dig yourself on the beach while camping. (The clams you buy in a fish market have already been purged.) Be sure to dig clams only on beaches specified for public digging. Don't dig during a red-tide warning.

1. Rinse the clams well with water to remove outside sand.

2. Place the clams in a 5-gallon container and fill with clean water. Let them relax for an hour, then sneak up on them and bang the bucket. Repeat 3 times, changing the water each time.

3. Cook the clams over a fire in a large clam cooker, or take them home on a bed of ice in an ice chest covered with damp burlap sacks.

Steamer Clam Soup

This makes a light broth-based first-course soup, very easy and very good, or it can be served with steamed rice and a cucumber salad for a light lunch.

> *1 ¼ pounds small clams*
> *4 cups cold water*
> *Hon-Dashi to taste (a powdered soup base available at Japanese and*
> *   specialty food stores)*
> *4 small strips lime peel*
> *Fresh cilantro*

Scrub and rinse the clams well. Place in a saucepan. Add the water. Bring to a boil. Skim off the foam. Add a little Hon-Dashi to taste. Divide the clams into 4 bowls. Pour in the hot broth. Garnish with lime strips and fresh cilantro.

Serves 4

Hap's Clam Chowder

For traditional Northwest clam chowder, fresh clams are best, but good-quality canned clams can be substituted. Small steamer clams, steamed open, also can be used. If you are using a larger clam, such as a razor or geoduck, remove the stomach and then grind the rest of the raw clam. (The large neck of the geoduck must also have the heavy outside skin removed.) The soda crackers thicken the soup to a nice consistency.

½ cup finely diced bacon

4 tablespoons butter

½ cup diced yellow onion

½ cup diced celery

1 cup diced potatoes (I like the texture of russet potatoes)

1 bay leaf

3 cups bottled clam juice

1 cup half-and-half

½ cup to 1 cup crushed unsalted soda crackers (crush them in a food processor)

2 cups chopped fresh clams or small whole steamed clams

¼ cup minced parsley

Freshly cracked pepper

In a sauté pan, sauté the bacon, drain on paper towels, and set aside. In a large enameled soup pot, melt the butter. Add the onion, celery, potatoes, and bay leaf and cook for several minutes. Add the clam juice and continue to simmer until the potatoes are tender. Add the half-and-half. Thicken the broth to the desired consistency by stirring in the crushed soda crackers, a little at a time. Add the clams and sprinkle with the cooked bacon, parsley, and freshly cracked pepper. Cook just to heat—do not boil—and serve immediately.

Serves 6

Pinot Gris Steamed Clams with Garden Herbs

Oregon pinot gris and fresh herbs add a delicious flavor to the small steamer clams.

4 tablespoons butter

¼ cup chopped fresh parsley, thyme, marjoram, and dill

1 to 2 tablespoons minced garlic

¼ teaspoon crushed red chile pepper

1 cup pinot gris

1 cup water

Juice of ½ lemon

4 pounds small steamer clams

Salt and pepper to taste

In a large pot with a tight-fitting lid, place the butter, herbs, garlic, and crushed chile. Simmer over medium heat for 2 to 3 minutes. Add the pinot gris, water, lemon juice, and clams. Cover. Bring to a boil and boil for 3 to 5 minutes, until all of the clams have opened. (Discard any that have not opened in 5 minutes.) Adjust the seasoning with salt and pepper to taste.

Serve in shallow bowls with crusty French bread for dipping into the delicious juices.

Serves 4

Steamed Clams with Parsley Butter

The parsley butter drizzled over the clams makes them look shiny and gives them a delicious taste. The butter mixes in with the juices. The most important thing is to serve the clams steaming hot (and sand-free).

2 pounds steamer clams

1 cup water

5⅓ tablespoons (⅓ cup) butter

¼ cup minced fresh parsley

Place the clams in a colander and rinse under cold, running water.

Transfer the clams to a 2- to 3-quart saucepan. Pour in the water. Cover, bring to a boil, and cook for several minutes (until the clams open).

Transfer the clams and juice to a 2-quart shallow serving bowl. Melt the butter immediately. As soon as the butter foams, add the parsley and drizzle the butter instantly over the clams.

Makes 4 first-course servings

Spaghettini with Fresh Steamed Clams, Parsley, and Parmesan Cheese

When we go to our beach house, I always take pasta, olive oil, garlic, fresh parsley, and Parmesan cheese, and cook this dish with freshly dug clams.

2 pounds steamer clams

1 cup water

3 tablespoons butter

5 tablespoons olive oil

½ cup chopped yellow onion

2 cloves garlic, minced

¼ teaspoon crushed red pepper flakes

¼ cup white wine

½ to 1 cup reserved clam juice

½ pound spaghettini

Kosher salt and freshly ground black pepper to taste

2 tablespoons minced parsley

Freshly grated Parmesan cheese

Place the clams in a 4- to 5-quart pot. Pour the cup of water over them. Bring to a boil, cover, and steam for 3 to 4 minutes, until all the clams open. Drain off the liquid and reserve. Remove the clams from their shells.

In a large frying pan, heat the butter and 3 tablespoons of the olive oil and sauté the onion. Add the garlic, chile flakes, white wine, and clam juice. Bring to a boil and simmer for 2 to 3 minutes.

Cook the spaghettini just until tender in a large pot of boiling water. Drain well and add the noodles to the sauce. Add the clams. Simmer until the mixture is nice and hot. Drizzle over the remaining 2 tablespoons of olive oil. Transfer to a warm serving dish. Season with salt and pepper. Sprinkle with parsley and Parmesan cheese, and serve.

Serves 2

Razor Clam Fritters

This is a good way to use chopped razor clams.

1 ½ cups flour

2 teaspoons baking powder

1 teaspoon salt

½ cup clam juice

2 eggs, beaten

1 cup chopped razor clams

1 tablespoon melted butter

2 tablespoons grated white onion

Vegetable oil for deep frying

Tartar Sauce (page 258)

In a bowl, mix together the flour, baking powder, salt, clam juice, eggs, clams, butter, and onion. Heat oil in a large pot to 375°F and drop spoonfuls of the batter into the hot oil. Cook until golden. It's important not to make the spoonfuls too large or the fritter won't cook all the way through.

Serve with Tartar Sauce for dipping.

Makes 4 to 6 appetizer servings

Stir-Fried Geoduck with Vegetables

Judy Lew's recipe is a good way to cook geoduck so that it stays tender. The geoduck clam is also used to make chowder and is a favorite for sashimi.

1 medium geoduck clam

2 tablespoons white wine

½ teaspoon salt

¼ teaspoon pepper

1 teaspoon sesame oil

2 teaspoons cornstarch

3 tablespoons vegetable oil

2 cloves garlic, minced

½ pound snow peas (stringed, rinsed, and drained)

1 small onion, cut in wedges

1 tablespoon slivered fresh ginger

2 teaspoons soy sauce

2 tablespoons water

Slivered green onion for garnish

Pour boiling water over the neck of the clam until the skin separates from the neck. Run a knife around the inside of the shell to open the clam. Discard the stomach and pull off the neck. Cut off the tip of the neck and slice open lengthwise. Rinse carefully. Cut into thin ⅛-inch slices. Combine with 1 tablespoon of the wine, the salt, pepper, sesame oil, and cornstarch.

Heat a wok or heavy frying pan and add 1 tablespoon of the oil. Add half of the garlic and snow peas and onion. Stir-fry for 1 minute. Remove to a platter. Clean the wok. Heat again and add the remaining 2 tablespoons oil. Add the rest of the garlic, the ginger, and the clam slices. Stir-fry for 30 seconds. Add the soy sauce, water, and the remaining tablespoon of wine. Serve over the vegetables, sprinkled with green onion. (Don't overcook the geoduck, or it will become tough and rubbery.)

Makes 4 small servings for a first course

Fried Razor Clams

A true delicacy, razor clams are fun to gather because they dig to escape as you are digging after them. In late spring, many people head to the Washington and Oregon coasts to dig for razor clams and then enjoy a great feast afterwards. Razors have a very thin, lightweight shell with sharp edges that give them their name. They are time-consuming to clean.

To clean the clams, extract the clam from its shell. With a pair of kitchen scissors cut away anything that's dark, the tip of the neck, the gut muscle, and any sand residue. Cut each digger in half so that it will lie flat for frying. The soft, puffy meat inside the digger is the best part, so be careful not to scrape it away. Dry the clams well with paper towels.

To fry the clams, heat ½ inch of oil in a heavy frying pan. The fat must be quite hot so that the clams will brown quickly—*30 seconds on each side* is the rule. Dip each clam in dry pancake mix, then drop into the hot fat. Remove the clams from the pan with a slotted spoon, sprinkle with salt and pepper, and eat them right away. It's important not to overcook the clams or they will be tough.

Steamed Mussels

Twenty years ago in the Northwest, mussels were gathered by only a few people. Today mussel farms supply us with this sweet-tasting, blue-shelled delicacy almost year-round.

2 pounds mussels (about 40)

4 tablespoons butter

1 cup white wine

½ bunch finely chopped fresh parsley

6 finely chopped shallots

1 teaspoon fresh thyme leaves

1 teaspoon freshly ground pepper

1 bay leaf

Remove the beards from the mussels and scrub them. Put butter and wine in a 3-quart saucepan. Bring to a boil, and boil for 2 minutes. Add the mussels, parsley, shallots, thyme, pepper, and bay leaf. Cover tightly and cook until the shells open (about 2 minutes). Cook for another 30 seconds to firm the meat. Pour mussels and their broth into a warm serving dish.

Makes 4 servings

Captain Whidbey's Citrus-Steamed Mussels

The Captain Whidbey Inn is a unique log inn built in 1907. Located on beautiful Whidbey Island, it overlooks Penn Cove, one of the world's best mussel-growing areas. This recipe was created for the Penn Cove Mussel Festival to honor this tender and tasty shellfish.

1 cup water

¼ cup sugar

½ cup Johannisberg Riesling

1 tablespoon Calvados

Grated zest of 1 orange

Grated zest of ½ lemon

½ cup orange juice

½ cup grapefruit juice

½ cup lemon juice

3 pounds Penn Cove mussels

Combine the water and sugar in a saucepan, and bring to a boil over medium heat, washing down any crystals clinging to the sides of the pan with a brush dipped in cold water. Simmer for 5 minutes. Add the wine, Calvados, and citrus zest and juices. (This much may be done in advance.)

In a large pot, combine the wine-citrus mixture and the mussels and steam over high heat until the mussels are open and opaque.

Serves 6

Marinated Scallops with Salsa

I like to marinate the small Oregon scallops and serve them chilled. Mixed with fresh salsa, they make a favorite summer dish.

1 pound small Oregon scallops or other bay scallops

¼ cup fresh lime juice

¼ cup fresh lemon juice

1 to 1½ cups Krueger Pepper Farm's Salsa (page 256)

¼ cup olive oil

2 avocados, cut into bite-sized pieces

Salt and pepper to taste

Place the scallops in a glass bowl. Pour in the lime and lemon juices. Mix well. Cover with plastic wrap and refrigerate for 2 hours. Remove from the refrigerator and drain off the excess liquid.

Mix the scallops gently with the salsa, olive oil, and avocado. Season to taste with salt and pepper. Serve chilled in small glass dishes as a first course.

Makes 6 first-course servings

Gingered Oregon Scallops with Lemon Zest and Fresh Cilantro

Oregon scallops are very small and thus can easily be overcooked. They are best prepared sautéed quickly in butter.

1 small knob of fresh ginger

4 tablespoons butter

1 teaspoon grated lemon zest

½ pound fresh Oregon scallops

2 tablespoons fresh cilantro or parsley, chopped

Peel the ginger and cut into thin strips. Melt the butter in a 10-inch skillet over low heat. Add the ginger and lemon zest. Pat the scallops dry and add to the ginger butter. Sauté quickly, turning up the heat as the scallops cook. Transfer to a warm serving dish and sprinkle with fresh cilantro or parsley.

Serves 2

Singing Scallops Poached in Citrus

Pink scallops are served in the shell. They open when cooked and look like they are singing. This recipe is from Caprial Pence, who has established her own style in the Northwest. Her restaurant in Portland, Westmoreland Bistro, is very popular.

3 pounds singing scallops in the shell, washed (sea scallops may be substituted)

¼ cup each lime, orange, and grapefruit juice

½ cup white wine

3 shallots, chopped

4 cloves garlic, chopped

1 cup crème fraîche

1 teaspoon freshly cracked black pepper

Citrus segments and watercress for garnish

Place the scallops in a large, heavy saucepan with the citrus juices, wine, shallots, and garlic. Bring to a boil over high heat and continue to cook until the shells have opened. Remove the scallops with a slotted spoon and divide among 6 individual plates. Cover and keep warm. Simmer the cooking liquid until it is reduced by half, then stir in the créme fraîche. Season with pepper. Pour the sauce over the scallops. Garnish with citrus segments and watercress.

Serves 6

Rockers Iko

A Creole-style seafood stew created by H. Stuart ("Rip") Ripley.

Sauce

1 tablespoon olive oil

1 medium red onion, diced

1 medium red pepper, diced

2½ teaspoons ground cumin

2 teaspoons ground coriander

1 teaspoon dried thyme

2½ teaspoons diced fresh ginger

1 bay leaf

1 teaspoon chopped garlic

1 tablespoon chopped fresh chile pepper

1 tablespoon lemon juice

½ cup white wine

1 can (28 ounces) diced tomatoes in purée, or 2 pounds peeled and chopped fresh tomatoes

Seafood

2 tablespoons olive oil

½ red pepper, julienned

1 carrot, julienned

2 stalks celery, julienned

1 leek, julienned

*3 pounds seafood (a variety is best and should include clams, mussels, and crayfish; fish
cut in 1-inch squares that could include rockfish, cod, and salmon; and scallops,
prawns, and shucked oysters)*

To make the sauce, in a saucepan, heat the oil and sauté the onion and pepper until soft. Add the cumin, coriander, thyme, ginger, bay leaf, garlic, and chile pepper, and sauté for 30 seconds more. Add the lemon juice, wine, and tomatoes. Simmer for 15 to 20 minutes, until the flavors are well blended.

To prepare the seafood, in a large pan, heat the olive oil and sauté the pepper, carrot, celery, and leek. Add the sauce and bring to a simmer. Add the seafood, starting with the clams, mussels, and crayfish. Add the fish chunks when the clams start to open. Finally, after 3 or 4 minutes, add the scallops, prawns, and oysters. Let simmer for another 3 or 4 minutes, or until done.

Serves 6

Cioppino

This is a traditional San Francisco dish that migrated north after it was celebrated in the popular West Coast magazine *Sunset*. It adapted extraordinarily well to our local seafood and is now found on many Northwest restaurant menus.

4 cloves garlic, finely minced

½ cup chopped fresh basil

¼ cup chopped combined fresh oregano and thyme

½ cup chopped parsley

½ teaspoon crushed red pepper flakes

2 teaspoons freshly ground black pepper

1 to 2 teaspoons kosher salt

2 pounds clams in the shell, scrubbed

2 Dungeness crabs, or 3 pounds other hard-shell crabs, cleaned and cracked

1 dozen fresh crayfish, or 1 pound medium-sized prawns or large shrimp,
*   shelled and cleaned*

2 pounds firm-fleshed white fish (lingcod, halibut, or rockfish), cut into 2-inch pieces

1 cup clam juice

1 cup dry white wine

2 cans (28 ounces each) diced tomatoes, with their juice

¾ cup olive oil

In a medium bowl, combine the garlic, basil, oregano and thyme, parsley, red chiles, pepper, and salt to make an herb seasoning mixture.

Layer the clams in the bottom of a 10- to 12-quart stockpot. Add the cracked crab and crayfish to the pot. Sprinkle with half of the herb seasoning mixture. Add the white fish.

Mix together the clam juice, wine, tomatoes, and olive oil, and pour over the fish. Sprinkle with the remaining herb seasoning mixture.

Cover and cook on medium heat for 25 to 35 minutes, until the mixture comes to a gentle boil. Remove from the heat and serve in large bowls with toasted garlic bread.

Serves 6

FISH

Fish

Salmon

There are four species of wild salmon that come to the market each year. It's important to know the different qualities of each in order to cook them properly.

SILVER or COHO: Pastel salmon color. When cooked, it doesn't flake but tears, leaving a jagged edge. It can become dry if not cooked properly; best baked or poached.

KING: Ranges in size from 1 to 120 pounds. The color ranges from red to white. The Columbia River is the first to harvest in mid-February, and the last local harvest is from the Strait of Juan de Fuca, at the end of September. October through January all kings are harvested from Alaskan waters during winter troll fishing. This is the best salmon to barbecue.

SOCKEYE: The brightest red of all the species. The Copper River run in mid-May starts the season, which then finishes in August with the Puget Sound run. Sockeye is available "fresh frozen" the year around. The best method of cooking is oven-broiling or baking on an alder plank.

CHUM, also known as FALL or SILVER-BRITE SALMON: It is absolutely critical to look for a "hot pink" meat color in this fish. As the color of chum grows paler, the quality of its taste diminishes. Silvery skin is essential, as is firm flesh. Southeast Alaska is the best source.

Pacific cod
Known as "true cod." Excellent for fish and chips. Most of the harvest is processed and frozen at sea.

Lingcod
One of the best eating fish on the West Coast. Not a ling or a cod, but actually a greenling. Nice flavor and reasonably priced. Be sure to ask for longline-caught fish; they have been individually bled, gutted, and iced (or frozen) on board the boat. You will pay more, but it's worth it. Don't be put off by the slight greenish color of this fish's flesh. It cooks to a beautiful white.

Black cod
Not an actual cod. Its true name is sablefish. The soft white flesh is rather oily. A favorite way of presenting it is lightly smoked.

American shad
A delicious freshwater fish that takes great skill to bone. It is a member of the herring family. The roe is a delicacy fried and served with strips of bacon. Columbia River shad appears sporadically in the markets in May and June.

Smelt
February brings fresh smelt into the markets. Smelt are sold whole and average 3 to 8 inches in length. The eulachon, also called Columbia River smelt, is the major commercial species on the West Coast.

Sole
Authentic sole is imported fresh or frozen to the United States from England or France. In the Northwest the seafood markets offer a variety of "sole" that are actually small flounder. The most popular and the best quality of the Pacific flounder marketed under the "sole" name is Petrale sole. Other flounders available in the markets of the Pacific Northwest are sold as Rex sole (too thin to fillet, so it is cooked whole and then boned at the table), English sole (small fillets, bland in taste), butter sole, and sand sole.

Pacific halibut
Firm white meat, usually sold in fillets or steaks. Halibut cheeks are a real delicacy. This is a fish that is available fresh most of the year, from mid-March through November. Once you have eaten the fresh fish, it's difficult to enjoy the frozen. There is a remarkable difference in the texture.

Pacific sand dab

A small flounder with nice texture and good flavor. Wonderful pan-fried.

Rainbow trout

The trout you see in the seafood markets is usually farm-raised. It's a good buy, but not as delicious as fresh-caught river or lake trout. The flesh is not as firm or flavorful. However, it is available year-round in the markets and makes a nice dinner.

Steelhead

A sea-run rainbow trout. There are many rivers and streams with annual runs of steelhead in the fall and winter. This is the sportfisherman's dream fish and is delicious. A more muscular flavor than rainbow trout.

Sturgeon

The white sturgeon of the Columbia River is an excellent eating fish. It has a very firm texture, so it holds up well to grilling. It is often seen on restaurant menus in Seattle and Portland. Sturgeon is also smoked, both cold-smoked and hot-smoked. Columbia River sturgeon caviar is highly acclaimed. The demand far exceeds the supply.

Rockfish

More than 200 rockfish species can be found off the Pacific Coast. There is a great deal of confusion over the names given to the different species available in the markets. The most misleading is the term "red snapper." True red snapper is found only in the Atlantic Ocean and does not resemble the Pacific Coast rockfish, which range from the 1-pound rosethorn that the Chinese steam whole to the giant 60-pound yelloweye that goes into the sashimi market.

Surfperch

Usually caught by recreational fishermen. Sometimes available in the markets. (Ocean perch sold in the seafood markets is not really perch but rockfish.) Both fish are usually marketed in 1- to 1½ -pound size and are very good cleaned and oven-broiled.

How to Select Fresh Fish

The number-one rule when buying fish is to consider the source. We are fortunate to have access to excellent seafood stores where the quality of the fish is exceptional. I strongly recommend that you take the time to find the best one in your neighborhood. It is exciting to see that retail grocery stores all over the Northwest are upgrading the quality of the seafood for sale. Here are a few tips for selecting fish.

Fresh fish should never smell. A good seafood market should never smell fishy; this goes for restaurants too. If you have any doubt, don't hesitate to give a fish a good, up-close sniff. A briny "ocean" smell is good; a "fishy" smell is not.

If the skin looks too big for the fish, it's old fish. The skin should have 80 percent or more of its scales still on and should not have any exterior scars or marks.

Press the fish behind the head along the backbone; the flesh should be firm to the touch. Run your hand along the rib cage to make sure it's firmly attached to the flesh of the fish. If the fish is old, the flesh will have started to separate from the bones.

Fish fillets should have a translucent, glistening look. They shouldn't look dry; the flesh should be smooth and even, with no separations on the surface.

Alder-Planked Sockeye Salmon with Lemon Shallot Butter Sauce

This method of cooking salmon has become a Northwest favorite.

Olive oil

1 seasoned alderwood plank (see note)

Four 8-ounce sockeye salmon fillets, 1 inch thick, boneless and skinless

1 cup Lemon Shallot Butter Sauce (recipe follows)

Chopped chives for garnish

Rub the entire top of the plank with olive oil. Set the seasoned plank in a *cold* oven. Turn the oven to 350°F to preheat the plank. After 10 minutes remove the plank. Place the fillets, lightly brushed with olive oil, on the plank, and bake for 12 to 15 minutes, until cooked to desired doneness. Remove from the oven, place on plates, and spoon the butter sauce over the salmon. Garnish with chopped chives.

Note: Alder planks are available at most kitchen stores. Directions for seasoning the plank are included in the package.

Serves 4

Lemon Shallot Butter Sauce

2 tablespoons chopped shallots

1 cup white wine

2 tablespoons lemon juice

¾ cup heavy cream

¼ pound (1 stick) cold butter, cut into ½-inch pieces

Place the shallots, white wine, and lemon juice in a small saucepan. Simmer until reduced to ¼ cup. Add the cream and simmer until reduced by half. Slowly whisk in the cold butter pieces. When the sauce thickens, transfer to a bowl. Keep in a warm place.

Oven-Broiled King or Sockeye Salmon

My favorite way to cook salmon steaks or fillets indoors is by oven-broiling. This method combines broiling and high-heat baking. Normally, during broiling in an oven, the door is left slightly open; however, in oven-broiling the door is closed completely. This creates the interior heat that glazes the fish and seals in the moisture. Use this method if you have a top broiler mounted inside your oven.

¼ pound (1 stick) butter

1 tablespoon Worcestershire sauce

Juice of 1 lemon

Salt and pepper to taste

Four 6- to 8-ounce king or sockeye salmon fillets, skinless and boneless

Preheat the broiler. Melt the butter in a small saucepan. Stir in the Worcestershire sauce and lemon juice.

Place the salmon fillets on a broiler pan, lightly oiled. Brush the salmon generously with the lemon butter. Sprinkle with salt and pepper. Position the broiling pan so that the fish is 6 to 7 inches from the direct heat. Close the oven door and oven-broil for 5 minutes. Brush with more lemon butter and cook 2 to 3 minutes longer.

Serves 4

Whole Baked Salmon with Cucumber Sauce

My favorite way to cook a 5- to 6-pound silver salmon is to bake it whole. It's easy and makes a nice company dinner.

One 5- to 6-pound whole silver salmon (ask to have it boned)

1 medium-sized yellow onion, sliced

1 large lemon, sliced

1 orange, sliced

¼ pound (1 stick) butter, cut into 6 pieces

Cucumber Sauce (recipe follows)

Preheat the oven to 400°F. Lay the salmon on its side on a large piece of foil. Fill the cavity with the sliced onion, lemon, and orange. Place the pieces of butter evenly along the inside of the fish from end to end. Fold the foil over but don't seal it; leave it open along the cavity of the fish. Pinch both ends of the foil to close, and place the wrapped fish on a baking sheet. Bake in the oven for 1 hour. You will have a perfectly cooked salmon. Serve with the Cucumber Sauce.

Serves 8

Cucumber Sauce

1 English cucumber, peeled and cut in half lengthwise

1 cup water

1 tablespoon salt

¼ cup sugar

⅓ cup white vinegar

1 cup sour cream

1 teaspoon chopped fresh dill

Remove the seeds from the cucumber, and cut crosswise into thin slices. In a mixing bowl, combine the water, salt, sugar, and vinegar. When the sugar and salt are dissolved, add the cucumber. Refrigerate for 1 hour before serving. When ready to serve, drain the cucumber well and fold in the sour cream. Sprinkle with fresh dill.

Gravlax

This is the Scandinavian method for curing fresh salmon. It is delicious served with small cooked new potatoes and baby peas, and also makes an excellent lunch served with Swedish rye bread and the special Gravlax Mustard Sauce.

2½ pounds whole fresh sockeye salmon (or 2 center-cut fillets, same weight)

½ cup fine table salt

¼ cup sugar

20 coarsely crushed peppercorns

About ½ cup chopped fresh dill

Lemon slices

Gravlax Mustard Sauce (recipe follows)

If the fish is whole, bone it and cut it down the middle into two pieces, leaving the skin on. Wipe the fish dry. Score the surface of the skin in several places.

Mix the salt and sugar together in a small bowl. Sprinkle ¼ cup of the salt mixture in the bottom of a glass baking dish. Place half of the salmon, skin side down, in the dish and sprinkle generously with the crushed peppercorns, the dill, and ¼ cup of the salt mixture. Place the other piece of fish, skin side up, on top and sprinkle with the remaining ¼ cup salt mixture. Cover with plastic wrap and a light weight. Refrigerate for 48 hours. Turn the salmon over twice every day.

Remove from the brine and rinse under cold water. The cured salmon will keep for up to 1 week in the refrigerator. To serve, slice thinly on the diagonal toward the tail at a 45° angle, freeing the salmon from the skin. Garnish with lemon slices and serve with the Gravlax Mustard Sauce.

Serves 8

Gravlax Mustard Sauce

3 tablespoons oil

1 tablespoon red wine vinegar

3 tablespoons prepared mustard (yellow mustard is usually used for this because of the flavor and color, but you can use a Dijon style)

1 tablespoon sugar

½ teaspoon salt

2 tablespoons finely chopped dill

Whisk together the oil, vinegar, mustard, sugar, and salt and store in the refrigerator. Add the dill just before serving.

Smoked Salmon and Pecan Spread

A young friend of mine, Lynnie Schriock, gave me this terrific appetizer. It's a great snack to serve anytime.

> ½ cup finely chopped white onion
>
> 6 ounces hard-smoked salmon, broken into small chunks (see note)
>
> 8 ounces cream cheese
>
> 2 tablespoons cream-style horseradish
>
> 1 tablespoon lemon juice
>
> Salt to taste
>
> ½ cup chopped pecans
>
> 1½ tablespoons butter, melted

Place the finely chopped onion in a mixing bowl. Blend the salmon and cream cheese together in a food processor until well mixed. Add the horseradish, lemon juice, and salt. Stir the salmon mixture into the onion and then transfer to a serving bowl.

Sauté the pecans in melted butter until lightly toasted. Sprinkle over the top of the salmon spread. Serve with crackers.

Note: Hard-smoked salmon is smoked at a higher temperature than Nova Scotia–style cured salmon or lox and is more flavorful in this recipe.

Makes 2 cups

Creamy Scrambled Eggs with Smoked Salmon

This is a very good dish for brunch or for a light supper. Serve with a green salad and toasted sourdough bread. Slow cooking is essential to produce luxuriously creamy eggs.

> ¼ pound (1 stick) butter
>
> 12 eggs, beaten with a fork
>
> Salt and pepper
>
> ½ cup chopped green onion
>
> ⅓ pound thin-sliced cold-smoked salmon

Melt 2 tablespoons of the butter in a double boiler or a heavy enameled saucepan and pour in the eggs. Stir the mixture gently and continuously over low heat until the eggs begin to coagulate. Add the rest of the butter, bit by bit. When the eggs are creamy but not dry, put them immediately on a heated platter and sprinkle with salt, pepper, and green onion. Lay the slices of smoked salmon across the eggs. Serve right away.

Serves 6

Barbecued King or Sockeye Salmon

A good way to barbecue salmon is to buy a 3- to 4-pound side (one half of a fish) of king or sockeye salmon.

Light the charcoal. The charcoal should be going just off its peak, the coals hot and covered with gray ash. Measure the thickness of the salmon side at its thickest part and figure 10 minutes to the inch. Lay the fish on a piece of aluminum foil, allowing a 1-inch border. Turn up the edges of the foil to form a "boat." Brush the fish with Salmon Barbecue Sauce (recipe follows). Place the foil and fish on the grill, cover, and cook until done, basting occasionally.

Salmon Barbecue Sauce

Joyce Ingle doesn't claim that this sauce is her own invention; she thinks she found it in a newspaper years ago. But she recognized a classic and in the process has indelibly defined for her family what the flavor of barbecued salmon should be.

½ pound (2 sticks) butter

1 clove garlic, minced

¼ cup ketchup

¼ cup soy sauce

2 tablespoons prepared mustard

1 tablespoon Worcestershire sauce

1 tablespoon fresh lemon juice

Freshly cracked pepper

Melt the butter with the garlic in a saucepan. Mix the remaining ingredients and warm over very low heat to keep the sauce from separating.

Makes 2 cups

Salmon with Lemon Verbena and Tuberous Begonia Sauce

The Herbfarm is located 30 miles east of Seattle at Fall City. Lola Zimmerman began this lovely place as a hobby and now it has grown into a mecca for food lovers—400 varieties of herbs, 120 species of succulents, greenhouses, llamas, doves, and turkeys. The Herbfarm offers an extensive list of cooking and gardening classes. People from all over the country are sharing this "secret garden." Jerry Traunfeld, one of the Northwest's finest chefs, creates wonderful dinners for the Herbfarm. He shared his special recipe for this salmon.

Tuberous begonia petals have a citric tang ideally complemented by the lemon scent and flavor of lemon verbena. Combined, they create a salmon sauce fit for royalty.

Four 6-ounce king salmon fillets

Salt

Cayenne pepper

Few drops of lime juice

Lemon Verbena and Tuberous Begonia Sauce

6 tablespoons butter, cut into 6 pieces

2 shallots, minced

Juice of 1 lime

1 ½ tablespoons white port

2 tablespoons white wine

3 lemon verbena leaves

3 tablespoons heavy cream

Salt and white pepper

Cayenne pepper

1 tuberous begonia blossom (unsprayed)

To prepare the salmon, preheat the oven to 500°F. Remove the bones from the fillets with pliers. Cut diagonally into 4 equal serving pieces about ¾ inch thick.

Place the salmon on half of a 24-inch-wide piece of aluminum foil set atop a baking sheet. Season the salmon lightly with salt and a tiny amount of cayenne. Sprinkle with a few drops of lime juice and rub to spread it around. Fold the foil over the fish. Fold the edges twice to seal.

To prepare the sauce, in a small, heavy pan, melt 1 tablespoon of the butter, add the shallots, and cook until softened (don't brown). Add the lime juice, port, wine, and verbena leaves. Boil gently until reduced to a thick syrup.

Remove the leaves. Add the cream. Return to a boil. Turn off the heat. Whisk in the remaining 5 tablespoons butter, 1 tablespoon at a time, making sure each pat melts before adding the next. Season with salt, pepper, a tiny amount of cayenne, and more lime juice if needed.

Just before serving, with scissors, snip the tuberous begonia blossom into thin threads, allowing them to fall into the sauce. Stir.

To bake the salmon, place the baking sheet with the salmon in the oven and cook just until the foil starts to puff up—4½ to 5½ minutes. Remove from the oven. Serve on warmed plates with the sauce.

Serves 4

Trail Creek Pan-Fried Trout with Caper Butter

At Sun Valley, Idaho, you can ride in horse-drawn sleighs to Trail Creek Lodge and have this delicious trout.

> *Milk*
> *1 cup flour seasoned with salt and pepper*
> *¼ cup cornmeal*
> *4 fresh trout*
> *½ cup clarified butter*
> *2 lemons, cut into wedges*

Caper Butter

> *2 tablespoons capers*
> *Juice of 1 lemon*
> *¼ pound (1 stick) butter, softened*
> *2 tablespoons chopped parsley*

Prepare the caper butter several hours in advance. Mash the capers lightly with a fork. Squeeze in the lemon juice. Mix with softened butter until well blended. Stir in the parsley. Wrap in foil and shape into a roll about 1½ inches in diameter. Refrigerate for several hours. When ready to serve, cut into ¼-inch slices and place 2 slices on top of the just-cooked hot trout.

To fry the trout, pour the milk into a large shallow dish. Combine the seasoned flour and corn-meal in another shallow dish. Dip the trout in the milk, then in the seasoned flour mixture. Heat the clarified butter in a 10-inch frying pan until hot. Place the trout in the hot butter and cook until golden on one side; turn and quickly cook the other side and transfer to a heated serving dish. Serve the fish with the Caper Butter slices on top and lemon wedges on the side.

Serves 4

Grilled Whole Trout with Peppered Bacon

Grilling whole fish outdoors on a barbecue results in a crisp skin and moist, tender meat inside. I have lots of mint growing near my barbecue, so I add it to the trout. I like to use a hinged square metal rack to grill small whole fish. It makes turning the fish easier.

Peppered bacon gives this trout extra snap. It is dry-cured bacon that has had crushed pepper pressed into the fat side.

> *4 fresh trout*
> *Olive oil*
> *4 sprigs fresh mint*
> *4 slices peppered bacon or thick-sliced bacon*
> *2 lemons, cut into wedges*

Light a charcoal fire. Brush the trout lightly with olive oil. Place a mint sprig inside each fish. Wrap with a strip of bacon. Place in a hinged rack and cook over medium-hot coals for 5 minutes per side.

Serve with lemon wedges.

Serves 4

Salted and Broiled Fresh Small Fish

Mrs. George Tsutakawa generously shared her time with me to show me how to cook various types of fresh seafood. I had never before bought small whole fish (1 to 2 pounds), buying fillets instead. Now, having learned how to cook the whole fish, I find them hard to resist.

Have the fish cleaned or, if you are fishing and catch your own, clean it carefully, leaving the fins and tail on. Perch and small rockfish, in particular, are delicious cooked this way.

Make 3 diagonal slashes into the outside flesh of the fish on each side. This allows the fish to cook faster and have more flavor. Generously salt the skin sides of the fish. Lightly sprinkle the inside. If possible, salt the fish 15 minutes in advance of cooking.

If cooking indoors, preheat the broiler. Place the fish on a foil-lined baking pan about 8 inches from the heat source and broil for 5 minutes (see note). Turn and cook 5 minutes longer. Place the fish in a warmed shallow serving dish. The skin should be crisp and the flesh should pull away from the bone easily.

If you are cooking outdoors, simply cook the fish on the grill over moderate heat for 5 minutes on each side.

Note: If your broiler is mounted inside your oven, oven-broil the fish with the oven door closed.

Fried Smelt with Parsley Butter

In February, in La Conner, Washington, 2,000 to 3,000 people arrive to "jig" for smelt, a small silvery, slightly oily fish. "Jigging" refers to the method used for catching smelt. The fishing line has 10 to 11 hooks and a weight at the end of the line, so you can cast. The line is then pulled back in a jerky motion, basically snagging the fish.

> *24 smelt*
> *Salt and pepper*
> *Flour*
> *4 tablespoons butter*
> *¼ cup vegetable oil*
> *Parsley Butter (recipe follows)*
> *Lemon wedges*

To clean the smelt, make a cut from the top of the neck straight down through the backbone, being careful not to sever the throat. Then, grabbing the body in one hand and the head in the other, with a quick twisting and pulling motion, remove the insides of the fish.

To cook the smelt, sprinkle the smelt with salt and pepper and roll in flour. Heat the butter and vegetable oil in a heavy frying pan. When the oil is hot, add the smelt in batches. Pour out the oil-butter mixture and replace it with fresh when it starts to fill with flour particles.

Serve with Parsley Butter and lots of fresh lemon wedges to squeeze over.

Serves 4

Parsley Butter

¼ pound (1 stick) butter

3 tablespoons minced parsley

3 tablespoons lemon juice

Heat the butter over low heat until just melted. Stir in the parsley and lemon juice and drizzle over the hot fried smelt.

Pickled Herring

Our Scandinavian heritage in the Northwest is felt strongly in our fishing and in our baking. Pickled herring is traditional during the holiday season. A good Norwegian friend of mine adds 5 cocktail onions to each jar—for the martinis that go with the pickled herring!

10 pounds salted Icelandic herring, filleted (salted herring from Iceland are larger fish and have a higher oil content than domestic herring)

2 cups granulated sugar

1 gallon water

½ gallon white vinegar

5 large white onions, quartered and sliced

2 ounces pickling spices

¼ cup chopped fresh dill

Place the fillets in a 5-gallon bucket in a deep sink. Let the cold water run continuously, overflowing the bucket slowly. Stick your hand in the bucket and stir the herring around from time to time. Keep the fresh water running in this way for 2 hours. The herring will still taste salty, but once it goes into the pickling brine it will balance out. Remove the herring and drain in a colander. Cut into bite-sized chunks.

Heat the sugar and water to dissolve the sugar. Cool. Add the vinegar to complete the brine. In a large, heavy 5-gallon crock or plastic container with a lid (see note), place layer of herring, then onions, then a sprinkling of pickling spices; repeat until all ingredients are used.

Pour in brine to cover and shake the crock to eliminate any air pockets; sprinkle generously with the fresh dill. Cover and store in the refrigerator. After 2 weeks, the herring will be ready to eat. I like to pack it in large canning jars with hinged lids to give to friends. The herring should always be refrigerated.

Note: You can obtain 5-gallon crocks or containers at restaurant supply stores.

Makes enough for a large crowd

Yelloweyed Rockfish

Generally sold whole, yelloweyed rockfish must be bled immediately after it is caught to be of the highest quality. To check, look at the left gill plate for a white membrane that indicates that it has been bled. If it has been prepared properly, the quality of yelloweye merits the cost. Filleted yelloweye is unique in flavor and texture.

Ask the fishmonger to cut the fish in half, one half filleted and skin removed, the other half with the skin on and bone in. Cut the piece with the bone into 2-inch strips, crosswise, for use in this dish. A 2- to 2½-pound whole fish can be cut up to yield two firm, fresh fillets and two nice collar pieces that can be used to make a very good soup. The fillets can be steamed or sliced thinly for sashimi.

This makes a good first course.

> ½ cup soy sauce
>
> 2 tablespoons mirin or sake
>
> 1 tablespoon sugar
>
> 2 slices fresh ginger, cut into thin strips
>
> 1 whole yelloweyed rockfish, cut up as described in the recipe introduction
>
> Additional soy sauce
>
> Wasabi (Japanese horseradish powder)

Mix together the soy sauce, mirin or sake, sugar, and ginger in a 2-quart saucepan. Bring the mixture to a boil. Add the bone-in strips of fish, skin side up. Cover and cook over moderate heat (the mixture should be just barely bubbling) for 3 minutes. Turn the fish over and continue to cook for 3 or 4 minutes longer. Turn off the heat, but leave the fish in the pan, covered, for 5 minutes before serving. This allows the flavors of the cooking sauce to be absorbed into the fish. Serve the fish skin side up in individual serving dishes with a little sauce spooned over. Serve the uncooked filleted half of the fish as sashimi by cutting it into thin pieces and serving with soy sauce mixed with wasabi.

Makes 4 appetizer servings

Fresh Halibut Steaks in Caper Sauce

The best halibut of all is out of Alaska, and the farther north it is caught, the better the fish.

½ cup flour, seasoned with 1 teaspoon salt and ½ teaspoon pepper

2 whole eggs, well beaten

Two 8-ounce halibut fillets (½ inch thick)

5 tablespoons butter

2 tablespoons vegetable oil

½ cup dry white wine

1 tablespoon fresh lemon juice

1 tablespoon capers

Place the seasoned flour in a shallow dish. Place the beaten eggs in another shallow dish. Dip the halibut fillets into the seasoned flour, coating them lightly on both sides, then dip into the beaten eggs. Heat 2 tablespoons of the butter and the oil in a sauté pan. Sauté the halibut until golden and turn (cook 3 to 4 minutes on each side). Transfer to a heated platter. Pour off any oil remaining in the pan. Pour the wine into the same pan and bring to a boil. Boil for 1 minute. Remove from the heat and stir in the remaining 3 tablespoons butter, lemon juice, and capers. Pour this sauce over the fish and serve.

Serves 2

Cheri Walker's Grilled Fillet of White Sturgeon with Chanterelles and Cranberry-Port-Cream Sauce

1 pound fresh chanterelle mushrooms

4 cups fish stock

6 cups cranberries (reserve a few raw berries for garnish)

2 cups port wine

¼ cup sugar

½ cup brandy

2 cloves garlic (1 teaspoon minced)

1 tablespoon fresh tarragon leaves

¼ pound plus 2 tablespoons (10 tablespoons) butter

¼ cup red wine vinegar

½ teaspoon salt

⅛ teaspoon pepper
¼ cup heavy cream
Eight 7-ounce white sturgeon fillets
Tarragon sprigs for garnish

Light a charcoal fire.

To make the sauce, finely chop half of the chanterelles. Combine the fish stock, berries, port, sugar, brandy, chopped chanterelles, garlic, and tarragon in a large saucepan. Bring to a boil, then simmer for 20 minutes, or until the berries have popped. Mash the berries slightly to release their juice. Strain through a fine-mesh sieve, pressing lightly to purée the fruit. Strain again through cheesecloth if the juice is cloudy with seeds. Simmer until the 4 cups of juice are reduced to 3 cups.

In a separate saucepan, melt 4 tablespoons of the butter. Add the remaining whole chanterelles and sauté until heated through. Deglaze with the vinegar, add salt and pepper, and let simmer until the liquid is almost absorbed.

To the reduced stock, add the cream and let simmer until the sauce clears slightly. Add the remaining 6 tablespoons of cold butter in bits, stirring until the sauce thickens and clears. Add the mushrooms and vinegar reduction. Keep the sauce warm over simmering water as you grill the sturgeon.

Brush the sturgeon fillets with olive oil and grill for approximately 5 minutes on the first side; turn over and grill 3 to 4 minutes on the second side, or until just firm to the touch.

To serve, ladle sauce on top of grilled sturgeon fillets. Garnish with sprigs of fresh tarragon and a few raw cranberries.

Serves 8

Beer Batter Fish and Chips

I like the moist, flaky lingcod the best for this. The Seattle waterfront offers a number of opportunities to buy fish and chips and sit by the water on a nice day. High-quality hook-and-line-caught cod is also wonderful baked.

1 cup flour

1 teaspoon baking powder

1 egg, beaten

2 tablespoons vegetable oil

1 cup light beer

2 cups Panko crumbs

Peanut oil for deep frying

1 ½ pounds lingcod fillets, cut into 2-inch pieces

Tartar Sauce (page 258)

Lemon wedges

Chips (recipe follows)

In a bowl, mix the flour, baking powder, vegetable oil, egg, and beer together, using a wire whisk. Heat peanut oil in a deep-fat fryer to 375°F. Coat the fish pieces with batter, then roll in Panko crumbs. Drop 2 or 3 pieces at a time into the oil. Fry until golden brown, turning once. Drain well on paper towels. Serve with tartar sauce, lemon wedges, and Chips.

Chips

2 large russet potatoes

Salt

Scrub the potatoes well. Cut into thin French fries, about ½ inch thick. Rinse in cold water and pat dry. Drop into the hot fat (375°F) when the fish has finished cooking. Fry until golden brown. Drain on paper towels. Sprinkle with salt, and serve hot.

Serves 4

Parchment-Baked Lingcod with Chive-Tarragon Butter

This is an easy way to cook any white fish that is ½ to ¾ inch thick. The parchment seals in the flavors and steams the fish nicely.

Four 8-ounce fillets of lingcod

Kosher salt

¼ pound (1 stick) butter, softened

¼ cup chopped chives

1 tablespoon fresh tarragon leaves

4 lemon slices

Strips of carrot and celery, julienned

1 egg white, lightly beaten

Preheat the oven to 400°F. Sprinkle the fillets with kosher salt. In a small bowl, mix the butter with the chives and tarragon. Divide the butter mixture into 8 pieces. Place 2 pieces on each fillet. Place a lemon slice on each fillet and lay carrot and celery strips across the top.

Cut 4 pieces of parchment paper, each large enough to enclose a fillet. Place a fillet on one side of each piece of parchment, fold over, and seal by brushing the edge with egg white and then twisting and rolling to seal. Bake in the oven for 10 to 12 minutes. Cut the parchment open carefully to avoid being burned by steam.

Serves 4

Black Cod in Swiss Chard with Lemon Butter Sauce

Black cod is a fish with a high oil content that is gaining popularity. Many people have developed a liking for the velvety texture of black cod, and when cooked and served properly, it can be a real treat. It is often sold at fish markets lightly smoked, which adds flavor and texture to the fish. You simply take it home and finish it on your outdoor grill. Serve with boiled new potatoes.

Wrapping the black cod in Swiss chard adds flavor and contrasting texture to the soft flesh of the fish. Serve with steamed jasmine rice.

Four 6-ounce black cod fillets

Salt and pepper

12 tablespoons (1½ sticks) butter

4 large leaves Swiss chard, cleaned and stems removed

Juice of ½ lemon

¼ cup white wine

Preheat the oven to 400°F. Sprinkle the fish with salt and pepper. Place a pat of butter (1 tablespoon) on top of each fillet (reserve remaining butter for making the sauce). Wrap the fillets individually, each in a leaf of Swiss chard and then in foil, leaving the packets partially open on the top to let steam out. Bake for 10 minutes.

While the fish is baking, make the lemon butter sauce. Bring the lemon juice and wine to a simmer in a small saucepan and cook for several minutes. When the fish is cooked, cut the remaining 8 tablespoons of butter into pieces and quickly whisk them into the lemon-wine mixture (off the heat). Remove foil. Place fillets on plates and spoon lemon-butter sauce over them.

Serves 4

Sesame-Ginger Lingcod

Lingcod is fished from southern Oregon all the way up the coast to southeastern Alaska. Hook-and-line-caught lingcod gives you the best-quality fish.

The fillets should be white and have a good, clean, smooth surface and no separating or "gaping" in the flesh. A firm fish with a good texture, lingcod is typically used for fish and chips, but it is also delicious marinated and then grilled or baked.

½ cup soy sauce

2 tablespoons sesame oil

½ cup brown sugar

½ cup water

¼ teaspoon crushed red pepper flakes

1 teaspoon sesame seeds

1 tablespoon chopped green onion

1 clove garlic, minced

Four 6- to 8-ounce lingcod fillets

Additional sesame seeds

In a shallow dish, mix all of the ingredients together, except the fish and extra sesame seeds, to make the marinade. Let the marinade sit for several hours to blend the flavors. Transfer to a shallow dish. Marinate fish for 30 minutes on each side.

Preheat the broiler. Broil the fish 8 inches from the source of heat for 8 to 10 minutes. Sprinkle with additional sesame seeds.

Note: You can also steam the fillets in a bamboo steamer for 6 to 8 minutes. Boil the remaining marinade for 1 minute while the fish is steaming, and spoon over fish before serving.

Serves 4

MEAT, POULTRY & GAME

Pork Aside, SOME PIGS HAVE NAMES

*T*he winter pig's name was Isolde, and her days were numbered. The summer pig's name had been changed from Winston to Food, and what was left of him could be found in the freezer.

When frigid winter weather blew up the mouth of the Columbia River, the warm pig Isolde and her three milk goat friends steamed in the morning light in the barnyard at Templehof Farm near Astoria in Oregon. Freezing weather meant an extra three-gallon bucket of traditional slops for Isolde. Otherwise, she'd burn her calories to keep warm and wouldn't put on weight. And raising a meat animal, after all, is all about putting on weight.

"Slops" sounds so unpleasant in and of itself. Yet it's a wholesome mixture of kitchen waste, old bread, the whey left over from cheese-making, soured yogurt, old cheese rinds, garden waste—anything, basically, that a pig would find edible, even palatable. This isn't to say that pigs aren't particular about what they eat. They like their slops cooked, or at least warmed. So twice a day Karin Temple finds herself cooking for a pig. She's done it, two pigs a year, for 25 years. It's how she eats meat.

"If I didn't have access to meat that was healthily and humanely raised," Temple says, "I wouldn't eat it. It's as simple as that."

Imagine, for a moment, cooking for a pig, then going to work. In Temple's case that meant teaching German, French, world literature, and writing at a nearby college. She'd spend all day with students and fellow faculty, would organize literary lectures and films for the film club for greater Astoria, edit the poetry magazine, then come back home to Templehof and, maybe humming a mindless tune, lean her body into the warm flanks of a milk goat and massage the milk out of the milk goat's teats and into a bucket. The greeting of Isolde and her porcine kind would have started with a grunted, rooting rumble only to rise in pitch and volume to something closer to a squeal. Pigs are such sentient animals that the greeting would have said as much about companionship as it did the happy feeling that slops are near at hand.

"It's hard," Karin Temple allows. "Raising meat animals for the table is hard. Pigs roll over to have their tummies scratched. So after six months, when it's time, there is definitely grief. It's not something you get used to, that goes away. Nonfarm types are amazed that I do this. The vegetarians I know have never been anything but respectful of me. I like to eat meat, and this is where it comes from."

There's a telltale German lilt to her spoken English, like the part of a song that remains in the air when the singing has ended. She was a child in Germany when the Second World War came to a close and hunger rose up out of the rubble. The little gardens people tended kept them alive, the few chickens they raised for eggs, the grass they gathered to feed rabbits in hutches in the basement. The lessons remain intact and important for Karin Temple.

"When it comes to feeding myself, I want to be able to do more than shop," Temple says. "I want to be able to contribute to my own table, to have that knowledge. Otherwise, I think, you lose touch a little. Western culture is so disdainful of other creatures. We feel we can use them any way we please, and when all we see is raw meat wrapped in plastic in the supermarket, why not? Meat like that has so little to do with animals. The hard part about raising meat becomes someone else's problem."

I know how she feels. I raised rabbits and egg-laying hens in a backyard in a Seattle residential neighborhood for a number of years. People weren't amazed in my case. They simply thought I had lost it. But it is such an old tradition, both urban and rural, this raising rabbits for the table, the gathering of eggs. You see the hutches near the gardens along railroad lines as you speed through the outskirts of French, Italian, German, and Dutch cities and towns. Little community gardens, and little hutches. In America that translates into weirdness.

There is nothing in our culture that demands of a meat eater the knowledge of how meat comes to the table. Even a little squiggle of knowledge. This may be a modern, if not unfortunate, definition of civilization. Without knowledge consumers can't make informed choices. They take what's served, or sold. The issue of product quality turns from how meat should really taste—there is a world of difference between the taste of a Templehof farm-raised ham and its Hormel cousin—to whether or not it's safe. The question is no longer "Will this roast or chicken inspire the aesthete in me?" but "Will it make me sick?" And somehow that has become acceptable.

I have heard meat eaters arguing with vegetarians. They like to point out that vegetables are living things, too, and that killing and food are inseparable. This is true, but only to a point. And the point is simple. Vegetables don't bleed. If you cut a head of lettuce from its stalk, it won't jet warm, sticky, thickening blood onto your hands. Vegetables never sigh a last, bubbly breath, because vegetables never have their throats cut. You don't feel in your hands the last spastic trembles of dying vegetables. You don't feel the animal warmth fade. Harvested vegetables don't smell like harvested rabbits or chickens or deer, the dead animals with which I am most familiar. With meat, food and the smell of death are inseparable.

On the occasions that priests of Ifa, Candomble, or Santeria make a blood sacrifice, an offering of a rooster, say, they do so because an Orisa, or spiritual entity, has asked for as much through a process of divination. At the moment of blood letting, which is dispassionate yet focused, anyone attending the ritual tugs at the skin of his own throat to commiserate with the plight of the feathered victim. How many of us do the same for the turkey that sits on our Thanksgiving table? We thank God with a grace. But what about the turkey?

We kill turkeys by the hundreds of millions in this country, reducing Thanksgiving and Christmas to holidays of savage excess. In numbers like that, where's the individual turkey to be found, its animal nature, its biological history, its sentient integrity, its voice? We're not eating turkeys at Thanksgiving. We're eating sentimental poultry food units spit out of the Big American Meat Factory.

There's talk of building an environmentally controlled hog farm in Nevada on such a grand scale that each day it will produce more sewage than all of Los Angeles. Is this weird, too? Or simply obscene? When society so loses track of the very basic integrity of domesticated farm animals, meat animals, giant factories make perfect sense. But then, so too does British beef that eats holes in your brain and kills you. The person who thinks it's acceptable to feed diseased sheep to beef cattle, no matter how finely ground those sheep might be, is the same person who thinks up the giant meat factories. It's the same person who thinks meat comes from the supermarket wrapped in plastic. It's the same person who is outraged by bacteria-tainted hamburger, and who can't understand why government doesn't do a better job of protecting the consumer from his own foolishness.

It needn't be so.

Doc and Connie Hattfield raise beef cattle in central Oregon and, along with twenty-nine other ranches, sell the meat under the Oregon Country Beef label. "We had a horse and beef cattle veterinary practice in the Bitterroot Valley in Montana years ago," Doc says. "Connie got into cattle on the side. But raising cattle there was like trying to grow palm trees in Seattle. Here's this wonderful animal designed to harvest rough forage, but we had to grow food for cattle in the Bitterroot Valley, which puts you in the loop of fossil fuels, high electricity use, additional labor, chemical fertilizers. What I was seeing as a vet was a result of all that. So we moved down here to Brothers 24 years ago because you can't grow anything here but cows. Not even a vegetable garden. Freezes too late in June."

For 10 years Doc and Connie raised cattle and took them to market like any other rancher. And when the bottom fell out of that market in the mid-1980s, they suffered right along with the rest. Such was the conventional wisdom of a generic marketplace where all beef ended up in one big pile regardless of how the cattle were raised, or how the rangeland and watershed were treated.

Connie drove from Brothers to Bend, the nearest big town. Part of what troubled her was the first wave of bad news about beef, that a diet that included red meat was sure to kill you. And then the European Union nations had refused to accept imports of American beef because they felt it was too loaded up with hormones and antibiotics. Doc and Connie used no hormones or antibiotics on their beef. Nor did they finish them on corn or grains that would add layers of fat to boost their weight just before the animals were sold for slaughter.

Connie found herself talking to the trainer at a gym in Bend. Ace was the local guy who knew all about health, about vitamins and protein and cardiovascular exercise. What exactly did he think about eating beef? Connie braced herself for the worst but was surprised to hear Ace say he had no problems with beef, that he encouraged his clients to eat beef three times a week unless they had specific health problems that suggested otherwise. The only problem he had, Ace said, was getting a consistent supply of Argentine beef in the local market. That got Connie's attention.

"They grow a natural product down there," Ace explained to her. "No chemicals in the feed, no antibiotics, no hormones. It's lean, not fatty. But you just can't count on finding it."

Connie asked Ace if he would speak to a group of ranchers if she pulled together a meeting, and Ace allowed as how he'd be happy to do just that. "When Ace showed up," Connie says, "we had ten thousand mother cows represented in that one living room." This is how Oregon Country Beef got up on its hind legs.

Member ranchers had to be willing to grow an all-natural product. And they had to agree to a set of guidelines about the land and the watershed. They also had to be willing to visit with consumers of their beef. "When you call Oregon Country Beef on the phone," Connie says, "you don't get an office or a broker or a processor. You reach a ranch."

Oregon Country Beef went into the marketplace and asked consumers what they wanted. This was radical behavior. This was living and working way outside a norm that dictated that as a rancher you provided the kind of animal the processors said they needed. "What Connie found out," Doc says, "is that people were looking for smaller cuts of beef, not just big old steaks. They wanted a leaner product and an environmentally sensitive product. And they wanted to know that the animals were being treated right."

It costs more per pound, Oregon Country Beef. The processor that handles their product accepts the 150 or so beeves Oregon Country Beef can deliver to market each Monday, keeping them separate, helping with the special marketing demands of the product. The same processor slaughters a thousand animals a day. Those thousand-a-day animals are anonymous. That doesn't make them bad, even suspect. But they are anonymous, and they will end up wrapped in plastic and sold in the generic market. Oregon Country Beef can be trailed from the meat case back to the ranch.

Short of raising a pig in the backyard, what's a meat eater to do? The trick is to eat like a peasant, be it European, African, or Asian. Look at meat as something exceptional,

MEAT TEMPERATURE GUIDE

Today, we are eating meat rarer than we used to; however, the meat thermometers have not changed their readings, so many roasts, sadly, are overcooked. Here is a current chart for easy reference.

Meat	Temperature
Poultry	170°–180°F
Lamb	130°–135°F *(medium rare)*
	145°–150°F *(well done)*
Pork	160°–170°F
Beef	125°F *(rare)*
	125°–130°F *(medium rare)*
	135°–140°F *(medium)*
	140°–150°F *(well done)*

Remember that the temperature will rise 5° to 10° after you remove the roast or the fowl from the oven.

not ordinary, not daily. Buy meat less often, but buy better meat. Use wonderful recipes to enhance the experience of meat.

Oregon Country Beef is a branded product: The label tells you about the origins of the product as well as the cost per pound. But Oregon Country Beef isn't the only player in this rapidly expanding niche. A search of Internet Web sites will tell you as much. There are Web sites where you can buy natural meat products directly from the people who raise the animals and make the meat. You pay more. But, as Karin Temple says, "You don't end up paying for and eating cruelty." And then there's the issue of quality.

"What we do as consumers is incredibly significant," Temple says. "Not everyone can live as I do, or would even want to. But we can all make choices. We can choose to support those people who are really trying to raise meat animals in humane and healthy ways. These may be small contributions. But small contributions really do count."

Each morning when she leaves her house, the fowl are there to greet Karin Temple at her front door: Muscovy ducks, the mixed flock of chickens that includes Barred Plymouth Rocks, Wyandottes, Arakanas, Rhode Island Reds, Black Astrolorps, and even a white-feathered Leghorn, the only hen that lays a white egg for Karin. They all want to be fed.

So do the milk goats, the goat wethers that will make meat in their time, the pig, the Black-Faced Scottish sheep. Karin Temple will feed them, and they will all feed her in one way or another. But the pigs do the yeoman duty. "I can barter with pork," Temple says. "There are fishermen who'll trade salmon, hunters who'll trade venison, and carpenters who'll trade labor. Smoked ham and bacon paid for the murals an artist painted on my barn doors."

What starts as slops ends as art, with only the winter or summer pig and Karin Temple standing in between.

Gwen Bassetti's Lamb Meat Loaf

Gwen Bassetti says, "I tend to make meat loaf the way I make bread: with whatever is on hand. The end result is good, fresh sandwich meat." Have the butcher use boned shoulder for the ground lamb. Packaged lamb patties available in many markets have too much fat and won't taste good. (Lamb is so much more tender than beef that a meat loaf made of ground lamb alone would crumble, which is why the ground beef is added.)

1 pound lean ground lamb
1 pound lean ground beef
1 cup fresh bread crumbs
½ cup finely chopped onion
1 egg, beaten
½ cup ketchup
1 teaspoon salt (seasoned salt if available)
½ teaspoon freshly ground pepper
Dried thyme (optional)

Preheat the oven to 325°F. In a bowl, mix together all of the ingredients, being careful not to overmix. If the bread crumbs are exceptionally dry, moisten them first with a little milk. Otherwise, adjust the moistness of the meat loaf with ketchup. Seasoned salt is nice to use. So is a little thyme.

Press the mixture into a large, ovenproof glass loaf pan, 8 by 3 by 4 inches. Bake for 1 hour. Remove from the oven and drain the fat off immediately. For the best results, let cool, remove from pan, wrap, and refrigerate overnight.

Serves 6

Medallions of Lamb with Pinot Noir and Hazelnut Sauce

Here Greg Higgins, an inspired Portland chef, uses the region's products to great advantage.

2½ pounds boneless lamb loins

Flour for dredging

Salt and pepper to taste

¼ cup vegetable oil

2 tablespoons minced shallots

1 tablespoon minced garlic

2 cups pinot noir

2 tablespoons red wine vinegar

¼ cup ground toasted hazelnuts

1 tablespoon coarse-grained mustard

6 tablespoons butter, cut into pieces

1 bunch spinach, cut into chiffonade (finely shredded)

Preheat the oven to 400°F. Dredge the lamb loins in the flour and season with salt and pepper. Heat the oil in a medium sauté pan. When the pan is quite hot, add the lamb loins and brown well on all sides. Transfer the lamb to a roasting pan and place in the oven for 10 minutes. Sauté the shallots and garlic in the same pan. Just as they begin to brown, add the pinot noir and vinegar, and reduce the heat to medium. Whisk in the nuts and mustard, and continue to reduce the liquid until it coats a spoon. Remove from the heat and whisk in the butter pieces.

Slice the lamb loins at a 45-degree angle to form 1-inch medallions. Arrange over the spinach chiffonade. Whisk the sauce until smooth and glossy and pour over the medallions.

Serves 6

Carré d'Agneau à la Provençale

This delicious creation by Susan Vanderbeek celebrates the spirit of French country cuisine. Use well-trimmed "frenched" lamb racks.

¼ cup olive oil

2 "frenched" racks of lamb, to serve 4

White wine

½ cup veal glacé (can be purchased at specialty food stores)

2 tablespoons Madeira

Chopped parsley

4 tablespoons (¼ cup) Compound Butter for Lamb (recipe follows)

Preheat the oven to 500°F. Heat the olive oil in a roasting pan on top of the stove and add the racks of lamb. Brown on the meaty side; turn. Place in the hot oven. Roast for 6 minutes, turn the meat over in the pan, and roast for 6 minutes more. Remove the lamb from the oven and keep warm.

Deglaze the pan with a little white wine. Add the veal glacé and the Madeira, and a little chopped parsley. Add the Compound Butter. Carve the meat and place on a warm plate. Pour the sauce over the lamb and serve.

Serves 4

Compound Butter for Lamb

¼ pound (1 stick) unsalted butter, softened

1 clove garlic, peeled and sliced

¼ cup Niçoise olives, pitted

2 tablespoons julienned basil

2 ounces sun-dried tomatoes in oil

Squeeze of lemon juice

Salt and pepper

Process all ingredients in a food processor. Roll into a log and wrap in plastic. Refrigerate until ready to use. Use ¼ cup in the sauce served with Carré d'Agneau à la Provençale and reserve the rest for serving on broiled salmon or steamed vegetables.

Butterflied Leg of Lamb

The addition of coriander and ginger to the marinade gives the lamb a delicious Middle Eastern flavor. Serve with Couscous Salad with Fresh Corn, Sweet Red Pepper, and Cilantro, page 146.

> *3 cloves garlic*
>
> *1 ½ teaspoons kosher salt*
>
> *1 teaspoon ground pepper*
>
> *1 teaspoon ground coriander*
>
> *½ teaspoon ground ginger*
>
> *2 teaspoons fresh rosemary, chopped*
>
> *2 teaspoons fresh thyme, chopped*
>
> *¼ cup olive oil*
>
> *2 tablespoons dry sherry*
>
> *One 4- to 5-pound boned and butterflied leg of lamb*

Crush the garlic. Mix together in a bowl with the salt, pepper, coriander, and ginger. Add the rosemary, thyme, olive oil, and sherry.

Carefully trim as much fat and silver connective tissue as you can from the outside of the leg of lamb. Spread half of the marinade on one side of the meat and half on the other. Marinate for 4 to 6 hours (or overnight).

To cook, prepare your grill ahead of time so that you have a nice, evenly heated bed of coals. Grill the lamb for 12 to 15 minutes on each side and serve immediately on a heated platter.

Serves 6 to 8

Roast Rack of Lamb

There couldn't be an easier or better dinner for two. The rack cooks perfectly every time. Following are two roasting methods. The first is for ovens that have a broiler; the second is a high-heat method for ovens without a broiler.

Using an oven broiler:

> *1 rack of standard domestic lamb, well trimmed of excess fat ("frenched")*
>
> *Kosher salt and freshly ground pepper*
>
> *1 tablespoon chopped fresh rosemary*

To broil in the oven, preheat the broiler. Place the rack of lamb on your broiler pan. Sprinkle with salt, pepper, and rosemary. Place the pan in the oven with the tops of the rack of lamb 8 inches from the source of heat. Close the oven door. Broil for 8 to 10 minutes, until the fat begins to burn slightly. Turn the heat down to 325°F, leaving the oven door closed, and cook 20 minutes longer.

Without an oven broiler:

1 rack of lamb

Kosher salt and pepper

1 tablespoon chopped fresh rosemary

4 tablespoons butter, softened

1 teaspoon chopped parsley

2 teaspoons Dijon-style mustard

Preheat the oven to 425°F. Sprinkle the rack with salt, pepper, and rosemary. Roast in the oven for 25 minutes.

Mix the butter, parsley, and mustard together and brush over the lamb after removing it from the oven.

Serve with oven-roasted potatoes and fresh spring asparagus.

Serves 2

Herbed Lamb Shanks

Lamb shanks are delicious when cooked slowly with herbs, onion, garlic, and orange peel.

4 lamb shanks

4 cloves garlic, cut into slivers

Kosher salt and freshly ground pepper

Fresh rosemary, chopped

½ yellow onion, cut into thin rings

8 strips of orange peel, 1½ to 2 inches long and ½ inch wide (orange part only)

Preheat the oven to 375°F. Lay each lamb shank on a 12-inch-square piece of brown paper or parchment. Make small incisions with the tip of a sharp knife and insert the garlic slivers. Sprinkle with salt, pepper, and fresh rosemary to taste.

Place a few rings of onion and 2 strips of peel on each shank. Fold the paper to seal tightly and place on a baking sheet. Bake for 1 hour. Unwrap and serve with new potatoes, fresh asparagus, and mint sauce.

Serves 4

Perfect Leg of Lamb

This method of cooking a leg of lamb works on any standard-sized leg of lamb, whether it's 5, 6, or 7 pounds, and it's delicious time after time. You don't even need to use a meat thermometer.

1 leg of lamb

1 lemon, cut in half

2 cloves garlic, cut into slivers

Salt and pepper

1 tablespoon each fresh rosemary, thyme, and marjoram

2 tablespoons butter

¼ cup flour mixed with 1 cup water for gravy

Preheat the oven to 425°F. Wash the leg of lamb and pat dry. Trim away any fat and silver tissue. Rub the leg all over with the cut lemon. With the tip of a sharp knife, poke small slits in the meat and insert the garlic slivers. Place the lamb in roasting pan. Sprinkle with salt, pepper, and herbs. Dot the top of the leg with butter.

Start roasting the lamb in the oven at 425°F for 15 to 20 minutes. Lower the temperature to 325°F and bake for 1½ to 2 hours. Remove from the oven and transfer to a serving platter, and let it rest until it reaches the desired temperature.

Pour off the excess fat and make the gravy on top of the stove by stirring the flour-water mixture into the roasting pan until the desired consistency is reached. Add the juices that have accumulated from the resting roast. Then carve the roast and serve. Fresh mint sauce goes well with this.

Serves 6 to 8

1, 2, 3 Irish Stew

The true flavor of an Irish stew is lost if carrots or turnips are added, or if it has too much liquid. There are really only three ingredients, plus liquid and seasonings.

1 pound yellow onions

2 pounds potatoes

3 pounds lamb stew meat

1 tablespoon chopped parsley

1 teaspoon dried thyme

2 teaspoons kosher salt

1 teaspoon freshly cracked pepper

2 cups water

Preheat the oven to 350°F. Peel and slice the onions and potatoes. Trim any fat off the meat. Put a third of the potatoes in a pan, sprinkle with half the parsley and thyme, and cover with half of the meat and half of the onions. Season with salt and pepper and repeat this once more, finishing with a layer of potatoes. Pour in the water, cover with foil, and bake in the oven for 2 hours. Check after 1½ hours and add a little more water if the stew seems to be getting dry.

Season to taste with additional salt and pepper. Serve with soft white bread to dip in the gravy, and hot tea with lemon.

Serves 6

Grilled Lamb Sirloin Steaks with Fresh Herb Crust

Ask your butcher to cut these steaks from the top of the leg. The crusty topping adds texture. These can be broiled entirely indoors, but if grilled over charcoal first, they are superb.

1 tablespoon lemon juice

½ cup olive oil

2 cloves garlic, mashed

2 teaspoons Dijon mustard

Six 8-ounce lamb sirloin steaks

Kosher salt and freshly ground black pepper

2 cups fresh bread crumbs

¼ cup chopped parsley

2 cloves garlic, minced

1½ teaspoons chopped fresh rosemary

¼ cup melted butter

Light a charcoal fire.

Mix together the lemon juice, olive oil, mashed garlic, and mustard. Marinate the lamb steaks in this mixture for ½ hour. Remove the steaks from the marinade and place on the hot grill. Sprinkle with salt and pepper. Brush with the marinade while grilling.

Preheat the broiler. In a bowl, mix together the bread crumbs, parsley, minced garlic, rosemary, and melted butter.

When the lamb steaks are cooked just to medium, about 4 to 5 minutes on each side, remove from the grill. Place on a baking sheet, top generously with the bread crumb mixture, and place under the broiler for 1 or 2 minutes, until the crumbs are crisp and golden.

Serves 6

Grilled Flank Steak

In the summertime in the Northwest, on nice sunny days, everyone moves outside. Barbecuing is a way of life through the season, and grilled flank steak is a favorite.

¼ cup vegetable oil

¼ cup soy sauce

3 tablespoons red wine vinegar

2 tablespoons brown sugar

1-inch piece fresh ginger, sliced

2 cloves garlic, sliced

1 teaspoon sesame oil

½ teaspoon red pepper flakes

1 teaspoon toasted sesame seeds

¼ cup chopped green onion

One 2-pound flank steak

In a shallow dish or resealable plastic bag, combine the oil, soy sauce, vinegar, brown sugar, ginger, garlic, sesame oil, pepper flakes, sesame seeds, and green onion. Add the flank steak and marinate for 1 to 2 hours. Broil in the oven or grill for 5 to 10 minutes on each side. Slice across the grain into ½-inch strips.

Serves 4

Calf's Liver with Sautéed Walla Walla Sweet Onions and Peppered Bacon

Calf's liver is delicious cut in strips, floured, and quickly sautéed. The peppery bacon and soft, sweet onions complement the liver. This dish is wonderful served with crisp matchstick fries and steamed rhubarb chard.

1 pound Walla Walla Sweet onions (or, in winter, use sweet yellow onions)

4 tablespoons butter

½ pound thick-sliced peppered bacon

1½ pounds calf's liver

Flour seasoned with salt and pepper

2 tablespoons oil

2 tablespoons red wine vinegar

Cut the onions in quarters and then slice thinly. Sauté in 2 tablespoons of the butter until soft. Reserve. Cut the bacon into ½-inch pieces and cook until crisp. Drain and save.

Cut the liver into 1½-inch strips. Pat gently with a paper towel. Shake in a paper bag with the seasoned flour to coat, then transfer to a wire strainer and toss gently to remove excess flour.

Heat the remaining 2 tablespoons of butter and oil in a large nonstick frying pan over moderate heat, and add the floured strips of liver. Turn up the heat and cook the liver quickly, adding more oil and butter if necessary, until browned all over. Add the vinegar. Transfer to a warm serving platter. I like to grind a little pepper over the liver just before topping it with the onions and bacon.

Serves 4

Stuffed Flank Steak

I like flank steak either stuffed or marinated and grilled. It's a good value, even though it's more expensive than it used to be.

> *¾ pound mild Italian sausage*
>
> *½ cup chopped yellow onion*
>
> *½ cup diced carrot*
>
> *1 Granny Smith apple, peeled and chopped*
>
> *2 cups seasoned bread stuffing*
>
> *1 egg, lightly beaten*
>
> *¼ cup chopped parsley*
>
> *2 cups beef stock*
>
> *One 2-pound flank steak (ask the butcher to butterfly it for you)*
>
> *Herb Sauce (page 259)*

Preheat the oven to 350°F. Break the sausage into small pieces and sauté in a frying pan over medium heat. Transfer to a bowl. Add the onion and carrot to the frying pan and sauté in the drippings until soft. Stir in the apple and cook for 1 minute longer. Add to the sausage. Stir in the bread stuffing, egg, parsley and 1 cup of the beef stock.

Lay the steak open and spread with the sausage mixture, leaving a ¼-inch border on all sides. Loosely roll the steak lengthwise and secure at intervals with string. Place in a roasting pan, seam side down. Pour in the remaining beef stock and bake, covered, for 1½ hours. Let cool 10 minutes before slicing. Serve with Herb Sauce.

Serves 6

Tenderloin of Beef with Red Wine, Walnuts, and Oregon Blue Cheese Butter

Karl Beckley, the creator of this dish, was one of the first chefs to create culinary excitement in the Pacific Northwest.

2 cups red wine

1 ½ cups veal stock

4 small tomatoes, chopped

2 bay leaves

1 ½ teaspoons fresh thyme

1 tablespoon black peppercorns

2 tablespoons chopped shallots

1 pound (4 sticks) unsalted butter, softened and cut in pieces

⅓ cup blue cheese

½ cup walnuts, broken into pieces

4 beef tenderloin steaks (filet mignon)

Place the wine, stock, tomatoes, herbs, peppercorns, and shallots in a saucepan and bring to a boil. Reduce the liquid by half and strain into another saucepan. Return to a boil and reduce to ¼ cup. Cool.

Place the butter, blue cheese, and walnuts in a mixing bowl and begin to whip at low speed. Slowly add the reduced liquid to the butter while whipping. When the ingredients are incorporated, roll the mixture into a log in waxed paper, and refrigerate until ready to serve.

Grill the steaks to the desired doneness. Top each with a slice of the blue cheese butter and serve.

Serves 4

Beef Brisket with Chili-Beer Sauce

Brisket has always been one of my favorite cuts of beef. This is an easy, flavorful way to cook it.

One 4- to 5-pound beef brisket

Flour

2 tablespoons vegetable oil

½ teaspoon salt

Pepper

1 cup chili sauce

1 can (12 ounces) beer

1 medium yellow onion, sliced into thin rings

Preheat the oven to 350°F. Flour the meat lightly. Heat the oil in a heavy frying pan. Brown the meat on all sides. Sprinkle with salt and pepper. Transfer to a baking dish.

Mix the chili sauce with the beer and pour over the brisket. Scatter the onion rings over the top. Place a piece of waxed paper on top of the meat. Cover and bake for 3 hours, or until the meat is tender. Uncover and let rest for 10 minutes before serving.

Serves 6 to 8

Anita's Swedish Meatballs

Anita Myrfors is the best Swedish cook I know. She loves to cook, and her kitchen is always filled with good things to eat.

¾ pound lean ground beef

¼ pound ground pork

1 slice white bread

1 cup heavy cream

1 egg

½ medium yellow onion, finely chopped and sautéed

1 teaspoon salt

¼ teaspoon ground white pepper

½ teaspoon ground allspice

Butter for frying

Gravy

¼ cup flour

1 cup water

¾ cup heavy cream

In a medium bowl, mix the beef and pork together. In a small bowl, soak the bread in the cream. Mix the bread and cream with the ground meat. Stir in the egg, onion, and seasonings.

Roll the meat mixture into small walnut-sized balls. Dip your hands into cold water now and then while rolling, so the meat won't stick to your fingers. Put the formed meatballs on a platter that you've rinsed with cold water.

Brown the butter until golden brown and nutty smelling. Fry the meatballs a few at a time, shaking the frying pan to make them roll around in the butter, browning them evenly. After the meatballs are all browned, return them to the pan and cover them. Cook over low heat until finished cooking (about 5 to 10 minutes). (You can also bake them on a baking sheet at 350°F for 10 to 15 minutes. Then sauté them in a little butter to add flavor and make drippings for gravy.) Transfer to a warm serving dish and make the gravy.

To make the gravy, sprinkle the flour into the frying pan used to cook the meatballs. Stir in the water. Let cook, stirring with a whisk, until you have a nice, velvety sauce. Mix in the cream.

Serve with boiled new potatoes, lingonberry or cranberry preserves, and pickles. *Väl bekomme!*

Serves 4

Bernie Manofsky's Cabbage Rolls

Stuffed cabbage leaves can be made any size. The smaller size is nice for a buffet or as an accompaniment to roast chicken; larger ones are substantial enough for a main course.

2 heads green cabbage

1 pound lean ground beef

½ pound lean ground pork

½ cup uncooked long-grain rice

½ onion, grated

1 clove garlic, minced

2 teaspoons salt

1 teaspoon pepper

1 large can (46 ounces) tomato juice

16 ounces sauerkraut, homemade or fresh store-bought

1 to 2 pounds kielbasa (Polish sausage)

To prepare the cabbage leaves, cut deeply around the core of the cabbage. Steam or parboil the cabbage until the leaves are soft enough to be removed. Separate the leaves and cool on paper towels.

In a medium bowl, combine the beef, pork, rice, onion, garlic, salt, pepper, and ½ cup of the tomato juice. Mix well.

Place 3 tablespoons of the meat mixture on the stem end of a cabbage leaf. Roll until the leaf is wrapped around the meat mixture. Tuck the sides in by pushing the excess leaf into the mixture with your index finger. Repeat until all of the meat mixture is used.

Preheat the oven to 350°F. Place a layer of sauerkraut on the bottom of a roasting pan, then add a layer of cabbage rolls, placing them side by side with the leaf end down. Continue layering. Pour in enough tomato juice to barely cover. Place the kielbasa on top. Cover and bake in the oven for 1½ hours.

Serves 6 to 8

Roast Veal with Morels

A good choice for a spring dinner, when morels are showing up in the woods and the markets. Serve with fresh asparagus and oven-roasted potatoes.

2 tablespoons butter

One 3-pound veal shoulder roast, well trimmed and tied

1 ½ cups chicken stock

½ pound fresh morels, brushed clean with a mushroom brush

1 ½ cups heavy cream

Salt and pepper to taste

Dash of nutmeg

Preheat the oven to 350°F. Melt the butter in a Dutch oven and brown the roast slowly on top of the stove. Add the chicken stock. Remove from heat. Lay a piece of waxed paper directly on top of the meat, and then cover the pot. Bake in the oven for 2 hours, or until the meat is tender.

Slice the morels and place in a sauté pan. Pour in the cream and simmer for 20 minutes, or until the cream has been absorbed by the mushrooms. Season with salt, pepper, and freshly grated nutmeg.

Remove the roast from the pan and place on a serving dish. Add ½ to 1 cup of the pan juices to the mushrooms, and heat and serve with the roast.

Serves 6

Roast Pork Tenderloin with Green Peppercorns

The following recipe is another creation of Susan Vanderbeek.

> Salt and pepper
>
> Two 1- to 1¼-pound pork tenderloins, exterior fat and silver removed
>
> ¼ cup olive oil
>
> ¼ cup apple juice
>
> 2 tart cooking apples, peeled and thinly sliced
>
> Sugar
>
> Pinch of salt
>
> 2 tablespoons white wine
>
> 3 tablespoons green peppercorns, in brine, rinsed and chopped
>
> 1½ tablespoons chopped fresh sage
>
> 6 tablespoons veal glace (or 8 tablespoons chicken stock or light, fruity red wine)
>
> 6 tablespoons butter
>
> Lemon juice

Preheat the oven to 500°F. Salt and pepper the meat. Heat the olive oil in a flameproof, ovenproof pan large enough to hold the tenderloins, and brown the meat on top of the stove. Place in the oven, uncovered, for 6 to 10 minutes, or just until done.

Remove the meat from the pan and keep warm. Place the pan on top of the stove; add the apple juice to the pan. Add the apple slices and dust with sugar and a pinch of salt. Brown the apple slices on both sides, caramelizing slightly. Deglaze the pan with a few tablespoon-fuls of white wine. Add the green peppercorns and fresh sage. Add the veal glace and butter, some lemon juice, and additional salt and pepper if desired.

Carve the meat, place on a warm plate, and pour the sauce around it.

Serves 4

Baked Black Diamond Ham

Oregon and Washington produce some delicious bone-in smoked hams that need no soaking or precooking and require a shorter roasting period than the older-style cured hams. I like baked ham for Sunday dinner with old-fashioned baked beans, creamy coleslaw, and pumpernickel bread.

> One 6-pound half ham
>
> 1 teaspoon dry mustard

¼ teaspoon ground cloves

1 cup brown sugar

¼ cup apple cider vinegar

Preheat the oven to 300°F. Place the ham, skin side up, on a rack in a shallow roasting pan. Do not add water. Do not cover. Bake for 20 minutes per pound at 300°F, or until the internal temperature reaches 155°F to 160°F. Three-quarters of the way through the baking time, remove the ham from the oven, peel off the rind, and with a sharp knife, score the surface of the fat.

In a bowl, mix together the mustard, cloves, brown sugar, and vinegar. Spread over the ham. Return the ham to the oven for about ¾ hour until nicely browned and glazed.

Serves 8 to 10

Pork Loin Roast with Sautéed Apple Slices and Fresh Sauerkraut

Cooking a pork roast on a bed of sauerkraut keeps it moist; the garlic permeates the meat and gives it a wonderful flavor.

One 4-pound double pork loin roast, rolled and tied (2 loins tied together)

3 or 4 cloves garlic

2 tablespoons vegetable oil

2 cups fresh sauerkraut, rinsed and drained

Kosher salt and freshly cracked pepper

1 cup apple cider

2 or 3 Granny Smith apples

3 tablespoons butter

2 tablespoons sugar

Preheat the oven to 350°F. Poke holes 1 inch deep into the pork roast with the tip of a paring knife. Peel the garlic and cut into slivers. Insert the garlic slivers into the holes in the pork. Heat the oil in a large skillet over medium-high heat. Brown the roast on all sides. Spread the sauerkraut in the bottom of a 4-inch-deep roasting pan, then place the browned roast on top. Insert meat thermometer. Sprinkle with salt and pepper. Bake in the oven for 1 hour. Add the cider to the pan. Continue cooking for 1 hour longer, or until the roast reaches an internal temperature of 165°F.

Toward the end of the roasting time, peel and slice the apples. Melt the butter in a skillet and sauté the apples. Sprinkle with sugar and, just before serving, put the pan under the broiler to glaze the apple slices. Remove the roast from the oven and let it rest 10 minutes before slicing. Serve the apples as a side dish.

Serves 6 to 8

Barbecued Pork Tenderloin

This is an example of our developing Northwest food tastes. It makes a great appetizer.

> ¼ cup brown sugar
>
> ½ teaspoon salt
>
> 2 tablespoons hoisin sauce
>
> ¾ teaspoon Chinese five-spice powder
>
> 1 clove garlic, minced
>
> 1 teaspoon grated fresh ginger
>
> ¼ cup white wine
>
> 2 tablespoons soy sauce
>
> 2 pounds boneless pork tenderloin
>
> Hot mustard
>
> Toasted sesame seeds

Mix together the brown sugar, salt, hoisin sauce, five-spice powder, garlic, ginger, wine, and soy sauce to make the marinade. Cut the pork lengthwise into 2½- by 2- by 7-inch strips. Marinate the pork strips for at least 2 hours, or overnight in the refrigerator. When ready to cook, light a charcoal fire and let it burn for 15 minutes. Separate the coals, pushing half to the left and half to the right. Place the pork strips on the grill rack, exactly in the center. Place the lid on the barbecue and cook slowly with the coals always off to the side, not directly underneath.

Allow to cool. Cut into ¼-inch slices. Serve with hot mustard and toasted sesame seeds.

Makes 8 appetizer servings

Homemade Italian Sausage

Donnie Vey was in the meat business for more than 30 years. Every year he, his family, and friends make fresh Italian sausage, which they then freeze.

If you are interested in making your own sausage, I would recommend looking into an electric stuffing machine. They are not too expensive and they make sausage-making fun, not a chore.

10 pounds pork butt (ask the butcher to grind it twice as for chili, and be sure the thyroid gland is removed)

3 tablespoons kosher salt

1 tablespoon red pepper flakes

3 tablespoons ground black pepper

2 tablespoons granulated, dehydrated garlic

3 tablespoons fennel seeds

1 cup red wine

Hog casing (soaked in cold water; change the water several times)

Mix the ground pork with the salt, red pepper, black pepper, garlic, fennel seeds, and wine. Cover with plastic wrap and refrigerate overnight.

Rinse the hog casing well. Squeeze off the excess water. Bunch a strip of casing all the way up on the stuffing nozzle. Tie a knot in the end and slowly start the machine stuffing. Don't overfill the casing—leave a little slack, so you can twist or tie the links every 4 inches.

Lay the sausages on a baking sheet lined with a cotton dish towel. Let rest, uncovered, in the refrigerator overnight to allow the skin to dry out before freezing. Then put the links in freezer bags, wrap in foil, and freeze.

Makes approximately 10 pounds of plump sausage links

Roast Turkey

This is the way James Beard taught us to roast a turkey without stuffing during one of his summer-session classes at Seaside, Oregon. It comes out golden and moist. Turkey roasted this way makes great sandwich meat.

One 11- to 13-pound turkey

1 lemon, cut

¼ cup melted butter

Salt and freshly ground black pepper

Preheat the oven to 400°F. Wipe the interior of the turkey with paper towels to absorb excess juices. Rub the inside with the cut lemon, squeezing out the juice as you rub.

Place the bird on a rack in a shallow roasting pan. Brush completely with melted butter. Sprinkle with salt and lots of pepper. Turn the bird on its side and roast in the oven for 30 minutes. Turn it onto the other side and roast for 30 minutes more. Turn it breast side up and baste with the pan juices. Roast for another hour. Test for doneness by inserting a meat thermometer into the thigh joint. At 170°F it's done. Take care not to overcook it.

Serves 6

Boppo's Turkey Dressing

Here is a wonderful dressing recipe that is 100 years old and was passed down by a grandfather to his granddaughters, with love. As he said, "After about 30 to 45 years, making dressing will come easy. Hope everything turns out 'A-OK' and you have a fine dinner. Will drink a toast to your success!"

1 large loaf of white bread, about 3 days old

Turkey giblets and neck

3 or 4 slices bacon

1 sweet yellow onion

Butter

1 cup diced celery

2 apples, peeled and cored and finely chopped

Salt and pepper to taste

20 or more almonds, ground

2 eggs, beaten

Tear the loaf of bread into small cubes the night before you make your dressing. Place the cubes in a large pan and leave uncovered to dry overnight. That same night, cook the neck, gizzard, heart, and liver in water. When cool enough to handle, remove the neck meat from the bone and remove the gristle and inside lining from the gizzard. Save the cooking juices for the dressing.

Dice the bacon into small squares and fry until slightly crisp. Run the neck meat and giblets through a meat grinder and add to the bacon; stir until well mixed. Set aside on a plate to cool.

The next step is somewhat messy. Finely chop the onion. Then fry it slowly in a large skillet in enough butter to avoid burning until it starts to brown. Add the celery to the onion. Add the apples to the onion-celery mixture. Cook on low heat for 2 to 3 minutes. Remove from the pan and set aside to cool.

While the ingredients are cooling, sprinkle the bread cubes with salt and pepper and mix with your hands. Mix in the ground almonds, and then the bacon mixture.

Add the onion mixture to the bread mixture, a little at a time. Taste for seasoning.

If the dressing seems dry, add some of the reserved cooking juices from the giblets by dipping your fingers into the liquid and stirring it into the dressing. Add the eggs the same way, being careful not to let the dressing get too soggy.

Rub a little salt into the rib cage and breast of the bird. Spoon the dressing into the cavity, but don't pack it in too firmly. It expands while cooking.

Makes enough dressing for an 11- to 13-pound turkey

Lynn's Baked Chicken Dijon

My good friend Lynn Nelson is one of the best home cooks I know. This is an easy dish to prepare ahead of time and serve for a dinner party.

> ¼ *pound (1 stick) butter*
>
> *3 tablespoons Dijon mustard*
>
> *1 clove garlic, minced*
>
> ¼ *cup minced parsley*
>
> *1 cup freshly grated Parmesan cheese*
>
> *2 cups fresh soft bread crumbs*
>
> *6 boneless, skinless chicken breast halves, lightly pounded to flatten slightly*

Preheat the oven to 350°F. Melt the butter in a small saucepan. Blend in the mustard and garlic, stirring until the mustard binds with the butter and starts to thicken. Pour into a shallow dish.

In a shallow dish, mix the parsley, Parmesan cheese, and crumbs, blending well. Dip the chicken breasts in the butter mixture, coating all surfaces, then in the crumb mixture, patting the crumbs onto the chicken to coat well. Place in a shallow baking dish.

The chicken may be refrigerated at this point for several hours, covered with plastic wrap and aluminum foil. Remove the chicken from the refrigerator 30 minutes before preparing.

Bake in the oven for 25 to 30 minutes, until golden brown.

Serves 6

Bon-Bon Chicken

Grilled chicken strips served with spicy peanut sauce for dipping are a favorite at our house. I serve a basket of fresh vegetables for dipping in the sauce along with the chicken. It seems that today, everyone is enjoying finger food. This fits right in.

> *6 boneless, skinless chicken breast halves, lightly flattened so that they are*
> *an even thickness, cut into strips lengthwise, and threaded on presoaked*
> *8-inch wood skewers*

Marinade

> *¼ cup soy sauce*
>
> *1 tablespoon sugar*
>
> *1 teaspoon sesame oil*
>
> *1 clove garlic, minced*
>
> *1 small piece of fresh ginger, sliced*

Peanut Dipping Sauce

> *3 tablespoons peanut butter*
>
> *¼ cup hot chicken stock*
>
> *2 tablespoons soy sauce*
>
> *1 teaspoon sugar*
>
> *1 teaspoon sesame oil*
>
> *1 teaspoon chile oil*
>
> *2 teaspoons rice vinegar*
>
> *2 cloves garlic, minced*

1 teaspoon grated fresh ginger

¼ cup chopped green onion

In a large, shallow dish, mix together the marinade ingredients. Marinate the skewered chicken at room temperature for 30 minutes. In a serving bowl, combine all ingredients for the Peanut Dipping Sauce. Grill skewered chicken strips, turning once, for 2 to 3 minutes on each side. Remove and serve with the dipping sauce.

Serves 6

Gretchen Mather's Roast Chicken with Walla Walla Sweet Onions

Walla Walla Sweet onions are exceptionally sweet, large onions that have too short of a summer season. They are legendary in the Pacific Northwest. "You can eat them like an apple," many claim. My father always made onion sandwiches with them. I slice them, sauté them in a little butter, and keep them in freezer bags, so we can enjoy them year round.

3 Walla Walla Sweet onions (or substitute Vidalia onions)

Two 2½- to 3-pound chickens

¼ cup melted butter

¾ cup white wine

Salt and pepper to taste

Preheat the oven to 400°F. Cut the onions in quarters, then slice thinly. Stuff the inside of each chicken with some of the sliced onions. Sprinkle the remaining onions in an 11-by-13-inch baking pan, forming a bed for the chickens. Place the chickens on the onions and brush with the melted butter. Bake in the oven for 50 minutes.

Remove the chickens to a warm serving platter. Pour the juices and browned onions into a saucepan. Add the wine and cook quickly over high heat for 5 minutes. Season to taste with salt and pepper. Cut the chicken into serving pieces and pour the sauce over them.

In the summertime, I like to roast a chicken the Italian way: Slice a lemon and place it inside the cavity of the chicken, brush with melted butter, and roast at 400°F for 50 minutes. Serve with a summer salad, crusty bread, and fresh berries and cream for dessert.

Serves 6

Charbroiled Curried Quail with Spicy Noodles

Northwest chef Tom Douglas created this spicy dish. Quail are available at Uwajimaya market. They are moist and tender cooked this way, and the spicy noodles make a good accompaniment. If you can't get quail, you can substitute 4 chicken breast halves.

8 quail

6 ounces canned unsweetened coconut milk (available at specialty food stores)

2 tablespoons Thai curry paste (the hot yellow variety)

10 grinds coarse black pepper

4 cloves garlic, mashed

Spicy Noodles (recipe follows)

Split the quail in half and remove the backbone. Mix together the coconut milk, curry paste, pepper, and garlic, and marinate the quail overnight in the refrigerator. (Make the Spicy Noodles ahead of time to give them time to chill.)

When ready to grill the quail, light a charcoal fire. Grill the quail over medium-hot coals for 3 minutes, turn them over, and grill for 2 minutes more.

Serve the quail with the cold Spicy Noodles—a great contrast.

Spicy Noodles

3 tablespoons peanut butter

2 tablespoons water

2 tablespoons soy sauce

3 tablespoons well-stirred tahini or peanut butter

1½ tablespoons soy oil

1½ tablespoons Asian sesame oil

1½ tablespoons dry sherry

1½ tablespoons rice vinegar

2 tablespoons honey

¾ teaspoon minced garlic

¾ teaspoon crushed red pepper flakes

¾ teaspoon grated fresh ginger

8 ounces Chinese egg noodles

¼ cup chopped green onion

In a bowl, stir together the peanut butter and water. Add the soy sauce, tahini, soy oil, sesame oil, sherry, rice vinegar, honey, garlic, red pepper flakes, and ginger, whisking the mixture well after each addition. Chill, covered.

Cook the egg noodles according to the instructions on the package, then rinse under cold water. Drain well and chill, covered.

Mix the noodles and sauce together and sprinkle with green onion just before you are ready to grill the quail.

Serves 4

Grilled Quail on Seasonal Greens with Kalamata Olive Vinaigrette

This is another simple, delicious recipe from Marianne Zdobysz.

> *1 cup olive oil*
>
> *¼ cup white wine*
>
> *1 tablespoon chopped fresh rosemary*
>
> *1 tablespoon chopped shallots*
>
> *4 quail (have your butcher bone them)*

Kalamata Olive Vinaigrette

> *¼ cup kalamata olives*
>
> *2 tablespoons sherry vinegar*
>
> *Salt and pepper*
>
> *¾ cup olive oil*

———

> *Seasonal greens: Bibb lettuce, radicchio, watercress, endive*
>
> *¼ red pepper, julienned*

Combine the olive oil, wine, rosemary, and shallots. Place the quail, skin side down, in a shallow baking dish and pour in the marinade. Set aside at room temperature to marinate for 2 hours.

To make the vinaigrette, pit and coarsely chop the olives. In a bowl, combine the vinegar and salt and pepper to taste. Whisk in the oil and add the olives.

Light a charcoal fire. Remove the quail from the marinade. Grill, skin side down, for 4 minutes. Turn and grill for 4 minutes longer. The quail can also be quickly sautéed over high heat in a heavy-duty pan with 2 tablespoons oil, but the grilled quality will be lost.

Toss the greens with the vinaigrette and place on a plate. Place the quail on the greens and garnish with the julienned red pepper.

Serves 2 to 4

Slow-Baked Pheasant with Sweet Onions and Chanterelles

In the fall in the Pacific Northwest, many a young man's fancy turns to bird hunting: pheasant, quail, ducks, geese. If you are fortunate enough to have a hunter in your family, you can enjoy the bounty of a successful hunt.

In this recipe, the slow cooking makes the pheasant fall off the bone, and the sweet flavor of the onions gives a rich savor to the dish.

> 2 tablespoons olive oil
>
> ¼ pound plus 4 tablespoons (1 ½ sticks) butter
>
> 3 pheasants, cut into pieces and lightly floured
>
> 4 cups red wine
>
> ¼ cup flour
>
> 1 tablespoon sugar
>
> 2 cups sliced yellow onions
>
> ½ pound sliced chanterelles

Preheat the oven to 350°F. Heat the olive oil and 2 tablespoons of the butter together in a skillet and sauté pheasant pieces in batches until browned all over. Transfer to a baking dish.

Pour the red wine into a saucepan and bring to a boil. Boil for several minutes to remove any harsh alcohol flavor.

Mix 4 tablespoons of the butter and the flour together until well blended. Stir into the boiling wine in small pieces, then turn the heat down and stir to thicken. Pour over the pheasant and place a piece of waxed paper directly on top. Bake in the oven for 2 hours.

When the pheasant has been baking for an hour, melt 4 tablespoons of the butter, and add the sugar and onion. Cook over low heat until onion is soft. Add to the pheasant. Cover with waxed paper and continue baking.

When the pheasant is done, melt the remaining 2 tablespoons of butter in a 10-inch skillet and add the sliced chanterelles. Turn up the heat and cook very quickly. (It's important to cook chanterelles in a large, open frying pan as quickly as possible; otherwise they "stew" in their own juices.) Pour the chanterelles over the baked pheasant and serve.

Serves 6

VEGETABLES, SALADS & DRESSINGS

The Double-Dug Life:
GARDENING, FOOD,
and VARIOUS HUNGERS

A marriage headed south took me into a community garden in Seattle, if only to have a place I could call my own. Eight years later, true love took me out.

I picked up and left for Bainbridge Island and the neat little condominium where I would live with my wife, Joyce Thompson, and her children, Alexandra and Ian. My son, Farrell, would join us from time to time on a regular schedule. But the food garden at the Interbay P-Patch that for so long had been so central to my life slipped into my own history. Shopping became my primary connection to food.

The eight years I spent in the Interbay P-Patch were filled with digging and raking and growing and healing. I weeded my garden, and I weeded myself. As disrupted as everything else in my world seemed to get, the garden kept me moving with the cycles, paying attention to the rain and the sun. I was unable to cut myself off from the world, try though I might. I was surrounded by too many gentle souls who could talk forever about soil and salad greens, leaving all the rest unsaid. It was a time I could rub shoulders with older generations and simply take solace in the way they counted and carried their years and kept themselves sane.

Old George, for example, was a mysterious and taciturn gardener with a stooped, bowlegged walk, giant Scandinavian ears, and a nose the size and shape of a small russet potato. He and I were often the first souls in the garden in the morning. If George was working, the most I'd get was a wave of recognition. He kept to himself, whether in the garden, on the bus, or back home in his tiny basement apartment to which I would give him the occasional lift. He grew beets, lettuce, onions, and beans in what he called his "charity garden." George gave away the food he didn't use. He told me he had been a captain of ore boats on the Great Lakes and had retired to Seattle to be closer to his children and grandchildren. I never saw them. In fact, I never saw George with anyone but one old gal who giggled a lot and did most of the talking. Her big, lipsticked lips looked like fields of red poppies. She and George ate potatoes, cabbage, and beets together, and the occasional pan-fried steak. They spoke a secret language of partial words and inconsequential phrases that didn't seem to mean much more than companionship.

There are no Georges in the local supermarkets. Buying food attracts a different population than growing food. It all gets very impersonal until you reach the cash register. If the community is small enough, recognition lights up the face of the checker at the checkout stand. Such is the case for my wife. I must still have years to go.

My disconnection from food grew with each season I didn't garden. I found little solace in the local farmer's market. It brought out envy in me. And I hated my incessant cringing at the price tags on lettuce, herbs, and root crops. I finally began looking around for a place to plant. I realized I could go back to gardening without all the emotional baggage that had taken me there in the first place. This time it would just be about food and dirt.

There's a small triangle of ground on one side of the concrete path that leads to the front door of our condominium. The landscapers had stuffed the plot with a single tree and too many shrubs and covered the ground with Beauty Bark to hide any sins. I watched the plot for two years, watched sun and shadow play with it, watched rain run off it. I watched the cat, Velvet Elvis, sleep on it on hot days, and watched Casper, the family mutt, lift a leg on his favorite shrub each morning that we trudged and scampered together up to the mailboxes for the newspaper. Joyce and I talked about the plot, about what to grow at the front door. And then, last year I tore out everything but the tree, transplanting the shrubs into spots where they'd do a lot better, cutting away the plastic mesh the landscape contractor had left binding the roots, digging holes into which their roots could grow and colonize.

It took two days to double-dig the small plot. I nicked the plastic sprinkler pipe twice and had to replace straight sections and elbow joints. My children studied me from the near distance.

The ground was terrible. First, a prehistoric glacier had scraped away any semblance of topsoil. That had been followed by bulldozers leveling the foundation. The landscape crew had simply mounded into beds what passed for dirt, and shoved their nursery product into the ground as best they could.

I could dig down about two-thirds the length of a garden spade. This is a heavy, forged iron tool. Before I started digging I put on steel-shanked boots. Then I sharpened the spade. Between the boots and the sharp edge, I could work the spade down another quarter length, but no more. It was very hard, very slow going, and it made absolutely no sense to my family or the occasional curious neighbor. But from this effort came three odd-shaped little beds sitting up a couple of feet higher than the surrounding ground, after all the digging and soil amendments. Given proper care and maintenance, the next time I dig down to rock bottom I should be able to go a spade and half, maybe a spade and two-thirds deep.

The best example I have ever seen of this making-soil-from-dirt phenomenon was in northern Mexico. I accompanied John McMillin of Land and Water Resources and a group of his college students from Seattle to an impoverished boarding school for deaf children in the Sonoran desert a couple of hours south of San Diego. The same crew had gone down the year before on a combination mission of mercy and student training exercise. Some school benefactor somewhere along the line had heard about John. He gets pleas for help every week, all of them coming from the poorest of the world's poor. And he does what he can when he can. "Mostly," he says, "what they want is drinking water and food." The Mexican school for the deaf, though poor by any normal standards, seemed a comparatively wealthy operation to McMillin. But it provided him access to a safe field experience for his students.

McMillin is unusual for being able to look at pollution and see nutrients. It's a matter of extraction. He looks at wasteland and sees fertile potential. Since he works with people who can barely afford clothes, let alone tools, the technology he employs to put food on the table is both simple and benign. The projects he designs demand no great capital investment.

In one village in Ethiopia, McMillin organized the children to poke holes with sharpened sticks in ground that would be turned for food gardens. Each morning it was their job to sweep out the family huts and to dump the sweepings into the holes. Then they peed in the holes. It was a big joke. In their local dialect they called their efforts "piss holes." But within a year, when the ground was first worked for intensive kitchen gardens, it wasn't hard and compacted like the surrounding earth. It was friable, alive, and ready to make food happen because of all the nitrogen and organic matter that had been worked into it.

In Mexico the ground was like pavement, void of vegetation, parched. You couldn't sink the tip of a pickax into it, let alone dig. Let alone double-dig, which means going down twice the length of a spade and mixing in compost. The purist in McMillin wanted to do it right, with a spade. But the practical field worker knew better. He found a farmworker with a tractor and chisel plow who dug two long beds four feet wide and two spade lengths deep. Next to the beds the farmworker used the backhoe to dig a deep trench the same length as the beds.

There was no compost on hand, so McMillin used whatever organic matter was available, everything from kitchen garbage to grape skins from a local winery, layering it into the beds, where it would heat up and rot out. The students lined the trench with PVC sheeting, then plastered the bottom with horse manure from a nearby stable. Once filled with water, there was every possibility of raising freshwater fish such as tilapia. The nutrients that leached into the water from the horse manure would feed the duckweed floating on the surface of the pond. A lot of the duckweed would end up in the garden beds, feeding the plants. A lot of the garden trimmings would end up in the pond, feeding the fish.

After two weeks, McMillin and his students left behind a well-organized and carefully planted bio-intensive garden. The deaf students would care for it, watering it by hand from the fish trench.

A year later the garden had become a natural feature of the landscape, a large rectangle of verdant green surrounded by the muted tones of the desert. The deaf students had been able to grow so much produce on such a small piece of land that they had opened a roadside stand to sell their surplus chiles. The fish trench didn't work out as a year-round system; the winters were too cold. But it would work as a grow-out pond for fish hatched elsewhere.

McMillin doesn't just show people how to grow food. His training is in business esoterica. Once he gets an organic engine up and running, he shows people how to turn it into a profit engine. He figured the school for the deaf had the opportunity to take advantage of the high-end resort hotels on Mexico's Pacific coast. If they raised fish, both the fish waste and the pond water would enhance the gardens, much as the waste from the gardens would feed the fish. So the potential was there to supply hotel kitchens with fresh fish as well as gourmet vegetables. Grown intensively, the vegetables would come to market weeks ahead of the normal crop cycle, enhancing their value. Adding a smokehouse to the equation to take advantage of the vinifera vines in the valley would make wine-smoked fish products a possibility. Adding Japanese quail would provide a manure source for the gardens as well as an exotic smoked food product. Expanding the double-dug beds and planting fruit crops could lead to a line of sorbets and fruit compotes, maybe natural fruit drinks, maybe carbonated fruit drinks. The growth could occur well within the capacities of the school to make it happen, bit by bit by bit. The deaf children's nutrition would improve, but so too would their job skills and prospects for survival.

Only one person running the deaf school garden project understood the potential, and he wasn't able to get his point across. So by the time McMillin and his students returned, the surrounding landscape had been plowed and planted with chile peppers fed by drip irrigation that turned the ground surrounding each struggling plant into cement. With no nutrients in the soil, the chile crop demanded substantial applications of chemical fertilizers, which in turn demanded substantial applications of pesticides to protect the weak plants. The financial outlays for all this had to have been considerable. All of this had happened because the students had harvested a bumper crop of chiles from their garden that earned serious money. It looked so easy.

"You can't tell people what to do," McMillin said. "You walk away. You go to the next project. There are just too many desperately poor, desperately hungry people out there. And who knows? Maybe one of those other groups will actually get it."

He told me to try to stick a spading fork into the ground outside the garden fence. The iron tines actually rang out as if I had struck them against solid rock. I came back into the garden. "Now try sticking the fork into the path right here," McMillin said, gesturing at the ground at his feet. This ground between the beds had never been dug up. If anything it had become even more compacted from the intensified foot traffic over the past year. But with no effort on my part the fork slipped right down into the ground the full length of its tines.

"That's what organic gardening does," McMillin said. "Its effects spread in all directions from the place where you do the initial work. It's not just about making garden beds. It's about making fertile soil, fertile conditions. Once you do that, you can make food that is nutritious. Give people the means to feed themselves, particularly lactating mothers and children under five, give them the means to have fish protein as well as vegetables in their diet, and you break the back of poverty. It's that simple."

Joyce and I grew herbs, flowers, basil, and salad greens in our small condominium garden. I'll double-dig it again this spring, and we'll plant more exotic salad greens and mustard greens than the year before, and probably expand the kitchen herbs. It's worth the effort. The nature of a salad picked from the garden and placed on the dinner table bears no resemblance to its various ingredients carefully arranged and sprinkled in supermarket displays. One glows, the other doesn't.

I didn't really understand the nature of the community garden in my life, the hole it had filled, until I had to leave the P-Patch. It was the end of a nasty spring day, the wind blowing up off Elliott Bay. The garden was deserted. The naked branches of the fruit trees I had planted rattled at me.

I walked around in the garden plot for a bit, poking at the soil here and there. The topsoil was a couple of feet deep on ground that had been like a parking lot when I started years before. I sat on the lid of the worm bin and felt an enormous wave of grief sweep through me. This was good-bye to a dear old friend who had seen me through some hard, hard times. The best kind of friend. Always there. I sat alone in the wind and blubbered out my thank-yous and farewells.

And then I left, walking off into a new life. The process of building topsoil simply never ends.

Vegetables & Salads

Fresh Produce Calendar

The last ten years have seen a steady growth in weekly farmer's markets throughout the Pacific Northwest. More and better organic produce is readily available. This list is taken from the weekly "fresh sheet" published by Seattle's Pike Place Market, the oldest farmer's retail market still doing business in America. It shows what is available during the year to Pike Place Market customers. There are highstalls in the market, tended by vendors of commercial fruits and vegetables shipped in from all over, and there are low tables where local farmers sell their wares. Sunday and Wednesday have become organic farmer days from mid-June through October. The market is open all year; however, January's offerings are limited due to cold weather.

February Russian red kale, Scotch curled kale, overwintered cabbage (January King), overwintered cauliflower (Inca), chives, leeks.

March Radishes, baby carrots, last of the broccoli raab, Napa cabbage, Swiss chard, spinach, leeks, shallots, collard greens, arugula, chicory, endive, dandelion greens, radicchio, French sorrel, wild nettle stalks, mâche, watercress, French tarragon, Italian parsley, horseradish root, garlic chives, rosemary, sage, thyme, false morels, turnips, rutabaga.

April Kale, green chard, asparagus, Skagit Valley cauliflower, red and green lettuce (Red Sail, green leaf, romaine), green onions, field-grown rhubarb, mint, oregano, black morels.

May Chinese mustard greens, yu choy, baby bok choy, pea vine (the top 6 inches of the pea vine, used in salads or cooked—a big product for the Indochinese Farming Project), Chinese broccoli, butter lettuce, pepper cress, lamb's-quarter, fennel, dill, calendula and viola (edible flowers), boletus mushrooms (porcini, cèpes).

June Sugar snap peas, daikon radish, sea asparagus (a wild succulent harvested in marine estuaries, also called sea bean—the green is vaguely bean shaped; it has an intense, salty flavor and is used as a pickle), English shelling peas, Chinese snow peas, haricots verts, zucchini, red kohlrabi, mustard greens, shungiku, fennel, savory, marjoram.

July Golden beets, vine-ripened tomatoes, sweet slicing cucumbers, kohlrabi, sweet corn, beans (Kentucky Wonder, Blue Lake, fava, Romano, Royal Purple), squash blossoms, Skagit Valley broccoli, baby scallop squash, red and white Swiss chard, Chinese spinach, chrysanthemum leaves, nasturtium (edible flower, peppery), basil, anise hyssop, Walla Walla sweet onions, baby red onions, German purple potatoes.

August Pickling cucumbers, purple cauliflower, lemon cucumbers, peppers (jalapeño, yellow wax, green bell, red pimento, peperoncini), eggplant (purple and white, Japanese miniature), haricots verts, baby yellow zucchini, pattypan squash, yellow wax beans, red and white shell beans, endive, cinnamon basil, fresh dill, chanterelles.

September Yellow pear tomatoes, peppers (Hot Portugal, Hungarian Hot Wax, Crooked Green Bell, Sweet Chocolate), squash (golden acorn, Sweet Dumpling, Green Hokkaido winter squash, buttercup), Jack-Be-Little miniature pumpkins, green tomatoes, fall asparagus, savoy cabbage, red cabbage, spinach, sauce tomatoes, Yellow Taxi tomatoes, okra, Romanesco broccoli, Russian red kale,

French sorrel, oregano, thyme, watercress, caraway, lovage, rosemary, epazote (peppery herb from Mexico), shiitake mushrooms, chestnuts, walnuts.

October
Siberian tomatoes, orange bell peppers, flowering kale, fall radicchio, brussels sprouts, leeks, hazelnuts.

November
Jerusalem artichokes, savoy cabbage, kale, chard, golden and red beets, Siberian kale, acorn squash, radicchio, escarole, turnips, parsnips, bulb fennel, Roja garlic (very spicy), chestnuts, walnuts.

December
Turnips, parsnips, salsify.

How to Select and Store Vegetables
Always buy firm, unblemished produce. The fresher it is, the shinier it looks. Zucchini is a perfect example. It should glisten. Store in your refrigerator and use right away. Of course, growing your own is the best.

Buy tomatoes in the late summer, when they are the real thing and are so sweet. Fresh corn and sweet fresh peas should be picked and eaten as soon as possible. Store Walla Walla sweet onions in panty hose in a cool place in your garage. Tie a knot in between each onion, then hang them high.

Freeze fresh berries in freezer bags. (Slice and sugar strawberries before freezing.) Freeze sliced peaches in plastic containers. Place in plastic freezer containers. Pour over orange juice and enjoy in mid-winter.

Fiddlehead Ferns

Gather the small, unopened fronds of ferns in the spring. Remove the papery brown wrapping. Wash the fronds carefully in cold water. Place in a saucepan. Cover with water, add a few drops of vegetable oil, and boil for a few minutes. Drain in a strainer. Sprinkle lightly with a little sugar. Place in a shallow serving dish and pour a small amount of light soy sauce over the fronds. Serve at room temperature. These have a "wild" taste, like wild asparagus, and an interesting texture.

Italian Sausage–Stuffed Mushrooms

Sometimes the market will have huge mushrooms, perfect for stuffing. I serve them with warm marinara sauce on the side.

4 ounces Italian sausage

1 clove garlic, minced

1 cup fresh bread crumbs

½ cup grated Parmesan cheese

2 tablespoons chopped fresh parsley

1 teaspoons chopped fresh marjoram

4 tablespoons butter

12 jumbo fresh mushrooms

¼ cup white wine

Preheat the oven to 375°F. In a skillet, sauté the sausage, remove the casing, and break into small pieces. Drain off excess grease. Add the garlic. Remove from the heat and stir in the bread crumbs, Parmesan cheese, parsley, and marjoram. Melt the butter and pour over the bread crumb mixture.

Remove the stems from the mushrooms. Fill the caps with the bread crumb mixture, mounding the filling in each cap. Place in a buttered shallow baking dish. Pour in the wine. Bake for 15 minutes.

Makes 4 appetizer servings

Baked Morels with Herb Crust

Springtime in the Northwest is morel season. This is the beginning of our Northwest bounty, which runs well into September. Serve with roast chicken or meat.

1 pound fresh morels (or you can substitute fresh cultivated mushrooms)

¼ pound (1 stick) butter

½ cup heavy cream

2 cups fresh bread crumbs

1 tablespoon chopped fresh thyme

1 tablespoon chopped chives

Preheat the oven to 375°F. Slice the mushrooms. Melt 4 tablespoons of the butter in a skillet, and sauté the mushrooms. Place in a 9-inch glass quiche pan or pie dish. Pour in the cream. Mix together the bread crumbs, thyme, and chives. Melt the remaining 4 tablespoons of butter and combine with the crumbs. Spread the crumbs over the mushrooms and bake for 25 minutes, until crisp and golden.

Serves 6

Green Beans and Tomatoes

This is a dish for July and August, when the green beans are crisp and sweet and tomatoes are at their peak. In winter, you can substitute canned tomatoes, but it won't be quite the same.

1 pound fresh green beans

2 cloves garlic, sliced

⅓ cup olive oil

4 large, fresh tomatoes, seeded and chopped (or 1 large can chopped tomatoes)

Wash and trim the green beans. Snap in half. In a large skillet, warm the garlic in the olive oil. Add the beans, coating them well with olive oil, and sauté for 5 minutes. Add the tomatoes. Cover partially and simmer over low heat for 15 minutes, adding a little water if necessary.

Leave the lid slightly ajar to prevent condensation from forming inside the lid, which can discolor the beans, turning them a dull grey color.

Serves 4

Buttered Peas with Fresh Mint

The peas grown in Seaside, Oregon, were James Beard's favorites. Once peas are picked, the sugar turns to starch and the flavor fades. In an ideal world, you can pick, shell, and eat your peas all in one summer evening without cooking. If you must cook them, or have enough left to cook, here's how!

> 4 cups shelled fresh peas
>
> 1 cup water
>
> ½ teaspoon sugar
>
> 4 tablespoons butter, softened
>
> 1 tablespoon chopped fresh mint

Put the peas, water, and sugar in a saucepan. Cover and cook for 5 minutes over high heat. Remove from the heat, drain, and stir in the butter and mint.

Serves 4

Skagit Valley Yellow Pea Soup

Skagit Valley is a fertile farmland valley one hour north of Seattle. One of its main crops is peas. You can buy bags of dried Skagit Valley peas and make a delicious soup. In Swedish homes in the Northwest, yellow pea soup is a traditional dish. Serve this soup with grilled ham and cheese sandwiches.

> 2 cups dried yellow split peas
>
> 6 cups cold water
>
> 1 large onion, chopped
>
> 1 ham hock, cut into 1-inch slices (see note)
>
> 6 whole allspice
>
> Salt
>
> Freshly ground pepper

Wash the peas and place them in a 4-quart stockpot. Add the water and bring to a boil. Boil for 5 minutes, turn off the heat, and let the peas soak for 1 hour. Add the onion, ham hock, and allspice, and simmer for 1½ hours.

Season to taste with salt and freshly ground pepper.

Note: You'll need to have your butcher cut through the ham hock with a meat saw, unless you are willing and able to wield a hacksaw at home.

Serves 4 to 6

Stir-Fried Baby Bok Choy, Shiitake Mushrooms, Sugar Snap Peas, and Yellow Peppers

This is a good-looking, stylish combination that takes full advantage of some of the produce we now routinely enjoy in the Pacific Northwest. The shiitake are part of the region's great mushroom bounty; baby bok choy (see note) has become increasingly popular in the Pacific Northwest; yellow peppers and sugar snap peas thrive in season here and are widely cultivated to meet market demand. The method of cooking is part of a long tradition of the Chinese immigrants who settled here.

High heat is the essential element of the stir-fry technique. The ingredients are quickly tossed and sautéed in a small amount of oil. The key to success is adding the ingredients in the right order, beginning with those that will take the longest time to cook.

Always do your stir-frying just before serving, and remember: the whole procedure should take only 3 to 5 minutes.

1½ pounds baby bok choy

2 large fresh shiitake mushrooms

½ pound sugar snap peas

½ red bell pepper

½ yellow bell pepper

1 tablespoon vegetable oil

1 clove garlic, peeled

1 small piece fresh ginger, peeled

1 to 2 tablespoons light soy sauce

1 to 2 teaspoons sesame oil

½ teaspoon black sesame seeds

Cut the bok choy into diagonal slices ½ inch thick. Slice the mushrooms into thin strips. String, rinse, and drain the sugar snap peas. Seed the peppers and slice into thin julienne strips.

Heat a heavy skillet or wok, add the oil, and fry the garlic and ginger for a few seconds and remove. Add the pepper strips and cook for 1 minute. Then add the sugar snap peas and cook 1 minute longer, always stirring and tossing the vegetables as they cook. Add the mushrooms and finally the bok choy. Transfer to a warm serving dish and sprinkle with soy sauce, sesame oil, and sesame seeds. Serve immediately.

Note: Bok choy is a member of the Brassica family, along with cabbage, kale, broccoli, and the mustards. A mainstay with many varieties, it has large, spoon-shaped leaves with thick white stems. Baby bok choy is a popular miniature version. It is difficult to get the leaves and stems to cook at the same rate, so it is best to settle for tender leaves with slightly crunchy stems.

Serves 6

Murphy's French-Fried Onion Rings

Serve these as an appetizer to your friends while they are waiting for dinner.

2 large Walla Walla sweet onions, or another type of sweet onion

1 egg, separated

1 cup milk

1 tablespoon vegetable oil

¾ cup plus 2 tablespoons flour

2 teaspoons salt

1 ½ teaspoons baking powder

2 cups Panko crumbs

Vegetable oil for deep-fat frying

Peel the onions and slice them about ½ inch thick. Separate into rings. Cover with cold water and soak for 30 minutes. Drain on paper towels.

In a medium bowl, beat together the egg yolk, milk, and 1 tablespoon oil. Mix together the flour, salt, and baking powder and add to liquid mixture, blending to a smooth batter. Heat vegetable oil to 350°F. Beat the egg white until stiff and fold into the batter. Dip the onion rings in batter, then in Panko crumbs, and fry in hot oil until golden, turning once. Serve in a napkin-lined basket. Sprinkle lightly with salt.

Serves 4

Onion Marmalade

The sweet-and-sour taste of this condiment complements roasts, cold meats, and game.

2 large Walla Walla sweet onions

4 tablespoons butter

¼ cup water

¼ cup sugar

1 teaspoon salt

¼ cup white wine vinegar

Preheat the oven to 275°F. Slice the onions crosswise, ½ inch thick. Heat the butter and water in a 10-inch cast iron skillet. Stir in the sugar and salt, then add the vinegar and onions. Bake, uncovered, for 1 hour. The onions will cook down and become lightly glazed.

Serves 4

Diane's Harvest Onion Soup

A fast, easy, and lighter version of the classic French onion soup. Serve with toasted slices of French bread—baguette size—to eat with the soup, rather than floating them in it. I like to serve this soup in mugs while everyone is still standing, as a signal that dinner's ready. It's a good soup for a thermos, too.

5 tablespoons butter

3 cups thinly sliced Walla Walla sweet onions

¼ cup chopped celery leaves

2 sprigs parsley

4 cups chicken broth

Salt and pepper to taste

Parmesan cheese

In a large skillet, melt the butter and add the onions, celery leaves, and parsley. Partially cover and cook over low heat until the onions are tender, 20 to 25 minutes. Let cool.

Put the onion mixture and broth in a blender and add salt and pepper to taste; process quickly. Reheat and serve sprinkled with Parmesan cheese.

Serves 8

Ellie's Dilly Green Beans

I give a jar of these beans and a quart jar of my homemade Bloody Mary mix to my friends for Christmas presents.

4 pounds whole green beans

Crushed red pepper flakes

½ teaspoon whole mustard seed

Fresh dill

7 cloves garlic, peeled

5 cups vinegar

5 cups water

½ cup pickling salt

Wash the beans and pack into sterilized pint canning jars. Add ¼ teaspoon hot red pepper flakes, ½ teaspoon mustard seed, a sprig of fresh dill, and a garlic clove to each jar. In a saucepan, bring the vinegar, water, and salt to a boil. Pour into the jars to within ½ inch of the top. Screw on sterilized lids and process in boiling water for 15 minutes to seal properly.

Makes 7 pints

Irene Jue's Pickled Walla Walla Sweet Onions

The Walla Walla sweet onion is so good it should be named the Washington State flower. The sad part is that the season is over much too quickly. Here is a way to stretch it through the winter.

> *2 pounds Walla Walla sweet onions, each onion cut into eighths*
>
> *4 cups water*
>
> *7 tablespoons kosher salt*
>
> *4 cups distilled white vinegar*
>
> *1 cup sugar*
>
> *8 whole chile peppers, or 1 per jar*

Put the onion sections into a large bowl. Combine the water and 6 tablespoons of the salt and pour over the onions. Cover and refrigerate overnight. Drain the onions; rinse with cold running water.

Bring the vinegar, sugar, the remaining 1 tablespoon salt, and the chile peppers to a boil; add the onions and simmer for 3 minutes. Pack into hot, sterilized pint canning jars and seal with sterilized lids. Process in boiling water for 15 minutes to seal properly. Cool to room temperature. Refrigerate until cold. Will keep up to 3 months unrefrigerated.

Makes 8 pints

Walla Walla Sweet Onion and Cheddar Cheese Strata

A wonderful side dish with baked ham or leg of lamb.

6 eggs

2½ cups half-and-half

1 teaspoon Dijon mustard

1 teaspoon Worcestershire sauce

1 teaspoon kosher salt

5 cups firm-textured white bread cut in ¾-inch cubes (crust can be left on)

2 large Walla Walla sweet onions, quartered and thinly sliced

2 cups grated cheddar cheese

Preheat the oven to 350°F. In a medium bowl, beat together the eggs, half-and-half, mustard, Worcestershire sauce, and salt. Place half of the bread in a 2-quart soufflé dish. Layer half of the onions, then half of the cheese, in the dish, and repeat. Slowly pour the egg mixture over the top. Let set in refrigerator for at least 2 hours, or as long as overnight. Bake in the oven until golden brown on top, 50 to 60 minutes.

Serves 6

Golden Marinated Carrots

These are a good accompaniment to smoked meats, or pack them along on a picnic.

2 pounds carrots

1 green pepper

1 white onion

½ cup vegetable oil

¾ cup apple cider vinegar

1 can (10¾ ounces) tomato soup

¾ cup sugar

1 teaspoon Dijon mustard

Peel the carrots and slice diagonally into ½-inch slices. Cook in simmering water until just tender. Drain and cool. Seed the green pepper and cut into thin strips. Cut the onion into slices ½ inch thick. Mix the vegetables together. In a blender, thoroughly blend the oil, vinegar, soup, sugar, and mustard. Pour over the mixed vegetables and refrigerate overnight.

Serve as a condiment, like pickles.

Labor Day Corn on the Cob

Every Labor Day we visit close friends in Ellensburg, Washington, and feast on fresh corn. James Beard thought that fresh corn was the perfect first course. We put the pot on to boil, then go and pick the corn. We drop it in the boiling water and eat it within a half hour of its being picked, an annual treat.

Freshly picked ears of corn
Large pot one-third full of boiling water
Butter
Salt and pepper

Husk the corn. Drop into boiling water and cover. Cook for 3 minutes. Remove the corn with tongs and serve immediately with lots of butter, salt, and pepper.

Cauliflower with Tillamook Cheddar Cheese

Cauliflower is a major crop in the Northwest, especially in the Skagit Valley in northwestern Washington. Tillamook cheddar cheese is a regional cheddar from Oregon and a great favorite.

1 small head cauliflower
4 tablespoons butter, softened
1 cup grated Tillamook cheddar cheese
Pepper

Trim the cauliflower but leave the head whole. Plunge into boiling water, cover, and cook for 10 to 12 minutes, until a knife inserts easily into the center of the head. Drain well. Break the head into pieces over a warm serving bowl. Spread with the soft butter and add a few grinds of coarse pepper. Sprinkle with the grated cheddar cheese.

Serves 6

One-Minute Asparagus

I like to have everyone seated before cooking the asparagus. To me, asparagus in the spring is a star and deserves full attention at the right moment.

> *1 pound asparagus*
> *4 tablespoons butter*
> *1 lemon, cut into wedges*

Trim or break the white ends off the asparagus. Wash well. If you have early spring asparagus, you won't need to peel it; otherwise, give each spear several strokes with a vegetable peeler, rotating the spear on a cutting board as you go. Place the asparagus in a shallow frying pan and cover with lukewarm water. Bring to a boil, uncovered, and cook for exactly 1 minute. Drain immediately and place on a cloth napkin to absorb excess moisture, then transfer to a warm serving dish.

Meanwhile, quickly melt the butter in the same pan and, just when it begins to bubble and turn a golden brown, pour it over the asparagus. Serve immediately with lemon wedges.

Serves 4

Baked Spaghetti Squash with Parmesan Cheese

You can add a cup of grated raw zucchini to the cooked spaghetti squash. It adds a sweet flavor and a nice green color.

> *1 spaghetti squash, weighing about 2 pounds*
> *6 tablespoons butter*
> *1 cup grated raw zucchini (optional)*
> *Salt and pepper*
> *Dash of ground nutmeg*
> *½ cup grated Parmesan cheese*

Preheat the oven to 375°F. Place the whole spaghetti squash in a baking pan and bake in the oven for 1 hour, or until soft to the touch.

Remove from the oven and let the squash cool until it can be handled. Cut in half lengthwise. Remove the seeds. Scrape out the spaghetti-like strands of squash into a shallow baking dish. Toss with the butter. (Add the zucchini at this point if desired.) Add salt, pepper, and nutmeg to taste. Sprinkle with freshly grated Parmesan and serve.

Serves 6

Baked Acorn Squash

Nothing says fall is here better than baked acorn squash for dinner.

2 acorn squash

4 tablespoons butter

½ cup brown sugar

Preheat the oven to 400°F. Cut the squash in half, remove the seeds and strings, and then fill each half with 1 tablespoon butter and 2 tablespoons brown sugar. Place in a baking dish, cover with foil, and bake for 40 minutes. Remove the foil and bake 10 minutes longer.

Serves 4

Odessa's Yellow Summer Squash

If you have a garden in the Northwest, you usually have an abundance of yellow summer squash. This method of cooking seals in the moisture so that you don't end up with a watery concoction.

1 small red bell pepper

1½ pounds summer squash

1 small yellow onion

3 tablespoons butter

Kosher salt and pepper to taste

½ teaspoon sugar

2 eggs, well beaten

1 cup half-and-half

½ cup grated cheddar cheese

Preheat the oven to 325°F. Dice the pepper into small pieces. Cut the squash in half lengthwise, then slice it ½ inch thick. Dice the onion. In a skillet, melt the butter and sauté pepper, squash, and onion briefly. Season to taste with salt and pepper. Transfer to a buttered shallow baking dish.

Mix together the sugar, eggs, half-and-half, and cheese, and pour over the vegetables in the dish.

Bake for 45 minutes, or until set and golden brown on top.

Serves 6

Baked Butternut Squash with Nutmeg and Maple Syrup

Butternut squash has a smooth and creamy consistency. It makes wonderful soups.

1 butternut squash

1 cup apple juice

Nutmeg

4 tablespoons butter, melted

¼ cup maple syrup

Preheat the oven to 400°F. Cut the squash in half and remove the seeds. Place the squash, cut side down, in a baking dish. Pour the apple juice around the squash and add a few gratings of nutmeg. Bake in the oven for 45 minutes to 1 hour, until fork tender. Cut into serving pieces, combine the melted butter and syrup, and pour over the squash.

Serves 6

Butter-Steamed Beets and Carrots

Make this from the last remnants of a summer garden. The sweetness of the carrots adds to the earthiness of the beets.

4 or 5 small beets

6 to 8 small carrots

4 tablespoons butter

½ cup water

Salt and pepper to taste

Peel the beets and cut into wedges. Peel and slice the carrots. Place in a saucepan with the butter and water, and cover with a tight-fitting lid. Simmer gently for 12 to 15 minutes. Sprinkle with salt and pepper and serve. This also makes a delicious purée.

Serves 4

Pickled Beets

Serve these chilled during the winter holidays and on summer picnics.

    3 to 4 pounds medium-sized beets

    2 cups sugar

    2 cups water

    2 cups vinegar

    1 lemon, thinly sliced

    1 tablespoon ground cinnamon

    1 teaspoon ground cloves

    1 teaspoon ground allspice

Cook the beets in boiling water until just tender and the skins slip off easily. Cut into slices or chunks. Pack into sterilized jars.

Simmer the rest of the ingredients in a 3-quart saucepan for 15 minutes.

Bring the syrup to a boil and pour over the beets, leaving ½ inch of room at the top. Screw on sterilized lids and process in a water bath for 20 minutes.

Makes 6 to 8 pints

Beet and Sausage Soup

A hearty, sweet-and-sour soup that is delicious in the fall.

    4 tablespoons butter

    2 medium-sized onions

    1 clove garlic, crushed

    1 can (28½ ounces) canned tomatoes, diced (including juice)

    4 quarts rich beef broth

    1½ pounds new potatoes

    1 pound spicy country-style breakfast sausage

    2 pounds medium-sized beets

    ½ head cabbage

    ½ cup red wine vinegar

    1 tablespoon sugar

    Sour cream

    Chopped chives

In a large soup pot, melt the butter over medium heat. Add the onions and sauté slowly. Add the garlic and cook just until the onions are soft. Add the tomatoes and beef broth.

Dice the potatoes and add to the pot. In a skillet, crumble the sausage, lightly brown, and drain. Add to the soup.

Wash, peel, and grate the beets and put them in the pot. Shred the cabbage and stir in. Add the vinegar and sugar and cook for 30 minutes. This soup is best served the same day, because the color of the beets will fade overnight. Serve with sour cream and chives.

Serves 8

Skagit Valley Sauerkraut

My good friend Father Mike Schmidt used to make sauerkraut every fall, which he served at a potluck supper for at least 60 people in October. Everyone loved it! And everyone who knew him misses him.

> 6 to 8 heads green cabbage
>
> ½ tablespoon kosher salt per ½ head of cabbage, or 3½ tablespoons salt for every 4 to 5 pounds of cabbage
>
> Caraway or dill seed
>
> Small russet potato, grated

Shred 3 to 4 heads of cabbage into a 5-gallon crock. Add the salt and mix with your hands. Pound the cabbage with your fist until juice starts to appear. Add 3 or 4 more heads of shredded cabbage and repeat until the crock is almost full. Put a large plate on top and place a heavy rock on top of the plate to weight down the cabbage.

Ferment the cabbage for 10 to 14 days in a 60°F room. Skim off any impurities every 2 days. Then freeze in half-gallon milk cartons. Makes enough to fill 6 to 8 cartons.

To serve, simmer 1 quart of sauerkraut with 1 tablespoon caraway or dill seed for 50 minutes. Add the small russet potato, grated, and simmer 10 minutes longer. Serve with good German-style sausage and boiled potatoes.

Sweet-and-Sour Sauerkraut Slaw

This is a delicious accompaniment to corned beef and makes a great Reuben sandwich.

4 cups sauerkraut, well drained

1 cup chopped celery

½ cup chopped red pepper

½ cup chopped green pepper

1 cup chopped green onion

1 cup sugar

¼ cup vegetable oil

¾ cup white vinegar

In a large bowl, combine the sauerkraut, celery, red and green pepper, and green onion. Mix well. Blend the sugar, oil, and vinegar together and pour over vegetables. Cover and refrigerate overnight.

Serves 8 to 10

Sweet-and-Sour Cabbage

Cabbages from the Skagit Valley and crisp apples from the Okanogan region combine to perfectly complement pork, duck, or sausage—all of which make a hearty fall dinner. It's also a tradition with Thanksgiving turkey in many homes.

4 tablespoons butter

½ yellow onion, cut into thin slices

1 medium-sized head red cabbage, cut in quarters

½ cup white wine vinegar

½ cup water

2 tablespoons red currant jelly

Salt and pepper to taste

2 Granny Smith apples, cut into thin slices (unpeeled)

In a large enameled pan, melt the butter and sauté the onions. Thinly slice the cabbage and add it to the pan. Add the vinegar, water, red currant jelly, salt, and pepper. Stir until well mixed. Cover, leaving the lid slightly ajar, and cook over low heat for 25 minutes. Add the apples and cook for 10 minutes longer.

Serves 6

Roasted Vegetables

Roasting vegetables caramelizes the sugars and gives a sweet, toasted flavor.

Roasted Beets

Cut the tops off the beets, leaving 1 inch of stems. Place on a baking sheet and roast at 400°F until tender, 45 to 50 minutes. Insert the tip of a knife to test whether they are cooked all the way through to the center. Let cool, then remove the outside skin. (In the markets in France, they sell beets already roasted and peeled.)

Roasted Corn

Remove the cornhusks and silk completely from each ear of corn. Place on a barbecue and roast for 1 minute, roll a quarter turn, and roast for another minute. Continue for a total of 4 minutes. Remove from the heat. Slather with butter. So sweet!

Roasted Garlic

This recipe comes from South Bay Farm, near Olympia.

> 1 large bulb garlic
>
> 1 tablespoon olive oil
>
> ¼ teaspoon dried basil
>
> ¼ teaspoon dried thyme
>
> Freshly ground pepper to taste

Preheat oven to 350°F. Cut ¼ inch off the top of the garlic bulb. Remove the loose outer leaves. The bulb should remain intact. Pour the olive oil over the bulb. Sprinkle with basil, thyme, and pepper. Place in a garlic baker. For a medium to large bulb, bake for 50 minutes. For an extra-large bulb, bake for an additional 10 minutes. Separate the cloves and squeeze out the garlic.

Serve with warm, crusty bread.

Roasted Asparagus

> 2 bunches fresh Washington asparagus (about 2 pounds); stalks should be the size of your index finger
>
> ¼ cup olive oil
>
> Kosher salt to taste
>
> Freshly ground black pepper

Preheat the oven to 425°F. Snap the tough ends off the asparagus spears. Place on a baking sheet. Pour the olive oil over the asparagus and stir with your hands to coat each spear, especially the tips. Sprinkle with salt and pepper to taste.

Roast for 10 minutes, until very lightly browned. Serve warm or at room temperature.

Serves 6

Cooking with Potatoes

We have wonderful potatoes in the Pacific Northwest: small red potatoes the size of walnuts, wonderful half-pound (and larger) russets for baking, Yellow Finns, buttery and delicious, and the favorite all-purpose potato, the Yukon Gold.

It's important to use the right potato for the desired results.

Russets
Use russets for making baked potatoes, hash browns, and mashed potatoes.

Small Red Potatoes
Small red potatoes are so sweet and delicious I could eat them a different way every day.

Yukon Golds
These have a good texture for mashing, boiling, or frying. They are great in potato salads. You can even bake them.

Yellow Finns
These are becoming increasingly more available. They are a buttery yellow color and are best when boiled and then used like a new potato. Do peel them after cooking. They make a wonderful salad with sliced Walla Walla sweet onions and Malt Vinegar Dressing, page 138. Serve with thick slices of garden-ripe tomatoes and a nice roast chicken.

White Rose Potatoes
Also called boiling potatoes, these make good potato salad and are also good sliced and pan-fried with onions.

To make baked potatoes:

Preheat the oven to 400°F. Scrub the potatoes (russets) well. Pat them dry or air-dry them completely. Poke the potatoes several times with a fork to keep them from exploding in the oven. Bake for 1 hour (you can leave them in the oven longer if you are not ready to eat yet). Remember that a good baked potato is like a soufflé—as soon as it is removed from the oven it starts to cool; it starts to steam and collapse inside the skin, becoming dense and compact. If you won't be serving them right away, leave the potatoes in the oven. The outer edge of the potatoes will continue to cook and will have a wonderful crisp texture. Don't turn the heat down! This will cause the potatoes to collapse.

To open a potato, cover it with a towel and strike it with your fist. The potato will burst open, fluffy and dry. Let everyone help themselves to lots of butter, sour cream, chopped chives, and freshly grated Parmesan cheese—and lots of freshly cracked pepper.

To make golden hash browns:

Cook your potatoes the day before, as follows: Place unpeeled russet potatoes in a large pot. Cover with cold water, bring to a boil, turn down the heat, and continue boiling gently. Cook for 20 minutes. Drain. Leave in the pot until cool. Refrigerate overnight.

The next morning, peel and grate the potatoes. Heat 3 tablespoons each of butter and oil in a heavy 10-inch skillet. Add 6 cups of grated cooked potatoes, lightly pressing them into the pan. Cook one side of the potatoes until golden brown, then flip them out onto a plate. Add additional butter and oil to the pan. Return the potatoes to the pan and cook on the other side. Sprinkle with salt and freshly cracked pepper. Serve with crisp bacon and warm applesauce.

To make fluffy mashed potatoes:

Peel russet or Yukon Gold potatoes and cut into quarters. Cook in boiling salted water until soft; drain. Shake them in the pan over low heat until white and mealy. (I use a heavy enameled pan.) Mash with a potato masher. To 3 cups mashed potatoes add ½ cup hot milk and ¼ cup soft butter. Continue mashing until smooth and fluffy.

To boil potatoes:

Always start them in cold water, then cook until soft. I test with the tip of a small paring knife. Drain off the water, and shake the potatoes in the pan over low heat, covered, for several minutes. This tightens the skin and keeps it from falling off in potato salads.

I never peel the small red potatoes, because the skin is so tender and colorful. Once they are boiled, I love to serve them with a fresh fish dinner, tossed with melted butter and fresh chives from the garden. You can also steam them or simply put them in a casserole with a lid, drizzle them with a little olive oil, sprinkle them with chopped shallots, and bake, covered, until tender.

Good hot or cold, they make a delicious cold potato salad. Cut them up and fry them in butter for wonderful fried potatoes, or use them in a good corned beef or chicken hash.

Potato Gratin

This is the best potato dish I've ever made. Ellie Chasey, who lives in the south of France, shared it with me. It's on my top ten list of favorite recipes.

> *2½ pounds Yukon Gold potatoes*
> *2 beaten egg yolks*
> *1½ cups half-and-half*
> *1 teaspoon salt*
> *½ teaspoon ground white pepper*
> *1½ cups grated Gruyère cheese*
> *2 tablespoons butter*

Preheat the oven to 375°F.

Peel and thinly slice the potatoes. Arrange in a buttered casserole. (I recommend an oval baker 9 inches by 14 inches, 2 to 3 inches deep.)

In a separate bowl, whisk together the egg yolks, half-and-half, salt, pepper, and ½ cup of the cheese.

Pour over the potatoes and top with the remaining cheese. Dot with the butter and bake until the cheese is bubbly and golden brown (about 1 hour). The potatoes should be soft and easily pierced with a knife.

Note: You can also use new red potatoes, thinly sliced—and you don't even have to peel them.

Serves 6

Oven-Roasted Potatoes

These are nice to serve with a roast leg of lamb, roast veal, or roast chicken.

4 russet potatoes

4 tablespoons butter

¼ cup vegetable oil

Salt and pepper

Preheat the oven to 375°F. Peel the potatoes and cut each crosswise into 4 pieces. In a small skillet, melt the butter and add the oil. Place the potatoes cut side down in a 9- by 13-inch glass baking dish and pour in the butter-oil mixture. Make certain the potatoes are well coated by turning them over several times. Sprinkle with salt and pepper and bake for 1 hour.

Serves 6

Baby Red Potatoes with Sautéed Walla Wallas, Cougar Gold Cheese, and Coarse Black Pepper

At the Pike Place Market in Seattle, we can find small red potatoes the size of walnuts. I keep a bin in the refrigerator filled with them. I can use them to make a wonderful potato salad, or I can boil them and then fry them in butter, or use them for clam chowder, hash, or in this recipe, which can serve as Saturday's lunch or a late snack. I like to serve something salty on the side—a dish of imported green olives, or smoked hard-shell clams or oysters—and a simple green salad.

12 small red potatoes

3 to 4 tablespoons butter

½ Walla Walla sweet onion, cut in crescent slices

Coarsely ground black pepper

Generous handful of grated Cougar Gold cheese or Yakima Gouda or Kasseri

In a saucepan, cover the potatoes with cold water (to prevent skins from bursting) and bring to a boil. Reduce the heat to a gentle boil and cook for 15 to 20 minutes, until the potatoes are tender. Pour off the water, leaving the potatoes in the pan, and cover. Leave covered for several minutes; this plumps the potatoes and makes the skin tight.

While the potatoes are cooking, melt the butter in a skillet and sauté the onion until soft and lightly browned.

Remove the lid from the pan and, while still hot, cut the potatoes into thick slices. Place in a small, shallow bowl, and pour over the onions. Coarsely grind black pepper over the top, and sprinkle with the grated cheese.

Serves 2

Scalloped Potato and Cheese Casserole

I serve these cheesy, creamy potatoes with a bone-in baked ham and tender green beans.

> *3 pounds russet potatoes*
> *1 tablespoon salt*
> *3 tablespoons butter*
> *2 tablespoons flour*
> *¼ teaspoon freshly grated nutmeg*
> *2¼ cups milk*
> *3 cups grated Swiss cheese*
> *Chopped parsley*
> *4 slices lightly cooked bacon*

Preheat the oven to 375°F. Peel the potatoes and cut into slices ½ inch thick. Place the potatoes in a large saucepan and cover with boiling water. Sprinkle in 2 teaspoons of the salt and cook, covered, for 5 minutes. Drain. Melt the butter in a saucepan and blend in the flour, nutmeg, and the remaining teaspoon of salt. Gradually add the milk. Cook, stirring, until the mixture thickens and forms a smooth paste.

In a buttered 9- by 13-inch glass baking dish, place half of the potatoes and pour half of the sauce over them. Sprinkle with 2 cups of the cheese. Add the remaining potatoes and sauce. Cover with foil and bake for 45 minutes. Remove the foil and sprinkle with parsley and the remaining 1 cup of cheese. Lay the strips of bacon across the top. Bake, uncovered, for 20 minutes longer, or until the potatoes turn a light golden brown.

Serves 6

Swedish Roast Potatoes

If you put a chicken in to roast at the same time as these potatoes, you'll end up with a delicious dinner.

6 medium-sized Yukon Gold potatoes

¼ pound (1 stick) butter, melted

Salt and pepper

Paprika

Preheat the oven to 400°F. Wash and peel the potatoes. Slash them crosswise, thinly, about ¾ of the way through, leaving the bottoms whole. Coat the potatoes with the melted butter and place in a baking pan. Sprinkle with salt and pepper. Bake until crisp and golden, about 1 hour and 15 minutes, basting occasionally with the butter from the baking pan. Sprinkle with paprika.

Serves 6

Potato Pancakes

I usually serve these with pan-fried pork chops, warm applesauce, and a dollop of sour cream.

4 large russet potatoes, 6 to 8 ounces each, boiled with the skin on for 10 minutes and cooled

3 eggs, beaten

1 teaspoon salt

¼ teaspoon pepper

2 tablespoons flour

2 tablespoons vegetable oil

2 tablespoons butter

Peel and grate the partially cooked potatoes. Put in a large bowl and add the eggs, salt, pepper, and flour. Mix well. Heat a large nonstick frying pan and add the oil and butter. When the oil is sizzling hot, drop in several spoonfuls of the potato mixture and form small pancakes. Turn when golden brown. Drain on paper towels. Serve hot.

Serves 4

Irene Hlueny's Potato Lefse

Lefse is Norwegian for a large, thin potato pancake served buttered and folded. Lefse dough needs to be well chilled before rolling, and you want to be sure to roll it as thin as possible.

> 5 large boiling potatoes
>
> ½ cup heavy cream
>
> 3 tablespoons butter
>
> 1 teaspoon salt
>
> ½ cup flour for every cup of mashed potatoes

Boil the potatoes and mash well, adding the cream, butter, and salt. Beat until light, then let cool. Add the flour and roll the dough into a ball, kneading until smooth. Form into a long roll and slice into pieces about the size of a large egg, or larger, depending on the size of lefse desired. Chill the dough.

Roll each piece out like a pie crust, as thin as possible. Do not grease the griddle. Bake on a lefse griddle or pancake griddle over moderate heat, turning once. When baked, place between clean cloths or waxed paper to keep the lefse from becoming dry.

Spread with butter, sugar, and cinnamon. Cut each lefse in half or fourths and roll up before serving.

Serves 6 to 8

Cougar Gold Cheddar and Potato Soup

Cougar Gold is a delicious, medium-sharp cheddar cheese, with a wonderful texture, developed and sold by Washington State University. It slices, crumbles, and melts beautifully. The cheese is sold in a 30-ounce tin.

> 4 tablespoons butter
>
> 1 yellow onion, thinly sliced
>
> ¼ cup flour
>
> 1 teaspoon dry mustard
>
> 3 cups chicken stock
>
> 1 cup peeled, grated carrot
>
> 3 cups peeled, sliced potatoes (½-inch slices)
>
> 2 cups half-and-half
>
> 3 cups shredded Cougar Gold cheddar cheese

Salt and pepper to taste

Finely chopped celery leaves

In a skillet over moderate heat, melt the butter and sauté the onion until soft. Stir in the flour and dry mustard. Cook for several minutes, stirring continuously. Transfer to a soup pot and stir in stock, whisking until smooth. Add the carrots and potatoes.

Simmer over moderate heat for 30 minutes. Add the half-and-half. Reduce the heat to low and stir in the cheese until melted. Season with salt and pepper to taste. Sprinkle with chopped celery leaves.

Serves 6

20-Minute Potato-Sausage Soup

Throughout the winter we always have a large sack of russet potatoes on hand. Baked, mashed, or made into this creamy soup, they are a mainstay of our winter menus.

> *6 medium-sized russet potatoes*
>
> *4 cups chicken stock*
>
> *1 or 2 leeks*
>
> *4 tablespoons butter*
>
> *2 cloves garlic, chopped*
>
> *2 cups half-and-half*
>
> *½ pound precooked smoked sausage, cut in half and then sliced*
>
> *2½ teaspoons kosher salt*
>
> *¼ teaspoon white pepper*
>
> *Dash of cayenne*

Peel and dice the potatoes. Cook them in the chicken stock until tender. Set aside to cool.

Trim off the tough tops of the leeks. Cut the leeks in half lengthwise. Rinse carefully under running water to remove any silt. Pat dry. Cut into ½-inch pieces. In a skillet over moderate heat, melt the butter and sauté the leeks. Add the garlic and cook until soft.

Purée the potatoes with the chicken stock in a food processor, in batches if necessary. Transfer to a saucepan, add the half-and-half, and reheat. Stir in the leeks and sausage. Cook 5 minutes. Season with salt, pepper, and a dash of cayenne.

Serves 6

Baked Yams with Toasted Hazelnuts

Yams are usually served only for Thanksgiving, yet they are delicious all year round with venison or roast pork.

6 yams, cut in quarters

¼ pound (1 stick) butter, softened

2 tablespoons maple syrup

1 cup chopped toasted hazelnuts

Preheat the oven to 375°F. Bake the yams with the skins on until tender. Peel and place in a 2-quart casserole. Mash the yams with a fork and mix in the butter and maple syrup. Sprinkle with nuts and bake for 25 minutes.

Serves 6

Mom's Baked Beans

Baked beans from scratch do take time, but they will get nice and soft if you cook them in a crockpot. Slow, easy cooking is what they like.

1 pound small navy beans

1 tablespoon salt

¼ pound uncooked bacon, diced

½ yellow onion, chopped

¼ cup brown sugar

6 tablespoons molasses

1 teaspoon dry mustard

½ teaspoon ground ginger

½ teaspoon ground coriander

1 can (16 ounces) diced or stewed tomatoes, with juice

¼ cup ketchup

Cover the beans with cold water, add the salt, and soak overnight. The following day, rinse the beans. Place in a large saucepan, add 2 cups cold water, and simmer, covered, for 1 hour.

Put the beans and any remaining liquid into a crockpot. Mix in the bacon, onion, brown sugar, molasses, seasonings, tomatoes, and ketchup. Cover and cook on the low setting for 6 to 8 hours, until the beans are soft. Remove the cover for last half hour of cooking.

Serves 8

Nina's Bagna Cauda

Try this outdoors in the summertime. It's fun to eat and goes well with barbecued meats.

Have on the table a tray or basket of fresh vegetables cut into dipping-sized pieces. The following are my favorites: red pepper strips, cauliflower pieces, fresh mushrooms, fresh green beans, rolled napa cabbage leaves, cherry tomatoes, and zucchini strips. A basket of sliced French bread is also a good accompaniment for catching the flavorful drips.

½ pound (2 sticks) butter, softened

⅓ cup olive oil

3 cloves garlic, thinly sliced

1 can (2 ounces) flat anchovy fillets, well drained

Fresh vegetables for dipping

Sliced French bread

Put the butter, olive oil, and garlic in a 6- to 8-cup enameled saucepan. Heat slowly. Chop the anchovies and add to the butter mixture. Stir until the mixture bubbles. Keep the heat low enough so that the mixture doesn't burn.

To serve, set the pot over a warming candle or low flame to keep warm. Swirl vegetable pieces in the bagna cauda (literally, "hot bath"). Use bamboo skewers or fondue forks to keep from burning your fingers.

Serves 6

Smoked Bacon and Fresh Corn Chowder

My father likes to add a small jar of raw oysters to this recipe for an oyster-corn chowder.

3 strips smoked bacon

¼ cup finely chopped yellow onion

3 cups fresh or frozen corn kernels

2 tablespoons butter

2 tablespoons flour

2 cups milk

1 teaspoon salt

½ teaspoon pepper

2 cups half-and-half

Cut the bacon into ½-inch pieces. Fry in a sauté pan until it begins to crisp. Add the onion and cook until soft. Put the corn in a food processor and process lightly, leaving some texture. Add the corn to the onion and bacon, and simmer until corn is hot. Add the butter, then stir in the flour. Cook slowly over low heat for 3 minutes. Transfer to a saucepan and add the milk, salt, and pepper, and cook until thickened. Then add the half-and-half and stir over low heat until steaming hot.

Serves 6

Fresh Corn Chowder with Cheddar Cheese and Tomato Salsa

Gilman Village in Issaquah (a town 20 minutes east of Seattle) is a favorite outing for visitors. Small houses built in the 1920s, all refurbished, form a village of shops and restaurants. At Sweet Additions restaurant, this delicious soup is served during fresh corn season.

4 tablespoons butter

½ cup chopped onion

3 cups fresh corn, removed from the cob (or frozen or packaged corn)

1½ cups peeled, diced russet potatoes

1 cup chicken stock

3½ cups half-and-half

1 teaspoon salt

Freshly cracked pepper

1 to 2 teaspoons Tabasco sauce

1 ½ cups finely grated cheddar cheese

1 cup Krueger Pepper Farm's Salsa (page 256)

Fresh cilantro

In a large skillet over moderate heat, melt the butter and sauté the onions. Coarsely purée the corn in a food processor. Add to the onions, and heat. Transfer to a soup pot. Add the potato, stock, half-and-half, salt, pepper, and Tabasco. Cook over medium-low heat until the potatoes are cooked and the soup thickens slightly.

Sprinkle each serving with a little cheese, and add a dollop of salsa and some fresh cilantro.

Serves 6

Sydney Moe's Chilled Summer Yakima Tomato Gazpacho

In summer, when the tomatoes in Yakima are plump and red and ripe, I make a big pitcher of this gazpacho and keep it in the refrigerator.

4 to 6 ripe tomatoes

1 small green bell pepper

½ white onion

1 English cucumber

1 bottle (32 ounces) good-quality Bloody Mary mix

¼ cup olive oil

6 tablespoons wine vinegar

1 avocado

1 small can salted roasted almonds

Remove the stem end from the tomatoes. Cut into large chunks. Seed the green pepper and cut into large pieces. Coarsely chop the white onion. Cut the cucumber in half. Cut one half into thick slices, and finely chop the other half for garnish.

Put 2 cups of the Bloody Mary mix in the food processor with the oil and vinegar. Add half of the vegetables and process until smooth. Transfer this mixture to a large pitcher. Process the remaining vegetables briefly so that they still have some texture, and then add them to the puréed mixture. Stir in the remaining Bloody Mary mix.

When ready to serve, dice the avocado. Garnish the soup with avocado, almonds, and chopped cucumber.

Serves 8

Tillamook White Cheddar–Beer Soup

We have friends who serve this as their house soup at their ski cabin in the winter. It's hearty and good with Granny Smith apples and giant pretzels.

4 tablespoons butter

1 ½ cups chopped yellow onion

1 cup peeled, sliced carrot

1 cup chopped celery

2 cups diced new potatoes

2 cups chicken broth

½ cup flour

2 cups milk

3 cups grated Tillamook white cheddar cheese (or Cougar Gold)

1 teaspoon dry mustard

⅛ teaspoon cayenne

½ can beer (the remaining half is for the cook)

Melt the butter in a heavy 6-quart saucepan. Add the onion, carrot, celery, and potatoes, and sauté briefly. Pour in chicken broth and simmer for 30 minutes. Mix the flour and milk together until smooth, then blend into the soup. Stir and cook until well blended. Add the cheese, mustard, and cayenne. Stir until the cheese melts, then stir in the beer.

Serves 6

Garden Minestrone Soup

This is a variation of a soup developed by Professor Angelo Pellegrini, remembered by food lovers for his devotion to his garden and his cookbooks. I serve it with homemade bread and Apple Grunt (page 168) for dessert.

4 slices bacon, cut in ½-inch strips

½ cup olive oil

3 cloves garlic, minced

3 cups chopped yellow onion

4 stalks celery, chopped (including tops)

Freshly ground black pepper

4 cups chopped Swiss chard (including leaves and stalks)

½ cup chopped parsley

2 cups small zucchini, sliced

2 cups green beans, cut in thirds

¼ cup fresh basil

2 cups shredded, chopped cabbage

4 carrots, peeled and sliced

2 cans (28 ounces each) chopped tomatoes with juice

6 to 7 cups beef or chicken broth

2 cups canned, drained white cannellini beans, or 2 cans (11½ ounces each) bean with
*   bacon soup (depending on how thick you like your soup)*

Chopped fresh parsley for garnish

Freshly grated Parmesan cheese

In a large pot, sauté the bacon until just brown, and drain off the fat. Add the olive oil. Stir in the garlic, onion, and celery, and sauté over medium heat until soft. Add several grinds of fresh black pepper. Stir in the chard, chopped parsley, zucchini, green beans, basil, cabbage, and carrots, and cook for 5 minutes. Add the tomatoes, broth, and white beans. Simmer for 30 minutes and serve, sprinkled with fresh parsley and Parmesan cheese.

Serves 8

Fresh Mushroom Soup

When I was growing up, my father always had a pot of soup on the stove in winter, which changed from day to day depending on the leftover vegetables he added after dinner. When I came home from school, I'd add a cup of water to the pot to thin the mixture, boil it for a few minutes, and enjoy Dad's "soup du jour."

4 tablespoons butter

1 pound fresh white mushrooms, thinly sliced

2 cups quartered, sliced onion

1 bay leaf

3 tablespoons flour

5 cups fresh chicken broth

1 tablespoon uncooked rice

1 cup half-and-half

Salt and pepper

Tabasco sauce to taste

Chopped parsley

In a 10-inch frying pan, melt the butter and, over very low heat, sweat the mushrooms, onions, and bay leaf by placing a circle of waxed paper directly on the mushrooms and weighting it with a saucer to prevent excess condensation. Continue cooking over very low heat for another 10 minutes. Remove the waxed paper and sprinkle the flour over the mushrooms. Mix well. Transfer to a 4-quart saucepan and add the chicken broth and rice. Simmer over low heat for 15 minutes. Add the half-and-half and season to taste with salt, pepper, and a dash of Tabasco. Sprinkle each serving with chopped parsley.

Serves 6

Chinese Vegetable Soup (*War Mein*)

This light soup can be served as a first course.

> *4 ounces Chinese noodles*
>
> *3 cups chicken broth*
>
> *¼ pound sliced barbecued pork*
>
> *1 cup green vegetables (such as snow peas or baby bok choy), cut into pieces if large*
>
> *4 water chestnuts, sliced*
>
> *1 green onion, sliced*
>
> *Soy sauce*

Boil the noodles until tender. Rinse, drain, and set aside. Bring the broth to a boil. Add the barbecued pork, vegetables, and water chestnuts, and boil for 2 minutes. Add the noodles and heat through. Serve, garnished with the green onion, and let each person add soy sauce to taste.

Serves 4

Lentil Soup from Alpenland

We are fortunate to have this cozy restaurant in our Mercer Island neighborhood. They serve delicious soups. (Lovage is an easy herb to grow and is particularly good in many soups.)

> *2 cups lentils*
>
> *4 cups chicken stock*
>
> *1 teaspoon salt*
>
> *1 clove garlic*
>
> *½ teaspoon pepper*
>
> *4 bay leaves*

2 celery stalks, trimmed

1 carrot, peeled

1 leek, washed thoroughly

1 sprig fresh lovage

1 cube chicken bouillon (optional)

2 tablespoons vinegar

1 smoked farmer's or precooked sausage, cut up

Soak the lentils in water overnight in an enameled, stainless steel, or porcelain-coated soup pot. The next day, drain the lentils, return them to the pot, and add the stock, salt, garlic, pepper, and bay leaves. Chop the celery, carrot, and leek, and add to the pot. Stir in the lovage, chicken bouillon cube (if desired), vinegar, and smoked sausage. Cook over low heat for 2 hours. This soup will keep well in the refrigerator for up to 3 days.

Serves 6

Glazed Turnips

Root vegetables come to the market in the late fall. These nicely glazed turnips are a good accompaniment to duck. This recipe is from Jane Wherrette, a well-known Northwest artist.

6 medium-sized white turnips

½ teaspoon salt

3 tablespoons butter, softened

1 tablespoon flour

½ cup chicken broth

Salt and freshly ground black pepper to taste

Chopped fresh parsley

Wash, peel, and cut each turnip into 6 to 8 wedges. Place in a saucepan, cover with water, add the salt, and cook the turnips, uncovered, just until tender, about 10 minutes. Drain well. Stir in the butter and let melt. Sprinkle with the flour and mix well with the buttered turnips. Add the chicken broth and cook over low heat until a sauce is formed. Season with salt and pepper and sprinkle with fresh parsley.

Serves 4

Northwest "Waldorf" Salad

A classic salad that's at home here because of our supply of good apples and walnuts. This version, with the addition of flavored nuts, orange zest, and a little apple butter in the dressing, is even more flavorful than the original.

> *2 tablespoons vegetable oil*
>
> *1 cup walnut halves*
>
> *1 tablespoon sugar*
>
> *1 teaspoon salt*
>
> *2 tablespoons apple butter*
>
> *½ cup mayonnaise*
>
> *1 teaspoon lemon juice*
>
> *3 or 4 Granny Smith apples, cut into bite-sized chunks*
>
> *1 cup chopped celery*
>
> *1 teaspoon grated orange zest*

Heat the oil in a heavy skillet. Add the walnuts. Sprinkle them with the sugar and salt and cook over medium-high heat until the sugar caramelizes and coats the nuts, about 2 to 3 minutes.

Mix the apple butter, mayonnaise, and lemon juice in a medium-sized bowl. Add the apples and celery and coat well. Chill until ready to serve. Just before serving, sprinkle with the orange zest and caramelized walnuts.

Serves 6

Oregon Blue Cheese, Bartlett Pear, and Hot Walnut Salad

This fall salad works well as a first course and eloquently, if simply, showcases Pacific Northwest products.

> *½ cup walnut oil*
>
> *3 to 4 tablespoons sherry vinegar*
>
> *Salt and a pinch of sugar to taste*
>
> *3 tablespoons butter*
>
> *1 cup walnuts*
>
> *5 heads Bibb lettuce, washed carefully and dried*
>
> *2 or 3 Bartlett pears, cored and sliced*
>
> *2 to 3 ounces Oregon blue cheese, crumbled*

Make a dressing by whisking together the oil, vinegar, salt, and sugar. Melt the butter in a skillet over low heat, and sauté the walnuts.

Divide the lettuce among 6 salad plates. Arrange the sliced pears on top. Pour the dressing over the fruit and lettuce, and sprinkle with the blue cheese and hot walnuts.

Serves 6

Oregon Blue Cheese Crumble

This recipe, a winner in a recipe contest sponsored by the *Mercer Island Reporter*, has become the most popular hors d'oeuvre I serve. It's also delicious on grilled steaks or hamburgers and as a topping for salads. Serve it with sliced Granny Smith apples and wheat crackers as the fruit-and-cheese course at dinner.

> *8 ounces blue cheese, crumbled*
>
> *2 cloves garlic, minced*
>
> *⅓ cup olive oil*
>
> *2 tablespoons red wine vinegar*
>
> *1 tablespoon lemon juice*
>
> *½ cup chopped red onion (or chopped green onion)*
>
> *½ cup minced parsley*
>
> *Freshly ground black pepper*

Sprinkle the cheese into a shallow 6- to 8-inch dish. Mix together the garlic and olive oil and drizzle over the cheese. Combine the vinegar, lemon juice, red onion, and parsley, and pour over the cheese. Refrigerate for 1 hour. Sprinkle with pepper.

Serves 8

Dad's Potato Salad

This was a fixture of my childhood in Spokane, Washington, a traditional potato salad best made with French's mustard and Best Foods mayonnaise. You can add celery, pickles, or anything else you like. The most important thing is to use enough mayonnaise. That makes the salad moist and flavorful.

> 2 pounds White Rose or Yukon Gold potatoes, quartered and peeled after cooking
> (leave skins on if using small red potatoes)
> ½ pound Walla Walla sweet onions or other sweet onions, sliced in crescents
> 4 hard-boiled eggs
> 1 to 1½ cups mayonnaise
> 3 tablespoons mustard (I like the flavor of prepared yellow mustard best)
> Kosher salt and freshly ground black pepper

Boil the potatoes in water to cover until tender. Cool to room temperature. Cut into bite-sized pieces. Sprinkle with the sliced onions and refrigerate, covered with plastic wrap. Chill well. When ready to serve, cut up the eggs and add to the potatoes. Moisten well with mayonnaise and mustard. Season to taste with salt and pepper.

Serves 6 to 8

Yellow Finn Potato Salad

Add freshly cracked pepper just before serving, so that it retains its aroma and flavor.

> 2 pounds Yellow Finn potatoes (or small red potatoes)

Malt Vinegar Dressing

> ⅓ cup malt vinegar
> ⅔ cup vegetable oil
> 1 teaspoon Dijon mustard
> 1 teaspoon kosher salt
> 1 clove garlic, minced

> ———

> 1 bunch green onions
> Freshly cracked pepper

Gently boil the potatoes in water to cover for about 20 minutes, until fork tender. Drain and cool slightly, then peel and slice. Place in a bowl.

To make the dressing, whisk the malt vinegar, oil, mustard, salt, and garlic until well-blended.

Pour the dressing over the warm potatoes and marinate at room temperature for 1 hour. Mix carefully again. Sprinkle with green onions and several grinds of freshly cracked pepper.

Serves 6

Marinated Mushrooms and Walla Walla Sweet Onions

A great accompaniment to hamburgers and steaks.

> *½ pound fresh mushrooms, cut in thick slices*
>
> *1 Walla Walla sweet or other sweet onion, cut into crescents*
>
> *⅓ cup vegetable oil*
>
> *⅔ cup tarragon vinegar*
>
> *1 tablespoon chopped fresh tarragon, or 1 teaspoon dried*
>
> *½ teaspoon kosher salt*
>
> *2 tablespoons sugar*

Mix the mushrooms and onions together in a bowl. Combine the rest of the ingredients to make a marinade. Pour the marinade over the mushrooms and onions. Cover and place in the refrigerator. Let marinate for several hours, then serve.

Makes 4 cups

Wilted Lettuce Garden Salad

The dressing for this is equally good over spinach or boiled and sliced new potatoes.

> 1 head baby red leaf or green leaf lettuce
>
> 4 bacon strips
>
> ¼ cup sugar
>
> ¼ cup apple cider vinegar
>
> 2 tablespoons water
>
> Salt and freshly ground black pepper

Tear the lettuce leaves in half. Place in a large bowl. Cut the bacon in half-inch pieces and cook until crisp. Remove the bacon, leaving the fat in the pan. Turn the heat to low. Add the sugar and vinegar, stirring to dissolve the sugar. Add the water. Turn the heat up to medium. Just as the dressing starts to bubble, remove it from the heat and pour over the greens. Add the bacon and salt and pepper to taste. Toss and serve immediately.

Serves 4

Romaine, Carrot, Blue Cheese, and Walnut Salad

When you select romaine, find a head that smells sweet and fresh, not bitter, at the stem end. Your salad will taste much better.

> 1 head romaine
>
> 2 carrots, peeled and very thinly sliced on the diagonal
>
> 4 ounces blue cheese, crumbled
>
> ½ cup large walnut pieces
>
> ¼ cup red wine vinegar
>
> 1 teaspoon kosher salt
>
> ½ teaspoon sugar
>
> 1 teaspoon Worcestershire sauce
>
> 1 teaspoon freshly cracked pepper
>
> ½ teaspoon dry Colman's mustard

Cut romaine into bite-sized pieces. Put in a large salad bowl. Mix in the carrots. Sprinkle the blue cheese and walnuts over the top. Cover with plastic wrap and refrigerate until ready to serve. Whisk or shake together the vinegar, salt, sugar, Worcestershire sauce, pepper, and mustard. Toss the salad with the dressing just before serving.

Serves 6

Tomato, Cucumber, and Green Pepper Salad

This salad is excellent with barbecued fish or meat. The tomatoes taste much better when served at room temperature.

¼ cup white or red wine vinegar (tarragon vinegar works well, too)

¼ cup olive oil

1 teaspoon sugar

½ teaspoon kosher salt

½ green pepper, cut into thin strips

1 English cucumber, very thinly sliced

Minced fresh parsley

Freshly cracked pepper

3 tomatoes, cut into large chunks

Combine the vinegar, oil, sugar, and salt. Layer the green pepper and then the cucumber in a shallow dish. Pour the vinegar mixture over them and marinate, refrigerated, for 1 hour. Sprinkle with parsley and freshly cracked pepper.

When ready to serve, put the tomatoes in a serving dish. Top with the marinated pepper and cucumber.

Serves 4

Great Greek Salad with Anchovy Dressing

The anchovies in the dressing give this salad much flavor and character.

½ small head romaine lettuce, shredded

1 English cucumber

3 tomatoes

½ red bell pepper (or green if red is not available)

8 ounces feta cheese

12 Greek olives

Anchovy Dressing

1 small tin flat anchovies

1 clove garlic, cut in half

1 teaspoon dried oregano

¼ cup red wine vinegar

¾ cup olive oil

Wash the lettuce and place in a shallow salad bowl. Cover with moist paper towels and plastic wrap. Refrigerate.

Put the dressing ingredients in a food processor and process until smooth.

Trim the ends off the cucumber. Cut in half lengthwise. Scoop out the seeds with a spoon. Cut into ¼-inch slices and place in a small bowl. Cut the tomatoes into large chunks. Seed the red bell pepper and cut into thin strips.

To serve, sprinkle the cucumbers over the shredded romaine, then the tomatoes, feta cheese, pepper strips, and Greek olives. Pour the dressing over the salad and serve immediately.

Serves 6

Sweet-and-Sour Cucumbers

I like to serve this in the summer with barbecued salmon.

3 firm cucumbers (or 1 English cucumber)

1 cup water

¼ cup sugar

1 teaspoon kosher salt

⅓ cup white vinegar

Chopped chives

Peel the cucumbers and cut into thin slices. Place in a bowl. Mix the water, sugar, salt, and vinegar, and let sit until the sugar and salt dissolve. Pour over the sliced cucumbers and refrigerate for 1 to 2 hours. Sprinkle with chopped chives and serve cold.

Serves 6

Broccoli, Mushroom, Avocado, and Tomato Salad

The flavors and textures in this salad blend together extremely well.

1½ pounds broccoli

½ pound mushrooms, sliced

8 slices thick-sliced bacon, cut into ½-inch pieces and cooked until crisp

1 avocado, thinly sliced

½ pound cherry tomatoes

¾ cup mayonnaise

½ teaspoon sugar

½ teaspoon salt

1 tablespoon lemon juice

1 clove garlic, minced

1 teaspoon chopped shallots

½ teaspoon paprika

1 tablespoon grated carrot

1 tablespoon finely diced green pepper

Prepare the broccoli for salad by cutting off the florets and breaking them into small pieces. Peel the stalks and cut into thin slices. Put in a salad bowl along with the mushrooms, bacon, avocado, and tomatoes. To make the dressing, combine the mayonnaise, sugar, salt, lemon juice, garlic, shallots, paprika, grated carrot, and pepper.

Mix the salad with the dressing and refrigerate for at least 4 hours.

Serves 8

Tomato Salad with Fresh Basil

Spread in a glass dish and sprinkle with minced parsley to serve.

1 clove garlic, minced

1 to 2 tablespoons red or white wine vinegar

½ teaspoon sugar

Salt and freshly ground pepper

5 tablespoons olive oil

2 to 3 tablespoons finely chopped fresh basil

4 tomatoes

Just before serving, mix together the garlic, vinegar, sugar, salt, pepper, olive oil, and basil to make a dressing. Slice the tomatoes ½ inch thick. Overlap them slightly on a serving plate. Spoon the dressing over the tomatoes and serve.

Serves 4

Summer Tomato Rustic Bread Salad

We have great bakeries in the Northwest today. This Italian favorite is a popular summer salad using those good rustic breads.

4 or 5 slices rustic sourdough bread

3 large ripe tomatoes

½ English cucumber, chopped

½ green bell pepper, seeded and diced

½ cup fresh basil, torn into small pieces

¼ cup extra-virgin olive oil

2 to 4 tablespoons red wine vinegar

Preheat the broiler. Remove the crusts from the bread. Cut into large croutons. Place on a baking sheet and toast lightly under the broiler just until golden. You should have 2 cups of croutons.

Remove the stem end from the tomatoes. Cut into large chunks. Place in a salad bowl. Add the croutons, cucumber, green pepper, and basil. Toss well with olive oil and vinegar to taste, and serve. The ingredients can all be prepared ahead and assembled just before serving.

Serves 2 to 4

Marnie's Chutney-Spinach Salad with Red Delicious Apples

I like to serve this salad in the fall when the apples and walnuts are fresh. The dark green spinach leaves and the red apple slices make a pretty combination.

3 tablespoons lemon juice

⅔ cup vegetable oil

4 to 6 tablespoons mango chutney

1 teaspoon curry powder

1 teaspoon dry mustard

Salt to taste

2 bunches spinach

3 Red Delicious apples

⅔ cup walnuts

½ cup raisins

½ cup thinly sliced green onion

Mix together the lemon juice, oil, chutney, curry powder, mustard, and salt in a pint jar with a lid and shake well. Let stand at room temperature for several hours. Shake again before tossing with the salad.

Wash the spinach well to remove any dirt or sand. Remove the stems and tough ribs and cut into bite-sized pieces. Pat dry, or spin dry in a salad spinner. Cover with plastic wrap and chill in the refrigerator until ready to serve.

Just before serving, cut the apples in half and then crosswise into thin, crescent-shaped slices. Mix the spinach, apples, walnuts, raisins, and green onion, and toss gently with the dressing, coating the greens well.

Serves 6

Orange, Red Onion, and Cilantro Salad with Pomegranate Seeds

This is the sort of salad we love with a fall dinner that includes Pacific Northwest game birds.

6 oranges

1 red onion

1 bunch cilantro

1 teaspoon chili powder

¼ cup orange juice

¼ cup red wine vinegar

½ cup vegetable oil

½ cup pomegranate seeds

Peel and slice the oranges. Arrange on a shallow serving dish. Cut the onion in half lengthwise and slice thinly crosswise. Scatter the onion slices over the oranges.

Wash the cilantro and shake dry. Tear off the leaves and reserve. Beat together the chili powder, orange juice, vinegar, and oil, and pour over the oranges and onion. Scatter the cilantro leaves and pomegranate seeds on top of the salad and serve.

Serves 6

Couscous Salad with Fresh Corn, Sweet Red Pepper, and Cilantro

This colorful salad is terrific with roast chicken.

1½ cups water

2 tablespoons butter

1 cup quick-cooking couscous

⅓ cup vegetable oil

Juice of 1 or 2 limes

4 green onions

1 cup cooked fresh corn kernels

1 small red bell pepper

½ jalapeño pepper

¼ cup fresh cilantro leaves

Salt

Tabasco sauce

Put the water and butter in a 2-quart saucepan. Bring to a boil. Add the couscous, cover, and remove from the heat. Let sit for 5 minutes. Transfer to a small salad bowl. Stir in the oil and lime juice.

Chop the green onions and add to the couscous. Stir in the corn. Dice the red pepper and add to the salad.

Carefully remove the seeds from the jalapeño and dice finely. (Be sure to wash your hands afterwards. Remember, the smaller the pepper, the hotter it is, and you can burn your eyes easily.) Add the pepper to the salad. Coarsely chop the cilantro and sprinkle over the top. Mix gently until well blended. Season to taste with salt and a little Tabasco.

Serves 4

Mushroom-Bacon Salad

This is a perfect salad to serve with a delicious roast beef and twice-baked potatoes.

> *12 slices bacon*
>
> *1 pound medium-sized mushrooms*
>
> *⅔ cup olive oil*
>
> *¼ cup lemon juice*
>
> *1 teaspoon Worcestershire sauce*
>
> *½ teaspoon salt*
>
> *¼ teaspoon pepper*
>
> *½ teaspoon dry mustard*
>
> *6 butter lettuce leaves*
>
> *½ cup chopped green onion*

Cut the bacon into ½-inch pieces and cook until just crisp. Drain on paper towels.

Clean the mushrooms and slice ½ inch thick. Whisk together the olive oil, lemon juice, Worcestershire sauce, salt, pepper, and dry mustard until well blended. Pour over the mushrooms. Marinate for 30 minutes to 1 hour, but no longer.

Arrange the lettuce leaves on individual salad plates. Fill with marinated mushrooms. Sprinkle with bacon and green onion.

Serves 6

Japanese Cucumber Salad

This light, refreshing salad is wonderful for picnics.

> *1 English cucumber*
> *Kikkoman seasoned rice vinegar*

Peel the cucumber. Cut in half lengthwise and remove the seeds with a spoon. Cut into very thin crescent-shaped slices and put in a small serving bowl. Pour the seasoned rice vinegar over the cucumber slices. Chill.

Serves 6

Chicken and Apple Salad with Chutney-Lime Dressing

This simple recipe meets every expectation for a clean, fresh-tasting chicken salad. You can use leftover roast chicken.

> *2 pounds chicken breast*
> *2 or 3 Granny Smith apples*
> *1 cup homemade mayonnaise, or your favorite brand*
> *Juice of ½ lime*
> *3 tablespoons mango chutney*
> *6 green leaf lettuce leaves*

Poach the chicken and cool. Skin, bone, and cut the chicken into ½-inch strips. Put in a 2-quart serving bowl. Cut the apples into thin slices and add to the chicken. Blend together the mayonnaise, lime juice, and chutney and mix thoroughly with the chicken and apples. Serve on individual lettuce leaves.

Serves 4

Than's Shrimp and Shredded Cabbage Salad

This delicious slaw comes from Gretchen's Of Course, a popular Seattle catering company. The unusual combination of flavors, both exotic and different, is a real treat.

> *1 head red cabbage, finely shredded*
> *1 head green cabbage, finely shredded*
> *1 bunch cilantro, chopped*

½ cup chopped fresh mint

1 or 2 fresh jalapeño peppers, seeded

½ cup Tiparos Fish Sauce

3 cups white wine vinegar

½ cup sugar

Juice of 2 limes

1 teaspoon freshly ground pepper

1 ½ pounds fresh cooked baby shrimp (or the smallest available shrimp, cut in half)

Mix the cabbages, cilantro, fresh mint, and peppers together in a large bowl. In another bowl, whisk the fish sauce, vinegar, sugar, lime juice, and pepper together to make a dressing and pour over the salad. Toss well. Top the salad with the shrimp just before serving.

Serves 10 to 12

Mother's Coleslaw

My mother says that finely shredding the cabbage is the most important part of making a good coleslaw.

A menu of coleslaw, baked beans, and barbecued chicken says summer is here in the Pacific Northwest.

4 cups shredded green cabbage

½ cup mayonnaise

2 tablespoons lemon juice

1 tablespoon grated onion

1 tablespoon chopped pickled ginger

1 teaspoon sugar

½ teaspoon salt

¼ teaspoon black pepper

1 cup dry-roasted peanuts, chopped

½ cup diced red bell pepper

½ cup diced green bell pepper

Crisp the shredded cabbage in ice water for 1 hour. Drain well. In a large bowl, combine the mayonnaise, lemon juice, grated onion, pickled ginger, sugar, salt, and black pepper. Mix the well-drained cabbage with the dressing and the peanuts. Garnish with the diced red and green bell pepper.

Serves 6

Lynnie's Coleslaw

A nice tart slaw that's even good the next day.

> 1 large head green cabbage
>
> 1 large head red cabbage
>
> 1 Walla Walla sweet onion (or mild white salad onions), cut into quarters, then thinly sliced
>
> 1 cup chopped green onion
>
> 1 red bell pepper, seeded and cut into thin strips
>
> 2 cups red wine vinegar
>
> 2 cups light, fruity olive oil (or vegetable oil)
>
> 2 teaspoons sugar
>
> 2 teaspoons celery seed
>
> 2 cloves garlic, minced
>
> 1 teaspoon salt
>
> 2 teaspoons freshly ground black pepper

Finely shred the cabbages. Put in a large bowl with the onions and bell pepper. Mix together the vinegar, oil, sugar, celery seed, garlic, salt, and pepper. Pour over the cabbage mixture and mix well.

Serves 8 to 10

Dad's Hot Slaw

An assertively flavored slaw that holds its own with a good grilled steak. The anchovies dissolve in the hot dressing, which is poured over the crisp cabbage, wilting it slightly.

> ½ head green cabbage, shredded
>
> 6 thick slices bacon
>
> ⅓ cup olive oil
>
> ⅓ cup red wine vinegar
>
> 1 small tin flat anchovies
>
> 2 cloves garlic, thinly sliced
>
> Freshly ground pepper

Put the cabbage in a salad bowl. Cut the bacon into ½-inch pieces and cook until crisp. Drain and reserve.

Warm the olive oil in a small frying pan over medium heat. Add the vinegar, anchovies, and garlic. Mash the anchovies with a fork until dissolved. Turn up the heat and cook just until the mixture begins to boil. Pour over the shredded cabbage.

Sprinkle with the bacon and serve. Lots of freshly ground pepper brings all the flavors together.

Serves 4

Dungeness Crab Louie

A classic Northwest salad.

> *1 head iceberg lettuce*
>
> *2 cups mayonnaise*
>
> *½ cup milk*
>
> *2 tablespoons vinegar*
>
> *½ cup seafood cocktail sauce*
>
> *¼ cup grated Walla Walla sweet onion (or white salad onion)*
>
> *1 pound Dungeness crabmeat (shrimp may be substituted)*

Garnish

> *Tomato wedges*
>
> *Quartered hard-boiled eggs*
>
> *Avocado slices*
>
> *Jumbo black olives*

Just before serving, line a salad bowl with the outer leaves of the lettuce. Shred the remaining lettuce and place in a bowl to form a salad bed. Combine the mayonnaise, milk, vinegar, seafood cocktail sauce, and onion, and pour over the salad bed. Top with the crab and garnishes.

Serves 4

Dad's Anchovy Dressing

This is my house dressing, which works well on a simple romaine salad with croutons. I give bottles of this as Christmas gifts.

1 ounce blue cheese (or grated Parmesan)

¾ cup olive oil

1 small tin anchovies

¼ cup red wine vinegar

1 clove garlic

| Whirl all ingredients in a blender. Chill.

Makes 1½ cups

Honey-Lime Dressing for Fresh Fruit

Prepare a large bowl of fruit in the middle of summer and serve this dressing on the side.

⅔ cup sugar

5 tablespoons apple cider vinegar

1 teaspoon dry mustard

1 tablespoon lime juice

1 teaspoon paprika

1 tablespoon grated onion

1 teaspoon celery seed

1 cup vegetable oil

⅓ cup honey

| Mix all ingredients together well. Chill for several hours before using.

Makes 1¾ cups

My Favorite Oil and Vinegar Dressing

This tart and lively dressing came to me from my good friend Ann Wells. Her father was a great chef in London at Buckingham Palace, and Ann gave me his recipe years ago. I have enjoyed it ever since whenever an assertive dressing is called for, such as large, fat spears of cooked, chilled asparagus.

⅓ cup malt vinegar

2 teaspoons chopped shallot

1 teaspoon Colman's dry mustard

1 teaspoon salt

⅔ cup vegetable oil

Mix together the vinegar, shallot, mustard, and salt. Slowly whisk in the oil.

Makes 1 cup

Oregon Blue Cheese Dressing

Make this ahead. You can double the recipe and keep it on hand in the refrigerator. This is a heavy dressing, best with romaine lettuce or other sturdy greens to support it.

4 ounces Oregon blue cheese, crumbled into very small pieces

1 cup buttermilk

½ teaspoon dry mustard

1 teaspoon coarsely ground black pepper

1 teaspoon Worcestershire sauce

1 clove garlic, minced

1 teaspoon kosher salt

1 to 2 tablespoons lemon juice

1⅓ cups mayonnaise

Place all of the ingredients in a medium-sized mixing bowl. Stir together. With an electric mixer set at low speed to prevent splashing, mix together half of the dressing at a time, until well blended. Don't overmix. Refrigerate overnight. This dressing must sit 24 hours before serving.

Makes 2½ cups

Honey-Tamari-Sesame Dressing for Winter Salads

This complements the sturdy, colorful kales used in winter salads.

> *1 tablespoon honey*
> *1 tablespoon tamari*
> *1 teaspoon pure (not filtered) sesame oil*
> *⅓ cup safflower oil*
> *⅓ cup rice vinegar*

| Blend all of the ingredients together.

Makes 1 cup

Lemon Herb Dressing for Summer

Delicate and light for tender, summer garden greens.

> *⅔ cup light, fruity olive oil*
> *⅓ cup lemon juice*
> *½ teaspoon freshly cracked pepper*
> *½ teaspoon kosher salt*
> *1 teaspoon fresh lemon thyme*
> *½ teaspoon dried basil*
> *1 tablespoon minced shallot*

| Blend all of the ingredients together.

Makes 1 cup

Pear Vinegar, Walnut Oil, and Roasted Walnut Dressing for Fall

This dressing works well on a salad of mixed greens—a light sprinkle of blue cheese adds flavor.

⅓ cup walnut oil

¼ cup pear vinegar

Salt and pepper

1 cup toasted and salted walnuts

Blend the oil, vinegar, salt, and pepper together. Sprinkle the walnuts over the salad after the dressing has been well tossed with the greens. (Toasting makes the walnuts crisp and adds texture to the salad.)

Makes about ½ cup

TREE FRUIT

How the PEAR GOT in the BOTTLE, and OTHER DISTILLED MYSTERIES

Even though his work life was unimaginably good, Stephen McCarthy felt less than alive in his last business incarnation. He owned a manufacturing company in Oregon that made gizmos for the sport shooting industry: slings and swivels and scope mounts and holsters and the like. It had been his father's company, employing twenty people and grossing $1 million annually when McCarthy bought the old man out and took over. He had made some good business decisions over the years. Everything had clicked. Vast wealth and statewide political power reached out to caress his brow.

By the time he sold the company in 1989, McCarthy employed two hundred people. The company's gross income was fifteen times what it had been in his father's day, and he had expanded sales to Europe. But he let it all go to distill eau-de-vie from Bartlett pears. He was forty-four.

Some who know Stephen McCarthy think he's nuts to have given up a license to print money so he could run a barely profitable enterprise and make all his own sales calls. And yet, here in his current incarnation at Clear Creek Distillery in Portland, Oregon, where he is owner, distiller, fruit buyer, sales staff, and head swamper, Stephen McCarthy has never felt quite so alive, surrounded as he is with barrels of world-class eaux-de-vie and grappa of his own manufacture. And single-malt Scotch. Let us not forget the McCarthy's Oregon Single Malt Whiskey he will spring on the world sometime soon.

In his first ten years as a distiller, McCarthy failed to turn a profit, and he poured close to $2 million of his own cash into the business—$500,000, he says, before he even took a deep breath. His rewards, however, are visceral.

"When you go to New York to work with liquor sales reps,"

McCarthy says, "they're hungry. They're paying all their own expenses, so this isn't about taxis and expense account lunches. You're lugging your sample cases on and off subways with them, coming into the classiest restaurants through the basement, passing dirty laundry in the halls and piles of vegetables in the kitchen, then stepping into the splendor of the dining room, where you sit down with smart buyers and smart sellers to show the line. You go in the first time, the second time, the third time, and you're treated like dirt. But go back the fourth time, the fifth time, and it's like you're part of the family. You're old friends doing business. You get into a roll like no other, hitting the sidewalks and shouldering your way through pedestrian traffic, crashing along from one account to another."

He's talking about restaurants in New York like Le Bernardin, Aureole, Montrachet, Union Square Café—restaurants where the buyers have seen and tasted everything, where every liquor maker and sales rep in the world would like to get in, have a word, pour a taste. Treated like family. Old friends doing business.

"Stephen McCarthy has a beautiful, clear fruit product with loads of integrity," says Karen King, wine director for Union Square Café. "You can tell he puts a lot of passion and care into making it. And you can always trust that it will be delicious. I truly love his spirits." You have to wonder if there was ever an Austrian shooter who had as much to say about McCarthy's sling swivels.

He crushed his first Bartlett pear in 1985, and over the next two years he learned exactly how ripe the fruit had to be for the optimum taste and nose to turn up in the bottle. In fact, he learned how to all but ripen the fruit on schedule for the crush. The nine tons of crushed pears that fill the fermenting tank yield a hundred gallons of brandy, passing from tank to pot still in sixty-gallon batches that ultimately fill four-gallon glass carboys. It takes twenty-eight pounds of pears to fill a single bottle with eau-de-vie de poire. Between pears, apples, raspberries, and plums, McCarthy goes through four hundred tons of fruit in a year, and it all dribbles out of his pot still in a thin stream of clear, potent liquid.

One learns the art of distilling in the doing. Or one stands in a line of distillers reaching back several hundred years, as is often the case in the great eau-de-vie regions of Europe, receiving the knowledge and art like a mantle. McCarthy hired Jorg Rupf, a cordials distiller from Alameda, California, to show him how to assemble the still that had just arrived from Germany and, at $10,000 each, how to distill seven different eaux-de-vie.

"I have learned in the years since 1985," McCarthy says, "that there are three reasons for what I call my success. The first is product quality. If the stuff isn't really, really good, the next two factors won't help. The second is the passage of time, which is what it takes for word to get around and restaurants to take you seriously. Third: deep pockets. If you can't afford to wait for one and two to kick in, forget whatever notions you might have of a little distilling business."

He's a big, bearded man with clear, steady eyes magnified by thick glasses, a man with a quiet voice. He's the kind of man you want with you in the raft on the wild river, or holding down the other end of the rope as you climb a mountain. He's a man willing to take considered, deliberate chances at a time in life when most men simply want to settle in for the slow ride. He's also a man who understands the value of the considerable humbling that went on in the first five or six years of the business, when little went right. He was able to adjust accordingly and learn.

"I was an entrepreneurial genius when I started up Clear Creek Distillery," McCarthy explains. "Or so I had been told often enough. So no, I had no business plan to start. I *knew* what to do. Hell, I'd just taken this shooting company into the stratosphere. I didn't know how to make a wrong decision. And, of course, I just got clobbered. There's no other business in existence like the liquor business. Its folkways are peculiar unto themselves. I had to pull out of markets I was in, reduce my staff and overhead, and learn how to sell my product by myself."

McCarthy had first taken an interest in eau-de-vie in the late 1970s, while on sales trips to Germany for his shooting accoutrements company. Dinners with customers invariably ended with small glasses of the clear, magical liquor. He was particularly charmed by the pear brandy. His family had owned pear orchards in Oregon's Hood River Valley since the turn of the century. The lights went on, you might say, when McCarthy discovered that the pear the French call Williams Bon-Chrétien was the same as Oregon's Bartlett. The rest is an unfolding history.

And yet something of a mystery remains: Why so successful a businessman would throw it all over for a questionable niche in the distilled spirits industry. To get to the heart of that mystery is to understand Stephen McCarthy better, and to understand something of the nature of Oregon, a state unlike any other.

As a young lawyer Stephen McCarthy worked on the state's land-use legislation, a package of laws designed to protect forests, farmland, and rangeland from development. As an older lawyer and businessman, McCarthy well understood that no laws on any books would keep subdivisions away from farmland if that land didn't make money.

"Not a lot of money, mind you," McCarthy says. "But land use does have to pay. All I'm doing here is some very fancy packaging of Oregon and Washington state fruit. This is glorified pear marketing. It's another way for the land to make a little money, another way to keep the subdivisions back inside the city limits." Which is another way to say that in the making of eau-de-vie and the selling of eau-de-vie and all the effort it takes to be a successful distiller, Stephen McCarthy is taking an environmental stand, putting both money and labor on the line for something in which he truly believes.

He wanders through an orchard high up in the Hood River Valley, near orchard land that has been in and out of and back in his family since the time his grandfather headed west from Yale's forestry school. McCarthy's checking on Bartlett pears growing inside glass bottles that hang from spiderwebs of twine in the shaded branches of the trees.

"It's true in any business, but maybe more so in this one," McCarthy says. "You have to listen to the customer. And the customer wants pear brandy with a pear in the bottle. The trick is explaining to a fruit farmer that you will pay him to hang bottles in his trees."

The Bartletts growing inside the bottles look small and knobby. "When you put the liquid in," McCarthy says, "the pear appears to be bigger than it actually is—which is proof of the existence of God."

If there was any question, a single sip of eau-de-vie, as divine an essence as was ever crafted by mortal man, should settle the case quite handsomely.

Tree Fruit Varieties

Apples

Although Washington and Oregon are famous for RED and GOLDEN DELICIOUS apples, there are many other locally grown varieties available in markets and roadside fruit stands. Old favorites like MCINTOSH, ROME BEAUTY, and JONATHAN are common enough. Some other varieties include these:

MELROSE: A big, round, red apple with a flavor balanced between tart and sweet. The Melrose is harvested between mid- and late October, but will keep until March when properly stored. As good for cooking as it is for eating. Best for eating around Christmas, when it has had time to sweeten up in storage.

MUTSU: A Japanese eating apple that in some ways is like the Golden Delicious. This apple grows to enormous size and density. It weighs heavily in the hand. It is crisp and sweet, a great eating apple. Mutsu is harvested in mid- to late October and will store until March. Yellow skin with an occasional red blush.

GRANNY SMITH: Harvested in October. Bright green skin, tart and juicy. Excellent all-purpose cooking and eating.

SUMMER RED: This is not a keeper. Harvested from early to mid-September, Summer Red should be used immediately, either as an eating apple or for cooking. It is fine textured and firm, with a rich flavor. Solid red background, speckled with dots.

JONAGOLD: Harvested in mid- to late October, Jonagold is great for eating, cooking, and drying. The crisp, juicy flesh is sweet and rich. It keeps until Christmas. Red stripes over yellow-green skin.

GRAVENSTEIN: One of the all-time classics. The Gravenstein is harvested from early to mid-September. It is a large, crisp, juicy apple that is good for eating and for sauce. A summer apple, it doesn't keep. Red-striped skin over light green.

AKANE: Another apple from Japan. The Akane is harvested in mid-September and keeps for about a month. This is an all-time favorite eating apple, with crisp flesh and a flavor that is balanced between sweet and tart. Bright, solid red.

GALA: Harvested in early October, the Gala is a hard, crisp apple that keeps well and cooks well. The flesh is aromatic and semisweet. Bright scarlet striped over yellow.

IDARED: Transplanted from the eastern United States, this is a beautiful red apple of classic shape and color. It polishes up like glass. Harvested in late October, it keeps until spring. Idared is tart when first picked but sweetens with storage. A good cooking and eating apple.

FUJI: Available October to December. Greenish-yellow skin; sweet and juicy. Excellent for eating and cooking.

Some other interesting varieties include Chehalis, Lodi, Yellow Transparent, and Newtown Pippin.

Pears

The BARTLETT is ubiquitous. The RED BARTLETT is coming on strong. Other Northwest pears of interest include these:

BENNETT: A Bartlett type harvested in late August. It is a big pear with smooth skin and a buttery, sweet flavor.

COMICE: Harvested in early October, the Comice stores until Christmas. A large fruit that is greenish yellow when mature. Very aromatic and buttery.

BOSC: Harvested in mid- to late October. A good keeper with fine texture, a long neck, and a spicy flavor. Good for baking.

SECKEL: A small, sweet pear that is good fresh or in preserves. Intense flavor. Reddish brown over yellow.

ASIAN PEAR: Also called pear-apple, this fruit remains firm and crisp and juicy when ripe, much like an apple. The flavor and the texture, however, are nothing like an apple, and only vaguely resemble a pear. Go figure. Asian pears can be eaten either fresh or cooked; they retain their crispness after cooking. Colors range from light yellow to russet. Flavors range from light and sweet to highly aromatic and cinnamonlike. The most popular varieties planted in the Pacific Northwest include Chojuro, Nijiseiki (Twentieth Century), Hosui, Kikisui, Seuri, Shinsui, and Kosui.

Apricots

RILAND: A round, peach-colored fruit with a distinct red blush. The flavor is strong. MOORPARK: Large fruit. Brownish-red skin, yellow to orange flesh. Aromatic, sweet, rich flavor. ROYAL BLENHEIM: Good fresh, canned, or dried. Sweet, aromatic yellow flesh.

Figs

BROWN TURKEY: Rich flavor. Best fresh. DESERT KING: Cool-climate fig. Large fruit. Dark green skin. MISSION or BLACK MISSION: Large fruit with purplish-black skin. Excellent flavor. Good fresh, canned, or dried.

Peaches

HALE: Red over greenish-yellow skin. Yellow flesh. REGINA: Freestone variety. Good for baking, canning, or eating fresh. RED HAVEN: Brilliant red skin. Juicy, sweet yellow flesh. ROZA: Large, round fruit with excellent flavor. Good fresh or canned.

New varieties appearing at peak season: SUNCREST, GOLDEN MONARCH, and peaches that look like doughnuts, as well as white-fleshed peaches.

Nectarines

RED GOLD, SUN GOLD.

Plums

STANLEY: Italian prune type. Large, dark blue fruit. Good dried, fresh, or cooked. SHIRO: Yellow skin and flesh. Juicy and sweet. The most popular of the Japanese plums.

Quince

PINEAPPLE QUINCE: A Luther Burbank original. Aromatic. Excellent in sauces and preserves.

Cherries

BING: Crisp, wine-red to black. Great for eating fresh. When dried, these work well in sauces. RAINIER: Yellow-red in color. Sweet, apple-crisp. For cooking and canning as well as eating fresh. LAMBERT: Smaller than Bing. Later harvest. Bold flavor. MONTMORENCY: Best of the pie cherries.

Bing and Lambert make up 95 percent of the Northwest cherry crop. Other cherries that show up in the market include Black Republican, Black Tartarian, Royal Ann, Chinook, Burlat, and Deacon.

How to Select Fresh Fruit

Buy fruit in season, in your local area. Soft tree fruit is the hardest to get when it's just right. Peaches and apricots don't ripen off the tree, so if you buy them green they will only get mealy as they soften. Buy tree-ripened fruit, freeze it packed in orange juice, or dehydrate it. Nectarines are excellent dehydrated.

Pears, on the other hand, ripen nicely off the tree, so they mature successfully at home. They also dehydrate well.

If you aren't going to eat apples right away, refrigerate them overnight, but always let them sit at room temperature for several hours before serving. Ice-cold fruit has less flavor.

Cloud Mountain Apple Soup

This soup is delicious served cold as a first course.

> 1 pound Jonagold or Spartan apples, peeled, cored, and thinly sliced
>
> 3 cups water
>
> 1 teaspoon grated lemon zest
>
> 1 teaspoon grated orange zest
>
> 1 tablespoon lemon juice
>
> 1 tablespoon orange juice
>
> ½ cup honey (more or less to taste)
>
> ½ teaspoon ground cinnamon
>
> ½ teaspoon freshly grated nutmeg
>
> ½ cup sour cream blended with ¼ cup milk

Place the apples, water, lemon and orange zest, lemon and orange juice, honey, cinnamon, and nutmeg in an enameled or stainless steel saucepan, cover, and simmer for about 20 minutes, until the apples are mushy. Purée in a food processor or blender. Serve hot or cold with a little of the sour cream mixture drizzled over the top.

Serves 2

Apple Butter

I have a Gravenstein apple tree that is a prolific producer. This is an easy way to preserve the bounty.

> 3 quarts apple cider
>
> 8 pounds juicy ripe apples, washed, cored, and quartered
>
> 2½ cups brown sugar
>
> 2 teaspoons ground cinnamon
>
> ½ teaspoon ground allspice
>
> ½ teaspoon ground cloves
>
> ¼ teaspoon salt

Boil the cider in a large enameled kettle until reduced by half (approximately 30 minutes). Add the apples and cook over low heat until tender, about 30 minutes. Stir often with a wooden spoon. When completely cooked, force through a large-mesh strainer. Return to the kettle and add sugar, spices, and salt. Cook over low heat until the sugar is dissolved. Then continue cooking very slowly for 30 minutes. (Put a flame-tamer under the kettle to prevent sticking and burning.) Stir almost constantly at the end of the cooking time. Pour at once into ½-pint freezer containers and freeze.

Makes 8 pints

Baked Apples with Walnuts and Vanilla Cream Sauce

This is a good winter dessert. It's cozy and delicious.

> 6 medium-sized Rome Beauty or Fuji apples
>
> 1 cup crumbled macaroon cookies
>
> 6 tablespoons butter, softened
>
> ½ cup brown sugar
>
> 12 to 18 walnut halves
>
> 1½ cups apple juice
>
> 1 pint good vanilla ice cream

Preheat the oven to 375°F. Wash and core the apples. Remove about 1 inch of peel from the stem end. Place the apples in a glass baking dish. Mix together the cookie crumbs, butter, and brown sugar to form the filling for the apples. Fill the apples, mounding some of the filling over their tops. Press 2 or 3 walnut halves into the mounded filling of each apple.

Heat the apple juice to boiling and pour into the baking dish. Bake for 1 hour, basting 3 or 4 times. While the apples are baking, remove the ice cream from the freezer and let it melt. Transfer to a pitcher to serve as a sauce for the warm apples.

Variation: Stuff 3 mini-marshmallows or several raisins in the bottom of each apple cavity when the apples are firmly resting in the baking dish to seal the opening and prevent the filling from running out during baking.

Serves 6

Apple Grunt

This is one of my favorite recipes from James Beard's classes at Gearhart, Oregon. I have used it over and over again because it is so easy to prepare and is so delicious.

3 or 4 large Granny Smith apples, peeled and sliced

4 tablespoons butter

¼ cup sugar

Topping

⅓ cup white sugar

1 cup self-rising flour

1 cup heavy cream, whipped

———

Vanilla ice cream

Preheat the oven to 400°F. Place the apple slices in a well-buttered 9- by 5-inch loaf pan, filling it two-thirds full. Dot with the butter and sprinkle with the sugar.

To make the topping, mix together the sugar and flour, fold in the cream, and spread over the apples.

Bake for 40 to 50 minutes, or until golden brown and bubbly. Serve warm with vanilla ice cream.

Serves 6

Apple-Mincemeat Pie

The apples in this pie help to lighten the mincemeat. This is good served warm with vanilla ice cream.

Pastry for a two-crust pie (page 231)
4 cups peeled, sliced apples
2 cups prepared mincemeat
1 tablespoon lemon juice
¼ cup brown sugar

Preheat the oven to 400°F. Roll out half of the pastry and fit it into a 9-inch pie pan. Mix the apples, mincemeat, lemon juice, and brown sugar, and spoon into the pastry shell. Roll out the remaining pastry and place on top of the pie. Seal the edges. Cut 4 to 6 vent holes in the top crust. Place the pie on a baking sheet and bake for 40 to 50 minutes.

Makes 1 9-inch pie

Pear Marmalade

This is a fresh-tasting fruit topping for toast in the morning, and is a favorite on toasted English muffins.

3 cups peeled, diced pears
1 cup canned crushed pineapple, well drained
1 small orange, chopped and then processed in a food processor
1 package powdered pectin
4 ½ cups sugar

In a large saucepan, bring the pears, pineapple, orange, and pectin to a boil, stirring constantly. Add the sugar and boil 2 minutes longer. Pour into hot sterilized half-pint canning jars and seal. Process in a water bath for 5 minutes.

Makes 6 half-pints

Neil's Cranberry Pears

Winter pears take on a beautiful blush color and a nice tart flavor when poached in cranberry juice instead of red wine.

> 6 pears, peeled and cored
>
> 4 to 6 cups cranberry or cranberry-raspberry juice
>
> 3 to 4 tablespoons honey (depending on how sweet the pears are)
>
> Cinnamon stick, 2 inches long
>
> Heavy cream

Preheat the oven to 375°F. Put the pears in a 2½-quart casserole with a lid. In a saucepan, bring the juice, honey, and cinnamon stick to a boil. Pour over the pears and bake in the oven for 1 hour (until the pears are tender but not mushy and have a nice pink color). Let the pears cool in the juice. Serve in dessert dishes with a little of the juice and a pitcher of cream to pour over.

Note: To make a syrup to pour over the pears, you can reduce the cooking juices in the saucepan.

Serves 6

Pear and Cranberry Crunch

Although this version of fruit crunch calls for pears and cranberries, you can also make it with apples or peaches. One of my favorites combinations is nectarine and blueberry. This dessert is fast and simple to make. You can prepare a large batch of the topping and keep it in the refrigerator, all ready to go.

> 6 to 8 Bartlett pears
>
> 1½ cups cranberries
>
> 1 teaspoon grated orange zest
>
> ½ cup granulated sugar
>
> 4 tablespoons butter

Topping

> 1 cup flour
>
> ½ cup brown sugar
>
> ¼ pound (1 stick) butter
>
> 1 cup oatmeal
>
> 1 cup chopped pecans

Preheat the oven to 350°F. Peel, core, and cut the pears into 1-inch pieces. Mix together with the cranberries, orange zest, and sugar, and put in a 9- by 13-inch glass baking dish. Dot with the butter.

To make the topping, mix together the flour, brown sugar, butter, oatmeal, and pecans, rubbing between your fingers until well blended. Pack on top of the fruit. Bake for 45 to 55 minutes, until the pears are soft and juicy.

Makes enough to fill a 9-by-13-inch baking dish

Pear Streusel Pie

This is a favorite winter pie recipe that was given to me years ago and is always a show-stopper. Use Bartlett pears.

> *Pastry for a single-crust pie (use half of recipe on page 231)*
>
> *3 tablespoons flour*
>
> *¼ cup brown sugar*
>
> *¼ cup granulated sugar*
>
> *3 tablespoons lemon juice*
>
> *5 or 6 pears, peeled and sliced*
>
> *¼ teaspoon freshly grated nutmeg*
>
> *3 tablespoons butter, melted*

Streusel Topping

> *½ cup flour*
>
> *¼ cup brown sugar*
>
> *¼ cup granulated sugar*
>
> *5 ⅓ tablespoons (⅓ cup) butter, softened*
>
> *½ teaspoon ground cinnamon*
>
> ———
>
> *Vanilla ice cream*

Preheat the oven to 400°F. Roll out the pastry and fit it into a 9-inch pie pan. Mix together the flour and sugars. Add the lemon juice, pears, nutmeg, and melted butter, mixing well. Arrange in the pastry shell.

To make the topping, mix together the flour, sugars, butter, and cinnamon, and sprinkle over the pears. Bake for 40 to 50 minutes. Serve warm with vanilla ice cream.

Makes one 1 9-inch pie

Pear Butter Cake

The buttery richness of this cake makes it just right for a breakfast coffee cake.

¼ pound (1 stick) butter, softened

¼ cup sugar

1 teaspoon vanilla extract

1 egg

1 cup flour

½ teaspoon baking powder

¼ teaspoon salt

3 pears, peeled, cored, and cut into 1-inch pieces

¼ cup sugar mixed with ½ teaspoon ground cinnamon

1 cup heavy cream, whipped and lightly sweetened

Preheat the oven to 350°F. Grease a 9-inch springform pan. Using a mixer, cream the butter and sugar together until light and fluffy. Add the vanilla and egg, and mix well.

In a medium bowl, combine the flour, baking powder, and salt. Stir into the butter mixture until well combined. Spread the dough in the pan. Arrange the pears on top. Sprinkle with the cinnamon sugar and bake in the oven for 40 minutes. Cool. Remove the outside rim of the springform pan and cut into serving pieces. Transfer to individual dessert plates. Serve with a dollop of lightly sweetened whipped cream on top.

Serves 8

Peach Shortcake

I think shortcakes should always be served in shallow bowls so that you can get plenty of fruit around them. When James Beard made peach shortcake, he always added a little bourbon to the sliced peaches.

8 to 12 ripe peaches, sliced and sugared lightly ahead of time, with a little lemon juice squeezed over to prevent discoloring

1¾ cups cake flour

½ teaspoon salt

1 tablespoon baking powder

¼ cup sugar

¼ pound (1 stick) butter, cut into 6 to 8 pieces

¾ cup milk

Heavy cream, whipped and lightly sweetened

Preheat the oven to 425°F. Mix together the flour, salt, baking powder, and sugar. Add the butter and blend until the mixture resembles coarse crumbs. Add the milk. Mix until the dough follows the fork around the bowl. Pat out into a circle (½ inch thick) on a buttered baking sheet. Bake for 20 to 25 minutes. Cut into 6 wedges. Split and fill with the sugared peaches. Save a few slices for topping, together with the lightly sweetened whipped cream.

Serves 6

Fresh Peach Melba with Raspberry Sauce and French Vanilla Ice Cream

I like tree-ripened peaches best uncooked. The texture and flavor of the fruit seem to disappear during cooking.

4 peaches

French vanilla ice cream

Tamara's Raspberry Sauce (page 187)

Whipped cream (optional)

Peel the peaches with a vegetable peeler. Cut in half. Serve a scoop of ice cream with a peach half, and pour raspberry sauce over the top. Whipped cream can be offered on the side.

Serves 8

Jackie Clark's Peach Dumplings

These fruit dumplings are baked in a delicious sauce and served warm with a pitcher of chilled nutmeg cream to pour over.

3 peaches

Pastry

1 ½ cups flour

1 teaspoon baking powder

½ teaspoon salt

½ cup shortening

½ to ¾ cup milk

Sauce

¾ cup dark brown sugar

1 ½ cups water

4 tablespoons butter

¼ cup granulated sugar

½ teaspoon ground cinnamon

---

1 cup chilled half-and-half, sweetened with ¼ cup sugar and ½ teaspoon freshly grated nutmeg

Preheat the oven to 375°F. Peel peaches and cut in half.

To make the pastry, mix together the flour, baking powder, and salt. Blend in the shortening. Add just enough milk to hold the mixture together. Roll out on a floured board to ¼ inch thick. Cut into 6 squares. Place a peach half in the middle of each square, bring the corners together, and pinch to seal. Try to enclose the fruit completely.

To make the sauce, place the brown sugar, water, and butter in a heavy, ovenproof 10-inch skillet and boil for 5 minutes. Place the dumplings in the skillet with the sauce. Sprinkle with sugar and cinnamon and bake for 25 to 35 minutes.

Serve with the chilled nutmeg cream.

Serves 6

Plum Sauce Cake

This is a wonderful fall cake. The touch of cloves is a nice surprise. I like to serve it with Hot Spiced Cider (page 176).

¼ pound (1 stick) butter

1¼ cups brown sugar

1 egg, beaten

½ teaspoon each ground cloves, cinnamon, and nutmeg

1 teaspoon vanilla extract

1½ cups Plum Sauce (recipe follows)

1 cup raisins

½ cup chopped walnuts

2 cups flour

2 teaspoons baking soda

½ teaspoon salt

Cream Cheese Frosting (page 176)

Preheat the oven to 350°F. Using a mixer, cream the butter, sugar, and egg. Add the spices and vanilla. Stir in the Plum Sauce, raisins, and nuts. Sift together the flour, baking soda, and salt, and add to the plum mixture. Pour into a lightly greased 9- by 5-inch loaf pan or a 9- by 13-inch cake pan, depending on the shape you want. Bake for 50 minutes in the loaf pan or 35 to 40 minutes in the cake pan.

Plum Sauce

12 to 16 Italian plums

½ cup water

Stew the plums in a small saucepan with the water until soft. Remove the pits and purée in a food processor. (In the winter use canned plums.)

Cream Cheese Frosting

3 ounces cream cheese

¼ cup half-and-half

1 teaspoon vanilla extract

2½ cups powdered sugar, sifted

Using a mixer, mix the cream cheese and half-and-half together until soft. Mix in the vanilla. Gradually add enough powdered sugar to get a good consistency for spreading. Spread over the cooled cake or loaf.

Makes enough frosting for one 9- by 13-inch sheet cake

Hot Spiced Cider

We have wonderful fresh cider in the Northwest. It's good served icy cold, or take it hot in a thermos when you go skiing.

2 quarts apple cider

¼ cup lemon juice

1 teaspoon whole cloves

1 cinnamon stick

¼ cup brown sugar

Orange slices

Bring the cider, lemon juice, cloves, cinnamon stick, and brown sugar to a boil. Simmer, and serve with orange slices.

Makes 2 quarts

BERRIES

Berries

STRAWBERRIES: Shuksan, Puget Beauty, Hood, Rainier, Totems.

RASPBERRIES: Meeker, Willamette, Golden.

BLUEBERRIES: Bluecrop, Dixie, Jersey, Collins.

NATIVE WILD BLACKBERRY: The diminutive coast trailing blackberry is a native with an intense, sweet flavor. It is a tiny blackberry that is prized for pies and jams. It takes forever to fill a bucket, so pickers are known to keep their best patches top secret.

HIMALAYAN WILD BLACKBERRY: The large Himalayan blackberry is an import that now grows everywhere. The fruit is black and juicy and seedy and is best used in cobblers.

BOYSENBERRY: A blackberry-raspberry cross. Reddish-black fruit. Large, sweet, and juicy.

MARIONBERRY: A cross between wild and domestic blackberries, named for Marion County, Oregon, where it was developed. Medium-sized fruit that is longer than it is wide. Deep, dark red color.

LOGANBERRY: A red raspberry-wild blackberry cross. Large fruit with unique flavor and quality.

TAYBERRY: From Scotland, a red berry similar in shape to the boysenberry. A cross between loganberry and black raspberry.

CURRANT: Both red and black. Used in sauces, jellies, and juices.

GOOSEBERRY: A round, green berry protected by vicious thorns. The tart fruit is used in pies, jams, and sauces.

LINGONBERRY: Red, tart berry on a low-lying evergreen plant. Swedish pancakes without lingonberry syrup and without lingonberries stirred into whipped cream are simply not Swedish pancakes.

HUCKLEBERRY: For the Indians in the Northwest, this berry constitutes a major wild crop, and its arrival is celebrated with First Berry rituals. Sweet, musky blue huckleberries are found at higher elevations on the mountainsides, particularly where there has been fire or logging activity. The red, tart huckleberry is found in the Puget Sound lowlands.

Other Northwest Fruits

INTERLAKEN GRAPES: A golden grape, good for drying as raisins. SCHUYLER GRAPES: An extremely productive, sweet, juicy black grape for eating fresh and using for juice. CANADICE GRAPES: Red, seedless, with a spicy flavor. RED FLAME GRAPES: A red seedless variety.

CANTALOUPE: Some of the sweetest, richest-tasting cantaloupes come from Oregon and eastern Washington. A soft fruit that doesn't travel well. Short season.

CRANBERRIES: Cranberries are a big crop on the coast of Washington and Oregon.

RHUBARB: Rhubarb is one of those vegetables that always gets stuck in among the fruits. The majority of the U.S. crop is grown in the Puyallup Valley in the shadow of Mount Rainier. First come the hothouse varieties, then the field-grown rhubarb.

Hood River Cream Sauce with Berries

This is a light custard sauce that complements but doesn't overpower the fruit. Serve fresh berries in cut-glass dishes, then pass around a pitcher of this wonderful sauce.

¼ cup plus ⅓ cup sugar

2 pints freshly sliced strawberries, fresh raspberries, or blackberries

1 cup milk

½ cup heavy cream

1 vanilla bean

4 egg yolks

2 teaspoons cornstarch

Sprinkle ¼ cup of the sugar over the berries and chill. Meanwhile, in a medium-sized saucepan, combine the milk, cream, and vanilla bean, and bring just to a boil. Remove from the heat and let sit for 10 minutes. Using an electric mixer, gradually beat the remaining ⅓ cup sugar into the egg yolks until the mixture is light and lemon-colored. Beat in the cornstarch. Stir the milk mixture slowly into the beaten yolks. Return to the saucepan. Cook until the mixture is thick enough to coat a metal spoon, then cool. Remove the vanilla bean. Chill thoroughly.

Makes 1 ½ cups

Tukwila Blackberry Jam

We have a steep bank near our house that is covered with blackberry bushes. The fruit comes on in late summer. These are large, juicy blackberries that are simply too juicy to work in pies. They are best in cobblers and jam. (The smaller, trailing wild blackberry is the best for pies.)

3½ cups crushed blackberries

¼ cup freshly squeezed lemon juice

1 package powdered pectin

1 cup light corn syrup

4½ cups sugar

Lightly rinse the blackberries in cold water, then crush but don't purée in a food processor. Put the blackberries and lemon juice into a 4-quart kettle. Slowly pour in the pectin, stirring vigorously until it is dissolved. Let the mixture sit for 45 minutes, stirring occasionally. Add the corn syrup and mix well. Over very low heat, stir the sugar gradually into the crushed berry mixture. Using a candy thermometer, slowly warm to 100°F, but no warmer. When the sugar is dissolved, pour the jam into clean glass jars with tight lids. It will keep in the refrigerator for 2 to 3 weeks or in the freezer for longer periods of time.

Makes 8 cups

Overlake Farm's Spiced Blueberry Jam

Every August we look forward to fresh blueberries at the Overlake Blueberry Farm near Seattle. Five varieties grow there, and they all freeze well.

> 6 cups blueberries
>
> 2 tablespoons lemon juice
>
> 1 box powdered pectin
>
> ½ teaspoon each ground cloves, cinnamon, and allspice
>
> 5 cups sugar

Crush the washed berries (you should have 4 cups). Put into a 5-quart kettle. Add the lemon juice, pectin, and spices; mix well. Bring to a full boil over high heat, stirring constantly. Immediately stir in the sugar. Boil hard for 1 minute, stirring constantly. Remove from the heat and skim off foam. Stir and skim for 5 minutes to get rid of floating fruit. Ladle into hot sterilized canning jars. Cover with paraffin.

Makes 4½ pints

Forgotten Torte with Fresh Berries and Whipped Cream

If you gradually add your sugar after the soft peak stage when beating egg whites, they form a light, lovely meringue. My favorite fruit topping for this is a combination of peaches or nectarines and two or three different kinds of berries mixed together in a bowl and sprinkled lightly with sugar and a dash of kirsch.

1 cup egg whites (about 7 eggs)

¼ teaspoon salt

½ teaspoon cream of tartar

1 teaspoon vanilla extract

½ teaspoon almond extract

1½ cups sugar

1 cup heavy cream, lightly sweetened

4 cups marionberries, raspberries, strawberries, or sliced peaches, lightly sprinkled with
½ cup sugar

Preheat the oven to 450°F. Put the egg whites in a large glass or stainless steel mixing bowl and bring to room temperature. Beat until soft peaks form. Sprinkle in the salt, cream of tartar, vanilla, and almond extract and continue beating. Slowly add the sugar while continuing to beat until all of the sugar is added and a nice meringue has formed. Transfer to a standard-sized angel food cake pan buttered on the bottom only. Place in the oven and turn off the heat at once. Leave in the oven overnight. Next morning, turn out onto a serving plate. Chill, lightly covered with plastic wrap, in the refrigerator.

An hour before serving, whip the cream and use it to frost the cake. Spoon berries and/or peaches on each serving.

Serves 8

Blueberries and Cream Muffins

A moist muffin with a golden brown "cracked" top, full of plump blueberries.

¼ pound (1 stick) butter, softened

¾ cup sugar

2 extra-large eggs, at room temperature

1 teaspoon grated lemon zest

¾ cup sour cream

1 teaspoon vanilla extract

2 cups fresh or frozen blueberries

2 cups all-purpose flour

½ teaspoon baking soda

½ teaspoon salt

Preheat the oven to 375°F. Using a mixer, cream the butter and sugar together. Add the eggs, one at a time, beating well after each addition. Add the lemon zest, sour cream, and vanilla. Stir in the blueberries.

In a medium bowl, mix together the flour, baking soda, and salt, and fold into the creamed butter mixture with a spatula, being careful not to overmix.

Fill 12 paper-lined muffin cups. Bake for 25 to 30 minutes.

Makes 12 muffins

Mom's Strawberry Jam

My mother's jams are consistently wonderful. During berry season, she makes a batch of jam a day for a local bakery. She knows how to make jam.

7 half-pint jars and matching lids (use new lids only)

4 cups crushed strawberries (approximately 6 cups whole strawberries)

7 level cups granulated sugar

1 teaspoon butter

1 pouch (3 ounces) liquid pectin

Sterilize 7 half-pint canning jars by washing and rinsing them in the dishwasher without detergent. Keep them warm under cloth towels. Put the jar lids in a small pan, cover with water, and boil for 10 minutes. Turn off the heat but keep the lids warm.

Rinse the strawberries lightly, being careful not to bruise them. Drain. Completely cut away the green caps and any damaged portions of the fruit. Place a small amount of strawberries at a time in a food processor and pulse briefly, making sure to crush but not purée the berries. Repeat until all of the strawberries are crushed.

Measure 4 cups of crushed strawberries. Place the strawberries and sugar in a large kettle and mix thoroughly.

Open the liquid pectin pouch with scissors. Stand it upright in a cup while waiting for berries to boil. Bring the strawberry mixture to a full, rolling boil over high heat. Add the butter and continue to stir as it melts. Pour in the pectin all at once, stirring vigorously. When the mixture reaches a full, rolling boil again, stir for 1 minute.

Remove the kettle from the heat. Using a metal spoon, skim off any foam.

Fill the sterilized jars with jam, leaving ⅛ inch of room at the top. With a damp cloth, wipe the jar rims. (The rims of the jars must be impeccably clean or they will not seal properly.) Quickly place the lids on top and screw on tightly. Set the jars upside down on a dry towel. Cover and let stand for 5 minutes. Return to an upright position. Cover with a large cloth towel and set aside to cool for 8 to 15 hours. Check to make sure they are properly sealed. Store in a cool, dark place for up to a year. Keep opened jars in the refrigerator.

Makes 7 half-pints

Variations: Red raspberry jam: Follow the recipe for Strawberry Jam, using 6½ cups of granulated sugar and 4 cups crushed red raspberries.

Blackberry jam: Follow the recipe for Strawberry Jam, using 7½ cups of granulated sugar and 4 cups crushed blackberries.

Pasta & Co. Cranberry Sauce

Pasta & Co. operates five upscale take-home food stores in the Northwest. This is their recipe for one of my favorite additions to our Thanksgiving dinner.

1 bag (12 ounces) raw cranberries, washed, dried, and picked over

¾ cup dried sour cherries

⅓ cup sugar

⅔ cup red currant jelly

⅔ cup water

¼ cup dark rum

In a large saucepan, combine the cranberries, sour cherries, sugar, jelly, and water. Over low heat, bring to a low simmer and cook, stirring occasionally, for about 5 minutes. Remove from the heat. Stir in the rum. Refrigerate overnight to thicken the sauce. Return to room temperature before serving.

Makes 3½ cups

Cranberry-Apple Relish

I like the fresh, tart taste of the uncooked cranberries in this recipe. It complements the turkey and dressing.

2 Granny Smith apples, with skins on

1 orange, with the peel on

1 bag (12 ounces) cranberries

1 cup sugar

Wash all fruit. Quarter the orange and core the apples. Coarsely chop the cranberries, then the apples, and then the orange in a food processor. Add the sugar, stir, and chill for several hours in the refrigerator before serving.

Makes 4 cups

Steamed Cranberry Pudding with Butter Cream Sauce

Cranberries give a tart flavor to this moist holiday dessert. Serve warm with the hot Butter Cream Sauce poured over the top.

¼ cup shortening

⅔ cup sugar

1 egg

1½ cups all-purpose flour

½ teaspoon salt

1 tablespoon baking powder

⅔ cup milk

1 cup chopped cranberries

½ cup seedless raisins

½ cup chopped walnuts

1 teaspoon grated orange zest

Butter Cream Sauce (recipe follows)

Using a mixer, cream the shortening and sugar together. Add the egg and continue mixing. Add the flour, salt, baking powder, milk, chopped cranberries, raisins, walnuts, and orange zest, and stir until completely mixed.

Pour into a greased and sugared 1-quart mold. Cover. Put 1 inch of water in a large pot with a tight-fitting cover. Place the mold on a rack in the pot and cover the pot. Bring to a boil and then reduce the heat to low. The steaming should be slight. Add water as needed. Steam for 1½ hours. Remove the mold from the pot and let stand several minutes before unmolding. Serve with the Butter Cream Sauce.

Serves 4

Butter Cream Sauce

1 cup sugar, mixed with 1 tablespoon flour

½ pound (2 sticks) butter

½ cup half-and-half

1½ teaspoons vanilla extract

Place all of the ingredients in a heavy saucepan. Stir until well mixed. Simmer over low heat for 12 to 15 minutes, until thickened.

Cranberry-Orange Muffins

The tart cranberries are complemented by the orange. These muffins are moist and rise well.

1 teaspoon grated orange zest

1 cup orange juice

½ cup honey

2 extra-large eggs, beaten

¼ cup vegetable oil

2 cups coarsely chopped cranberries

2 cups all-purpose flour

1 tablespoon baking powder

½ teaspoon salt

Preheat the oven to 375°F. In a large bowl, mix together the zest, juice, honey, eggs, and oil. Stir in the cranberries.

Mix the flour and baking powder together and fold into the orange-cranberry mixture, just until mixed. Don't overmix.

Drop the batter into paper-lined muffin tins. Bake for 25 minutes.

Makes 12 muffins

Blueberry-Apple Chutney

This spicy, fresh-tasting condiment complements roast pork or roast chicken.

2 pounds blueberries

Grated zest of 2 lemons

2 cups sugar

3 Granny Smith apples, peeled, cored, and finely chopped

1 cup cider vinegar

Juice of 2 lemons

1 tablespoon red pepper flakes

1 tablespoon mustard seed

Combine the blueberries, lemon zest, and sugar, and leave overnight in the refrigerator. The following day, peel and chop the apples. In a heavy enameled saucepan, combine the apples, vinegar, lemon juice, red pepper flakes, and mustard seed with the blueberry mixture. Cook over low heat until the mixture thickens, about 30 minutes. Pour into ½-pint plastic containers. Cool, then freeze.

Makes 5 pints

Tamara's Raspberry Sauce

This is a very simple but elegant sauce. You may leave the seeds in (for instance, when you are pouring it over yogurt) or strain them out for sauce to serve with chocolate cake. The sauce freezes well and keeps for months in the freezer. You can substitute blackberries for the raspberries.

9 cups raspberries

2 cups sugar

Put the berries in a saucepan and mash slightly. Add the sugar and bring to a boil over moderate heat. Cook for 5 minutes. Cool and transfer to freezer containers. Freeze any sauce that you won't be using immediately.

Makes 6 cups

Blueberry Sauce

Very nice on blintzes for brunch.

 1 ½ cups blueberries
 ½ cup orange juice
 ¼ cup sugar
 1 tablespoon cornstarch
 1 teaspoon grated orange zest

| In a saucepan, cook all of the ingredients over low heat until thickened.

Makes 2 cups

Strawberry Butter

This is good on breakfast scones (very Northwest).

 ¼ pound (1 stick) butter, softened
 1 cup sliced strawberries
 1 tablespoon lemon juice
 Honey to taste

| Using a mixer, cream the butter. Add the strawberries, lemon juice, and honey. Continue
creaming until well blended. Strawberry Butter will keep, refrigerated, for 3 days.

Makes 1 ½ cups

Glazed Strawberry Pie

A beautiful pie that tastes like strawberries and cream.

 Pastry for single-crust pie (use half of the recipe on page 231)
 3 cups sliced strawberries

Topping

> *2 cups mashed strawberries*
>
> *½ cup cold water*
>
> *1 cup sugar*
>
> *3 tablespoons cornstarch*
>
> ———
>
> *Whipped cream*

Preheat the oven to 400°F. Roll out the pastry and fit into a 9-inch pie pan. Prick the bottom of the pie shell with a fork and bake for 20 minutes until the crust is golden brown. Cool.

Arrange the sliced berries in the baked pie shell. To make the topping, put the mashed strawberries, water, sugar, and cornstarch into a medium-sized saucepan. Stir over medium-high heat until the mixture thickens. Pour over the uncooked strawberries in the shell. Chill until set.

Serve with whipped cream.

Makes one 9-inch pie

Strawberry-Rhubarb Pie

Strawberries and rhubarb complement each other in this favorite pie.

> *1½ cups sugar*
>
> *¼ cup all-purpose flour*
>
> *¼ teaspoon salt*
>
> *Several gratings fresh nutmeg*
>
> *3 cups sliced rhubarb (½-inch pieces)*
>
> *1 cup sliced strawberries*
>
> *Pastry for two-crust pie (page 231)*
>
> *2 tablespoons butter*

Preheat the oven to 400°F. In a large bowl, combine the sugar, flour, salt, and nutmeg.

Add the fruit, mixing well; let stand for 20 minutes. Roll out half of the pastry and fit it into a 9-inch pie pan; spoon in the fruit mixture. Dot with the butter. Roll the remaining pastry ⅛ inch thick and cut into ¾-inch strips. Arrange a lattice crust over the fruit. Turn the edges of the bottom crust up and flute with your fingers to make a standing rim. Bake for 40 to 45 minutes.

Makes one 9-inch pie

Orange Scone Berry Cakes

This is a gold-medal recipe, one of my favorites in the book. It was given to me by a dear friend who couldn't remember the source but has been making them for many years. She made 200 once and froze them for a garden reception.

> 2 cups (less 2 tablespoons) all-purpose flour
>
> 1 tablespoon baking powder
>
> 1 teaspoon salt
>
> ½ cup plus 2 tablespoons sugar
>
> 5⅓ tablespoons (⅓ cup) butter
>
> 1 extra-large egg, beaten
>
> ½ cup heavy cream
>
> 2 tablespoons melted butter
>
> 1 tablespoon grated orange zest
>
> 1 quart sweetened strawberries
>
> Whipped cream

Preheat the oven to 425°F. In a large bowl, stir together the flour, baking powder, salt, and the 2 tablespoons of sugar. Rub in the ⅓ cup of butter with your fingers until well blended. Combine the egg and cream and add to the flour mixture. Mix until just blended together.

Turn out on a lightly floured board and knead for 1 minute. Roll out to a rectangle 8 inches wide and ½ inch thick. Brush with the melted butter. Sprinkle with the remaining ½ cup of sugar mixed with the orange zest. Roll up jelly-roll fashion, sealing the edge. Cut into 1-inch rolls.

Place cut side down on an ungreased baking sheet and bake for 12 to 15 minutes. Serve topped with sliced, sugared strawberries and whipped cream.

Serves 8

Huckleberry Cream Cheese Pie

I first tasted this at a roadside restaurant in huckleberry country and returned home determined to make one of my own.

Crust

> 1 cup all-purpose flour
>
> 2 tablespoons powdered sugar
>
> ¼ pound (1 stick) butter

Filling

3 ounces cream cheese

½ cup powdered sugar

½ teaspoon vanilla extract

1 cup heavy cream

Topping

3 tablespoons cornstarch

½ cup granulated sugar

2 cups fresh huckleberries

Preheat the oven to 425°F. To make the crust, blend together the flour, powdered sugar, and butter until they just crumble. Pat evenly into a 9-inch pie pan. Prick well with a fork and bake in the oven for 8 to 10 minutes. Cool.

Make the filling by beating together the cream cheese, powdered sugar, and vanilla. Whip the cream until stiff and fold into the cream cheese mixture. Turn into the pie shell. Cover with plastic wrap and chill.

Make the topping by mixing the cornstarch and sugar together. Stir into the berries in a heavy enameled saucepan and cook over medium heat until the mixture thickens and looks shiny and clear. Cool and spread evenly over the chilled pie.

Makes one 9-inch pie

Jan's Huckleberry-Nectarine Pie

This is a great treat for a Labor Day weekend gathering. The lattice crust allows some steaming to occur, but not too much, and is good for soft tree fruits, which overcook easily.

Pastry for a two-crust pie (page 231)

½ cup sugar

2½ tablespoons cornstarch

½ cup cold water

4 cups sliced, unpeeled nectarines

1 tablespoon lemon juice

1 cup huckleberries

Preheat the oven to 425°F. Roll out half the pastry and fit it in a 9-inch pie pan. Combine the sugar and cornstarch in a saucepan, add the water, and bring to boil, cooking for 1 minute. Cool. Combine the sugar-cornstarch mixture with the nectarines, lemon juice, and huckleberries. Pour into the pastry-lined pan. Roll the remaining dough ⅛ inch thick and cut it in ¾-inch strips. Arrange a lattice-style crust over the top of the fruit. Turn the edges of the bottom crust up and flute with your fingers to make a standing rim. Place the pie on a cookie sheet to prevent spills in the oven. Bake on lower rack of the oven for 30 to 40 minutes, until the crust is golden and you can see the fruit bubbling slightly.

Makes one 9-inch pie

Wild Blackberry Pie

You have to use the small wild blackberries for this pie. The big blackberries, while more abundant and easier to pick, simply yield too much juice.

> *Pastry for a two-crust pie (page 231)*
> *4 cups small wild blackberries*
> *¼ cup all-purpose flour*
> *1 cup sugar*
> *4 tablespoons butter*

Preheat the oven to 425°F. Roll out half of the pastry and fit it into a 9-inch pie pan. Fill the shell with the berries. Mix the flour and sugar and sprinkle over berries. Dot with the butter. Roll out the remaining pastry and fit it over the top of the pie. Seal the edges. Make 6 to 8 slits in the top crust. Bake on the lower rack of the oven for 45 to 50 minutes.

Makes one 9-inch pie

Willie's Blackberry Crisp

In August we make this dessert often, when jumbo blackberries are wildly abundant. This is my favorite way to utilize the very large, juicy Himalayan blackberries that hang in clusters from mid-July through Labor Day. Wear long sleeves and long pants when picking to avoid the sharp thorns or you'll be covered with scratches.

> *5 to 6 cups fresh blackberries*
> *¾ cup sugar*
> *2 tablespoons all-purpose flour*

Topping

1 cup all-purpose flour

1 cup sugar

1 teaspoon baking powder

1 egg, beaten

¼ pound (1 stick) unsalted butter, melted

———

Vanilla ice cream

Preheat the oven to 375°F. Place the blackberries in a medium-sized bowl. Sprinkle with the sugar and flour. Toss gently to evenly coat the berries. Transfer the berry mixture to a well-buttered 8- by 8- by 2-inch glass baking dish.

To make the topping, mix the flour, sugar, and baking powder in a bowl. Make a well in the center of the dry ingredients and blend in the egg, mixing until the topping is crumbly. Sprinkle over the berries. Drizzle the melted butter evenly over the crumbly topping. Place the baking dish on a baking sheet to prevent spillovers. Bake for 45 minutes.

Serve with vanilla ice cream.

Serves 6

Fourth of July Raspberry Summer Pudding

Sprinkling a little sugar over your berries and letting them sit in the refrigerator for several hours brings out the juice. Served with cream, they are just fine. This was the dessert James Beard had his cooking class serve for the Fourth of July picnic at Seaside, Oregon, where the classes were held.

¾ cup sugar

2 pints raspberries, rinsed with cold water

Thinly sliced white bread, crusts removed

¾ cup water

Whipped cream

Sprinkle the sugar over the freshly rinsed raspberries in a medium saucepan. Let sit for 30 minutes to draw out the juices. Line a 6-cup flat-bottomed bowl with white bread. Add the water to the berries and bring to a boil. Remove immediately from the heat and let cool. Pour half of the berry mixture into the bread-lined bowl. Add another layer of bread, then the remaining berry mixture, and finally cover with a last layer of bread. Lay a plate that will fit inside the bowl on top to weight the mixture down. Refrigerate for 4 to 6 hours. Invert onto a serving plate. Serve with whipped cream.

Serves 6 to 8

Huckleberry Slump

This is a colonial New England specialty that has become a part of the culinary tradition of the Pacific Northwest.

> *6 cups huckleberries (blueberries can be substituted)*
>
> *1 cup sugar*
>
> *1 teaspoon ground cinnamon*
>
> *½ cup water*
>
> *1½ cups all-purpose flour*
>
> *¼ teaspoon salt*
>
> *1½ teaspoons baking powder*
>
> *½ cup milk*
>
> *Lightly whipped sweetened heavy cream mixed with a dash of fresh nutmeg*

Combine the huckleberries, sugar, cinnamon, and water in a saucepan. In a bowl, mix together the flour, salt, and baking powder. Add the milk and mix lightly. Bring the huckleberry mixture to a boil. Drop the dough by spoonfuls onto the huckleberry mixture. Cover. Turn down the heat and simmer for 30 minutes. Serve warm with the sweetened, lightly whipped cream.

Serves 6

Gooseberry Fool

It takes time to pick the fuzzy ends off gooseberries, not to mention the needle-sharp jabs you suffer harvesting the fruit. But they are so wonderfully tart that a treat like this fool makes it worth the trouble.

   1 quart ripe gooseberries (or raspberries, huckleberries, rhubarb, marionberries,
      blackberries, or boysenberries)

   ¾ to 1 cup sugar, depending on the sweetness of the fruit

   ¼ cup water

   1½ cups heavy cream (the richer the better)

Combine the berries and sugar with the water in a saucepan. Cook over low heat until the fruit is soft. Taste for sweetness and add more sugar if needed. Remove from the heat and work the mixture through a strainer to make a smooth purée. Chill.

Whip the cream. Fold the chilled fruit purée into the whipped cream, just barely mixing them together to get a well-marbled appearance. Chill and serve in champagne-style dessert dishes with crisp shortbread cookies.

Serves 6

BREADS
& CAKES

FARM WIVES *and*
FIELDS *of* WHEAT

Before the ranchers and their cattle and the farmers and their plows, the southeastern corner of Washington State was covered with varieties of bunchgrass that grew as high as a horse's belly. That has since disappeared, most of it replaced by wheat, particularly in areas like the Palouse, where the soil is rich and the land rolls in upon itself like a steep, confused sea. Just to the west of the Palouse, in country called the Big Bend, the last of the state's native grasses grow on ground called scabland. It is a haunting landscape where wheat farms command the hilltops, and down low, where a glacial-era flood swept out of Montana and scoured the land clean of any topsoil, coarse, black volcanic rock erupts in long patches like slow-healing, crusty wounds. The land is too broken up into draws and hollows to run cattle, so there the bunchgrass continues to grow.

The Gray farm looks out at the scabland of the Big Bend country. Walter J. Gray, an Englishman, bought the farm in 1914 to retire from the dry goods business he had built up in Sprague, just to the north. Gray was a gentleman farmer. He wore jodhpurs and puttees and a tattersall vest. He oversaw 1,700 acres of cropland and 1,600 acres of pasture from the back of a horse while his hired man attended to the actual labor of farming. Walter Gray built his Ionic column–fronted house to look out over a formal orchard and farm buildings that could have been lifted and dropped into the Devonshire farm country of his youth. He kept a flock of sheep more as a visual counterpoint than for any practical purpose, such as profit.

Walter Gray was never without a pair of gloves or a riding crop. By beating time in the palm of one hand with the gloves or the crop, he could get his words past his profound stutter. Some say he was the black sheep of his family. Others say he knew well enough that as the younger son he would never inherit the family farm in England, which dated back to Norman times. So he sought his fortune elsewhere, first in Canada and then in the Washington Territory. One thing is known for sure: Walter Gray didn't like wet weather, and so he shied away from the west side of the Cascade Mountains in favor of the arid climate of eastern Washington.

Sometimes in the summer a hot northeast wind blows down on the Gray farm near the town of Washtucna, and even the casual observer can watch the wheat shrivel on the stalk. It can happen just before harvest, when the wheat needs another week or two to come to full fruit.

It must have come as a shock to Walter Gray when his two sons, John and Joe, decided on careers as farmers rather than businessmen. They had been sent off to school in England as little boys dressed in the style of Little Lord Fauntleroy. In later years governesses were shipped in to Sprague from Boston and England. Both of the boys attended Washington State College in Pullman, although John managed only a year while Joe finished. But none of the obvious attributes of British breeding stuck.

The newly arrived would never have guessed the two men had such a background, to see them as old farmers out in the wheat fields, one wearing striped coveralls, the other solid blue denim, and both with baseball caps pushed back on their heads as they rubbed wheat kernels in the palms of their hands, determining whether the time was right to start the harvest.

Their Britishness, particularly John's, showed in more subtle ways, like John's bearing with hired hands. He treated them like servants on the verge of dismissal. That the Gray brothers relied on hired hands at all set them apart from other farmers in the area, who approached the business of farming as a family ordeal. When John's son Walt ran the Gray farm, he maintained his own machinery. John Gray would have hired a mechanic.

Food and tradition also set the Grays apart. Chutney was a common condiment on the table, and continues to be in current generations of the family. So too are various curries, and Yorkshire pudding when beef is served, and mint sauce for lamb, made with wild mint and vinegar. The strange puddings common in British households are not unknown in the Gray family.

John's wife, Lilian, baked rice pudding in individual cups. Rice, tasting like it had been slow-cooked in cream, filled three-fourths of the cup, and a rich custard, browned on top from the heat of the oven, curled up and over the lip. To this dessert the lucky diner added a spoonful or two of rich heavy cream, fresh from the family cow.

Lilian may have learned her Yorkshire pudding and curry when she married into the Gray family, but she brought with her cooking skills unparalleled in the surrounding community. Her mother had learned her way around a kitchen from her own mother's Chinese cook in a Portland high-society home, and she passed her lessons on to her daughters. There were five of them, Lilian being the youngest. She began baking bread for the entire family when she was 12, and her baking skills were greatly appreciated on the Gray farm, particularly at harvest time. She cooked on a coal-burning stove until the late 1930s, when Roosevelt-era programs such as the Rural Electrification Administration forever changed the American farm kitchen. Lilian wasted no time switching to an electric stove and oven and moving in refrigeration and a freezer. Before electricity she had relied on a freezer locker in the Washtucna butcher shop.

It was the food that brought the same stiffs back to work the wheat harvest year after year under the baleful eye of John Gray. Lilian Gray served the best food around, and plenty of it. Other wheat farmers would pile on the steaks and sausage and bacon, the pancakes and eggs and biscuits, but it was cooked up carelessly and served like slop to hogs. Lunch was delivered to the field, and the men ate it sitting in the dirt. If they didn't like it that way, they could clear out. There were plenty of men looking for work in the Depression years.

But at the John Gray farm the standing order was feet under the table three times a day. Lilian set a proper table, positioned herself at the door, and sent away any man who had not washed the wheat fields out of his ears and off his forearms.

She was white-haired even then, with the snowy white hair that can come on a woman at an early age and shape her beauty. Her brown eyes could fill with backlighted mirth or, when she was crossed, snap out at the unsuspecting with summer heat lightning, something John Gray would discover from time to time when he lumbered into his wife's domain. Dinner was to be served at 12:30 each day, and if John Gray got in a little early and started badgering Lilian about laying out the meal on time, sparks would fly.

Her way was to have everything perfect. It mattered not that the man at the dinner table was nearly toothless and reeked of b.o. and Bull Durham, a stiff hired off the streets of Spokane for the six weeks of harvest that started in mid-July. Lilian was determined to set a perfect table and produce a special meal. She cooked for a dozen hired hands and family men during harvests through the 1930s: roasts and fried potatoes and creamed onions fresh from her garden. She had her daughters out picking vegetables before the sun came up because she had read somewhere that fruits and vegetables were the most nutritious picked at dawn. She didn't just churn butter and form it into a rough block; Lilian pounded the water out of her butter and shaped it until the edges were sharp and the sides were square. The ones who remember soften up when they try to explain the effect of Lilian's butter melting into one of Lilian's rolls. She was a proud cook, a fine baker.

John Gray started Lilian's stove each morning when he got up. Then he would milk the cow and harness the twenty-eight mules that pulled the combine during harvest. The Gray brothers didn't sell the mules and switch to tractor-pulled machinery until 1937. Most days the oven would be hot enough to bake biscuits by breakfast time. After breakfast Lilian would bake pies for the noon meal, using homemade lard for the crust.

In spring she would bake berry and cherry pies, and through the summer she would change to apple and peach. She baked bread as it was needed, but biscuits and muffins and rolls and hot cross buns were a constant. There were no measuring cups and spoons in her kitchen, and the best of her ingredients came from just outside the kitchen door. Lilian's sour cream was just that. And the sour milk was true clabber. Eggs came fresh from the chicken house.

Lilian's oldest daughter, Kathrine, complained that when she left the farm for college she had to learn to cook all over again, and food has never tasted quite the same since. Lilian's cream didn't simply pour from the pitcher. It finally plopped out after a good long wait.

In the days when John Gray drove a combine pulled by twenty-eight mules, wheat was sewn into sacks on the combine, and the sacks were dropped in clusters in the fields. The sack sewer was an important man on the combine, as was the jigger, the man who nudged the filling sacks with his knees to get that full 153-pound measure before lifting the sack over to the sewer. The header puncher, usually a local farm kid, manned an apparatus like a ship's wheel to raise and lower the combine's cutting blades. A good header puncher would leave behind an evenly cut field with foot-tall wheat stubble. The sacks of wheat were picked up by men in the field, loaded onto the back of a truck, and hauled down to a warehouse by the railroad tracks. Some of those sacks were handled eight times between the field and the train car. So the men who came to sit at Lilian's table were hungry and thirsty. They downed tall glasses of iced tea, refilling them over and over again. And they cleaned their plates. No one gained weight during harvest.

The size of the crew diminished with the change from mule to tractor, then shrank again when John Gray switched from sacked wheat to bulk. By then he had grandchildren who drove the wheat into town to the grain elevator. He would hire only one or two men who would sit with the family at the noon meal and eat off fine china with silver utensils.

Lilian and John Gray left the farm after forty-five years and settled in a retirement complex in Portland, where Lilian continued baking. The year before she went into the hospital, never to return, she still baked hot cross buns for the entire complex, just as though the residents were another harvest crew.

Breads & Cakes

Sharon's Tips for Better Yeast Bread Baking

When I make a bread recipe for the first time, I always use a little less flour than is called for. You can always knead in more flour if the dough is too sticky, but too much flour will lead to a dry, crumbly loaf. There are many variables in bread baking that can't be defined in a recipe, such as the kind of flour used or the humidity in the kitchen, both of which can affect the end result. To prevent over-rising on hot summer days, have the liquid at room temperature, rather than heating water.

When working with yeast dough, I knead the dough for two or three minutes on a lightly floured board, then cover it with the bowl while I clean up. That takes about five to ten minutes and gives the dough a chance to rest and the gluten a chance to relax, which makes the dough much easier to knead to a smooth, elastic consistency. This technique also prevents the dough from absorbing too much additional flour during the kneading process.

For the first rising, I always use a large plastic bowl with a tight-fitting lid. It provides a warm, moist, draft-free environment for the dough to rise in. I can guarantee that in this kind of bowl the first rising will usually be complete within 45 minutes.

After the first rising, lightly punch down the dough. Shape into a standard loaf, baguette, or round, depending on your recipe. Let it rise again for 30 to 40 minutes, and bake.

Bake the bread until the top is well browned. Remove the loaf from the pan and check for doneness by inserting an instant-read thermometer in the center of the bottom of the loaf. The temperature should be 200°F.

Oatmeal Bread

I love this bread for its moist, full texture, and for the ease with which it comes together. It makes great toast. Betsy Piper's grandmother passed on this recipe to her family.

2 cups boiling water

1 cup oatmeal (quick or regular)

2 tablespoons shortening

½ cup honey

1 package dry yeast

2 teaspoons salt

5 to 6 cups all-purpose flour

In a large bowl, pour the boiling water over oatmeal and stir to blend. Mix in the shortening and honey. Let cool until warm and no longer hot. Blend in the yeast. Let stand for 5 minutes. Add the salt and 4 cups of the flour and beat until blended.

Let the dough rest for 10 minutes on a floured board, then knead in the remaining flour, a bit at a time, until the dough is smooth and elastic. Let rise for 1 hour, or until doubled in bulk. Shape into 2 loaves, place in small, oiled bread pans, and let rise for 1 hour. Before baking, preheat the oven to 375°F. Bake the loaves for 40 to 50 minutes.

Makes 2 loaves

Pumpernickel Bread with Orange Zest

For the soup and salad dinner, this is the bread to serve. It has a special flavor, unlike anything you can buy.

2 packages dry yeast

¼ cup warm water

½ cup light molasses

1 tablespoon plus 1 ½ teaspoons grated orange zest

2 teaspoons crushed fennel seed

1 ½ teaspoons salt

2 cups buttermilk

3 cups pumpernickel or rye flour

2½ to 3½ cups all-purpose flour

Glaze

¼ cup water

1 tablespoon molasses

In a large mixing bowl, dissolve the yeast in the water.

In a medium-sized saucepan, heat the molasses, orange zest, fennel seed, and salt. Bring to a boil, stirring constantly. Remove from the heat, stir in the buttermilk, and cool to lukewarm. Stir the buttermilk mixture into the yeast, then gradually stir in the pumpernickel or rye flour. Mix in the all-purpose flour. Knead for 15 minutes. Cover and let rise for 1 hour.

Punch down the dough and divide it in half, shaping each half into a ball. Place on a greased baking sheet. Slightly flatten the loaves, cut an X across their tops with a sharp knife, and let rise for 1 hour.

Preheat the oven to 350°F. Mix together the water and molasses to form a glaze. Brush the loaves with the glaze. Bake for 45 to 50 minutes. Remove from the pans. Brush with glaze a second time, while the loaves are still hot. Cool on wire racks.

Makes 2 loaves

Basic Sourdough Starter

You can't achieve the flavor or texture of sourdough without a starter.

1 package dry yeast

1 tablespoon sugar

2 cups warm potato water (water in which you have boiled potatoes)

2 cups all-purpose flour

2 cups warm water

Combine the yeast, sugar, and potato water in a glass or porcelain bowl. Cover lightly with cheesecloth and let stand at room temperature for 24 hours, stirring occasionally.

After 24 hours, add the flour and warm water, cover lightly, and let the mixture sit out overnight. This is your basic starter. After using the starter in a recipe, replenish it and keep it stored in a glass or porcelain container with a lid in the refrigerator.

To replenish the starter, add to it 1 ½ cups flour and 1 cup warm water, beating until smooth. Cover with cheesecloth and leave out overnight, then stir down and refrigerate.

Makes 1 quart

Alfred Schissel's Sourdough Rye Bread

We first tasted this bread on a skiing vacation at Crystal Mountain. Alfred's daughter Dody baked it for us, and I have linked its lovely flavor with the Cascade Mountains ever since.

1 cup all-purpose flour

3 tablespoons sugar

2½ teaspoons salt

1 package dry yeast

1 cup milk

2 tablespoons butter

1½ cups Basic Sourdough Starter (page 204)

¼ cup rye flour

2½ cups whole wheat flour

Cornmeal

1 egg white, beaten with 1 tablespoon water

Caraway seeds

Combine the all-purpose flour, sugar, salt, and yeast in a large bowl.

In a small saucepan, warm the milk and butter to 110°F. Gradually add to the dry ingredients and beat for several minutes by hand until well blended, or beat for 2 minutes at medium speed in a mixer.

Add the starter and rye flour and mix well. Stir in the whole wheat flour. Turn the dough out onto a floured board, knead into a ball, and cover with a bowl for about 5 minutes. Continue to knead until smooth and elastic (10 minutes). Place in a greased bowl. Cover. Let rise in a warm place until doubled in size, 1 hour.

Punch the dough down and turn onto a lightly floured board. Divide in half. Let rest for 15 minutes.

Shape into 2 loaves and place seam side down on greased baking sheets sprinkled with cornmeal. Let rise for 1 hour, until doubled in bulk. Just before baking, carefully slash the tops of the loaves on the diagonal with a sharp knife.

Preheat the oven to 350°F. Brush the loaves with the beaten egg white. Sprinkle with caraway seeds. Bake for 40 to 50 minutes.

Makes 2 loaves

Sourdough White Bread

This bread has a smooth texture, a nice crust, and that characteristic sourdough flavor.

> 1 cup Basic Sourdough Starter (page 204)
>
> 1 cup water
>
> 5 to 6 cups all-purpose flour
>
> 1 package dry yeast
>
> 1 cup warm water
>
> 1 tablespoon salt
>
> 1 egg white, beaten with 1 tablespoon water

In a bowl, mix the starter, 1 cup water, and 2 cups of the flour, and let sit overnight.

In a large bowl, dissolve the yeast in the 1 cup warm water. Let stand for 10 minutes, then stir in the starter mixture. Add the salt and remaining 3 to 4 cups flour. Turn out onto a lightly floured board and knead for 10 minutes. Cover and let rise for 1 hour.

Punch down the dough and divide in half. Shape into 2 round loaves and place on a baking sheet, lightly sprinkled with cornmeal. Let rise for 1 hour. Preheat the oven to 450°F. Five minutes before baking, turn the oven temperature down to 375°F and carefully place a shallow pan with ½ inch of boiling water on the lowest rack of the oven. Cut slashes across the top of each loaf. Brush lightly with the beaten egg white. Bake for 45 minutes.

Makes 2 loaves

Honey-Whole Wheat Bread

This is our "house" bread; it makes great toast, is wonderful with bacon, lettuce, and tomato sandwiches, and makes a good dinner bread, too. To serve warm, simply reheat in the oven.

> 4 cups warm water
>
> 1 cup honey
>
> 2 packages dry yeast
>
> 4 cups whole wheat flour
>
> 1 cup wheat germ
>
> 1 tablespoon kosher salt
>
> ½ pound (2 sticks) butter, melted
>
> 5 to 6 cups all-purpose flour

Combine the water, honey, and yeast in a large bowl and let sit for 5 minutes. Add the whole wheat flour, wheat germ, and salt. Mix well. Add the butter and 4 cups of all-purpose white flour. Beat with a wooden spoon until well mixed. The dough will be sticky at this point. Stir in the remaining white flour, ½ cup at a time, until the dough no longer sticks to the sides of the bowl. Turn out on a well-floured board and cover with the bowl.

Let rest for 10 minutes, then knead the dough, adding more flour if necessary, until smooth and elastic. Cover and let rise in a lightly greased bowl for 1 hour.

Punch the dough down and divide into 3 equal pieces. Shape into loaves and place in buttered 9- by 5-inch loaf pans. Let rise, uncovered, until the dough comes above the edges of the pans (at least 1 to 1½ hours).

Preheat oven to 375°F. Bake the loaves for 40 to 50 minutes. Remove from the pans and let cool on racks.

Makes 3 loaves

Whole Wheat Nut-Raisin Yeast Bread

This recipe comes from Bob's Red Mill near Portland, Oregon, where the flour is stone-ground.

> *2 packages dry yeast*
> *2½ cups warm water*
> *1 cup regular oatmeal*
> *½ cup molasses*
> *2 tablespoons butter*
> *1 tablespoon salt*
> *½ cup milk*
> *1 cup chopped walnuts*
> *2 cups raisins, softened in boiling water and drained*
> *3 cups whole wheat flour*
> *3 cups all-purpose flour*

In a small bowl, soften the yeast in ½ cup of the warm water. In a large saucepan, bring the remaining 2 cups water to a boil and gradually pour in the oats, stirring constantly for 1 minute. Add the molasses, butter, and salt. Mix well. Stir in the milk and cool to lukewarm. Transfer the oatmeal mixture to a large bowl.

Add the dissolved yeast, and stir in the nuts and raisins. Add 2 cups of the whole wheat flour. Let rest for 30 minutes.

Add the remaining 1 cup whole wheat flour. Turn out onto a floured board and knead for 15 minutes. Divide in half, shape into loaves, and place each into a greased 9- by 5-inch loaf pan. Let rise for 1 hour.

Preheat the oven to 375°F. Bake loaves for 50 minutes, remove from the pans, and cool.

Makes 2 loaves

Squaw Bread

At Sunriver, Oregon, people line up early in the morning at the bakery to buy their favorite baked goods and at least two loaves of squaw bread. This is a version that I make at home, when I don't have any loaves left in the freezer. It's a slightly sweet, moist bread that makes wonderful toast and sandwiches.

> 2½ cups water
> ⅓ cup vegetable oil
> ¼ cup honey
> ⅓ cup light molasses
> 2 packages dried yeast
> ¼ cup warm water
> 3 cups whole wheat flour
> 2 teaspoons salt
> 1½ cups rye flour
> 2½ cups all-purpose flour
> ½ cup cornmeal

In a medium bowl, combine the water, oil, honey, and molasses. Mix well. In a small bowl, soften the yeast in the warm water.

In a large bowl, mix together the whole wheat flour, salt, rye flour, 1 cup of the all-purpose flour, and the cornmeal. Add the oil and honey mixture and the yeast to the flour mixture. Mix on low speed in a mixer for several minutes. Gradually add enough of the remaining 1½ cups all-purpose flour to make a soft dough. Turn out onto a floured board. Cover with a mixing bowl and let rest for 5 to 10 minutes. Then knead for 10 minutes, until smooth. Cover and let rise for 1 hour.

Punch the dough down. Shape into 3 round loaves and place on lightly greased baking sheets. Let rise for 50 to 60 minutes.

Preheat the oven to 375°F. Bake the loaves for 40 minutes. Cool on racks.

Makes 3 loaves

Mrs. Bastrom's Good Hot Dinner Rolls

This is the perfect hot dinner roll, a recipe handed down by my mother-in-law. A panful is a thing to behold. Pull them apart, watch the steam rise, and add the butter.

> *2 packages dry yeast*
> *1 cup warm water*
> *1 cup warm milk*
> *6 tablespoons sugar*
> *2 teaspoons salt*
> *¼ cup shortening*
> *1 egg, beaten*
> *6 cups all-purpose flour*
> *Melted butter*

In a large bowl, combine the yeast, water, milk, sugar, salt, and shortening. (The shortening will melt in the warm water.) Add the flour, mix, turn out on to a floured board, cover with the bowl, and let rest for 10 minutes. Then knead the dough for 10 minutes. Let rise for 1 hour.

Punch the dough down. Pinch off 24 equal-sized pieces of dough. Shape into balls. Place each one on the bread board, cover with a cupped hand, and roll with a circular motion. You'll feel the ball tighten up under your palm. If you've done it right, the balls will have a smooth surface and a crease on the bottom. Evenly space the rolls in a greased 9- by 13-inch baking pan, and let rise for 1 hour.

Preheat the oven to 325°F. Bake the rolls for 45 to 50 minutes. Remove from the oven and brush with melted butter.

Makes 2 dozen rolls

Raised Whole Wheat Buns

Here's a nice roll to serve with your favorite soup and a tray of fruit and cheese for a simple dinner. It also makes delicious sandwiches.

2 packages dry yeast

2 cups warm water

½ cup vegetable oil

¼ cup molasses

¼ cup honey

1 tablespoon salt

¼ cup sunflower seeds

¼ cup wheat germ

6 cups whole wheat flour

Dissolve the yeast in ¼ cup of the warm water in a mixing bowl. Add the oil, the remaining 1¾ cups water, molasses, honey, salt, sunflower seeds, wheat germ, and 4 cups of the flour. Mix well. Let rest for 30 minutes. Add the remaining 2 cups flour. Turn out onto a floured board and knead for 15 minutes. Cover and let rise for 1 hour.

Punch the dough down. Roll it out ½ inch thick on a floured board. Cut with a 2-inch biscuit cutter. Place on a greased baking sheet. Let rise for 45 minutes.

Preheat the oven to 375°F. Bake the buns for 20 minutes.

Makes about 3½ dozen buns

Oatmeal Crackers

I like to serve these crisp, nutty-flavored crackers with cranberry-quince jelly.

1 cup shortening

1 cup sugar

3 cups all-purpose flour

4 cups quick oatmeal

2 teaspoons salt

1 teaspoon baking soda, dissolved in 1 cup warm water

Preheat the oven to 350°F. Using a mixer, cream together the shortening and sugar. Mix in the flour, oatmeal, salt, and baking soda dissolved in water.

Roll the dough out on a lightly floured board to a thickness of ¼ inch, and cut into 2-inch squares. Place on a greased baking sheet and bake for 15 minutes.

Makes 2½ to 3½ dozen crackers

1-2-3 Banana Bread

A moist quick bread with a good banana flavor. It keeps well and slices easily.

> *½ cup margarine*
>
> *1 cup sugar*
>
> *2 extra-large eggs*
>
> *3 overripe bananas, mashed well*
>
> *2 cups all-purpose flour*
>
> *1 teaspoon baking soda*
>
> *¼ teaspoon salt*
>
> *¼ cup chopped nuts*

Preheat the oven to 350°F. Using a mixer, cream together the margarine and sugar. Add the eggs, one at a time. Mix in the bananas. Stir in the flour, baking soda, salt, and chopped nuts. Bake in a greased 9- by 5- by 3-inch loaf pan for 1 hour. Cool in the pan for 15 minutes, then remove from the pan and finish cooling on a rack.

Makes 1 loaf

Rhubarb Nut Bread

As virtually all rhubarb sold commercially in this country is grown in the shadow of Mount Rainier, this recipe embodies the Pacific Northwest in content as well as spirit.

> *2 cups finely chopped rhubarb*
>
> *1½ cups sugar*
>
> *2 cups all-purpose flour*
>
> *1 teaspoon salt*
>
> *4 teaspoons baking powder*
>
> *1 teaspoon ground cinnamon*
>
> *1 cup milk*
>
> *2 eggs, beaten*
>
> *3 tablespoons vegetable oil*
>
> *½ cup chopped nuts*

Preheat the oven to 375°F. In a medium bowl, mix the rhubarb with the sugar; let stand for 30 minutes. Combine the flour, salt, baking powder, and cinnamon in a large mixing bowl, then stir in the milk, eggs, and oil. Fold in the rhubarb and nuts. Pour into a greased 9- by 5-inch loaf pan. Bake for 1 hour.

Makes 1 loaf

Blueberry-Orange Bread

Serve this bread directly from the oven, with the juices from the berries flowing and mingling with the orange-scented crumbs.

> *2 tablespoons butter*
>
> *¼ cup hot water*
>
> *½ cup orange juice*
>
> *1 tablespoon grated orange zest*
>
> *1 teaspoon vinegar*
>
> *1 extra-large egg*
>
> *1 cup sugar*
>
> *2 cups all-purpose flour*
>
> *1 teaspoon baking powder*
>
> *¼ teaspoon baking soda*
>
> *2 cups blueberries*

Preheat the oven to 325°F. Melt the butter in the hot water. Add the orange juice, zest, and vinegar.

In a large bowl, beat the egg with the sugar until light and fluffy.

In a separate bowl, mix together the flour, baking powder, and baking soda. Add to the egg mixture alternately with the orange juice mixture. Combine completely but do not overmix. Fold in the blueberries.

Put into a well-greased 9- by 5- by 3-inch pan. Bake for 1 hour and 10 minutes.

Makes 1 loaf

Zucchini and Black Walnut Bread

This is a Labor Day ritual if you have zucchini in your garden. By that time of year the squash is usually too big to simply sauté. Next year, don't break the rule: one plant per family of five.

3 cups all-purpose flour

2 cups sugar

1 tablespoon ground cinnamon

1 teaspoon salt

2 teaspoons baking soda

1 tablespoon vanilla extract

1 cup vegetable oil

3 eggs, beaten

2 cups peeled, grated zucchini

½ to 1 cup chopped black walnuts

Preheat the oven to 325°F. Mix together all the ingredients in a bowl, being careful not to overmix. Divide into 2 lightly greased 9- by 5- by 3-inch loaf pans. Bake for 45 minutes.

Makes 2 loaves

Fresh Cranberry-Orange Bread

You'll find that this bread slices best the next day.

1 cup raw cranberries, chopped

1 tablespoon grated orange zest

¾ cup plus 2 tablespoons sugar

2 cups all-purpose flour

1 teaspoon baking soda

¾ teaspoon salt

1 extra-large egg, beaten

½ cup orange juice

½ cup water

3 tablespoons shortening, melted

1 cup chopped pecans

Preheat the oven to 375°F. In a bowl, combine the cranberries, orange zest, and 2 tablespoons of the sugar. In a large bowl, mix together the flour, baking soda, salt, and remaining ¾ cup sugar.

In a small bowl, combine the egg, juice, and water. Add to the flour mixture along with the melted shortening, cranberry mixture, and pecans. Stir just until blended. Put into a greased 9- by 5- by 3-inch loaf pan and bake for 1 hour.

Makes 1 loaf

Carpie's Graham Bread

A coarse-textured quick bread that's very moist, and especially good for breakfast.

1½ cups brown sugar

2 cups graham flour

1 cup all-purpose flour

1 teaspoon baking soda

1 teaspoon baking powder

1 teaspoon salt

2 cups buttermilk

3 tablespoons shortening, melted

Preheat the oven to 350°F. In a large bowl, mix the sugar, flours, baking soda, baking powder, and salt. Make a well in the middle and pour in the buttermilk and melted shortening. Mix lightly. Put in a lightly greased 9- by 5- by 3-inch loaf pan. Bake for 1 hour.

Makes 1 loaf

Gretchen Driver's Orange Rolls

A lovely, sweet breakfast roll with a wonderful orange flavor.

5 cups all-purpose flour

2 packages dry yeast

1¼ cups milk

½ cup shortening

⅓ cup sugar

1 tablespoon grated orange zest

¼ cup orange juice

1 teaspoon salt

2 extra-large eggs

Orange Glaze

1 cup powdered sugar

1 teaspoon grated orange zest

2 tablespoons orange juice

In a large mixing bowl, combine 2 cups of the flour and the yeast.

Warm the milk, shortening, sugar, orange zest, orange juice, and salt in a saucepan over low heat just until the shortening melts. Let cool to lukewarm and add to the flour and yeast mixture. Mix well. Beat in the eggs.

Stir in another 2½ cups flour. Knead on a floured board for 10 minutes, adding the remaining ½ cup flour if necessary. Cover and let rise for 1 hour.

Punch the dough down. Let rest for 10 minutes. Roll into a rectangle 18 by 10 inches and ½ inch thick. Cut into strips ¾ inch wide and 10 inches long. Loosely tie each strip into a knot. Place on a greased baking sheet. Let rise 30 minutes.

Preheat the oven to 375°F. Bake the rolls for 20 to 25 minutes, until golden brown.

While the rolls are baking, make the orange glaze by mixing the powdered sugar, zest, and juice together. Remove the rolls from the oven and brush the hot rolls with the glaze.

Makes 18 rolls

Cinnamon Rolls

These rolls stay soft as they sit, although it is unlikely they will last long enough for anybody to tell.

> *2 packages dry yeast*
>
> *1 cup warm water*
>
> *¼ cup sugar*
>
> *6 tablespoons butter, softened*
>
> *¼ cup powdered milk*
>
> *2 eggs*
>
> *4½ cups all-purpose flour*

Filling

> *4 tablespoons butter, melted*
>
> *2 teaspoons ground cinnamon*
>
> *½ cup sugar*
>
> *2 cups raisins, softened in hot water and drained (optional)*
>
> *1 cup chopped nuts (optional)*
>
> ———
>
> *Cream Cheese Frosting (page 176)*

In a mixing bowl, dissolve the yeast in the warm water. Let rest for 10 minutes. Add the sugar, butter, powdered milk, and eggs. Mix together. Add 4 cups of the flour and mix well. Turn out on a floured board, using the remaining ½ cup flour. Knead until smooth and elastic. Cover and let rise until doubled.

Roll the dough into a 10- by 15-inch rectangle. To make the filling, mix together the melted butter, cinnamon, and sugar. If you like, you can add raisins (softened in hot water) and chopped nuts as well. Spread over the dough. Roll up like a jelly roll, then cut into 1½-inch cross sections by sliding a thread under the roll, crossing the ends over the top and pulling tight. This way the dough isn't compressed. Place the rolls in a buttered 12- by 18-inch baking dish. Let rise for 30 minutes. Bake for 20 to 25 minutes.

While still warm, spread with the Cream Cheese Frosting.

Makes 12 rolls

LaRene Morrison's Breakfast Sticky Buns

This great way to start the day came from The Dune's Restaurant in Grayland on the Washington coast—home of LaRene Morrison, long regarded as one of the best breakfast cooks in the state.

¾ cup milk, scalded

½ cup granulated sugar

2 teaspoons salt

¼ pound (1 stick) butter

½ cup warm water

2 packages dry yeast

1 extra-large egg

4 cups all-purpose flour

Topping

2 cups brown sugar

1½ cups chopped pecans or black walnuts

¼ pound plus 4 tablespoons (1½ sticks) butter, melted

4 tablespoons butter, softened

To make the dough, combine the hot milk, sugar, salt, and the ¼ pound butter, and cool to lukewarm. Measure the water into a large, warm bowl, sprinkle in the yeast, and stir until dissolved. Then stir in the milk mixture, the egg, and 2 cups of the flour. Beat until smooth. Stir in enough of the remaining flour to make a stiff batter. Cover tightly with waxed paper. Refrigerate for at least 2 hours. (The dough can be kept in the refrigerator for up to 3 days.)

To make the buns, stir 1 cup of the brown sugar and 1 cup of the nuts into the melted butter. Spoon into a big 12- by 18-inch pan. Combine the remaining 1 cup brown sugar and ½ cup nuts and set aside. Divide the dough in half and roll out each half to a 12-inch square. Spread each square with 2 tablespoons of the softened butter, then sprinkle each with half of the sugar and nut mixture. Roll up like a jelly roll and cut into 1-inch slices. Place the rolls in the pan, pressing them down into the nuts, sugar, and butter. Cover and let rise for 1 hour.

Preheat the oven to 350°F. Bake the rolls for 25 minutes.

Makes 2 dozen

Blueberry Sour Cream Coffee Cake

The plump, juicy blueberries add pockets of flavor to this moist coffee cake.

    ¼ pound (1 stick) butter

    1 cup sugar

    2 extra-large eggs, beaten

    ½ cup milk

    1 cup sour cream

    1 teaspoon vanilla extract

    2 cups all-purpose flour

    2 teaspoons baking powder

    2 cups blueberries

Streusel Topping

    ⅔ cup all-purpose flour

    ½ cup sugar

    6 tablespoons butter

    ½ teaspoon ground cinnamon

Preheat the oven to 325°F. Using a mixer, cream together the ¼ pound of butter and the sugar. Add the eggs one at a time and continue beating until light and fluffy.

In a medium bowl, mix the milk, sour cream, and vanilla together. In another bowl, mix the flour and baking powder. Add the dry ingredients alternately with the sour cream–milk mixture to the egg mixture. Fold in the blueberries. Spread the batter in a greased and floured 9- by 13- by 2-inch pan.

Make the streusel topping, mix together the flour, sugar, 6 tablespoons of butter, and cinnamon until crumbly. Sprinkle the topping over the cake and bake for 50 minutes.

Serves 8

Cinnamon Sour Cream Coffee Cake

I think you should always serve a nice coffee cake for brunch. This is a favorite of mine. It has a good, moist texture.

¼ pound plus 4 tablespoons (1½ sticks) butter, softened

1½ cups granulated sugar

3 large eggs

2 teaspoons vanilla extract

3 cups all-purpose flour

1½ teaspoons baking soda

1½ teaspoons baking powder

¾ teaspoon salt

2 cups sour cream

Nut Mixture

1½ cups chopped walnuts

2 tablespoons ground cinnamon

2 tablespoons cocoa powder

1½ cups brown sugar

Preheat the oven to 350°F. Using a mixer, cream together the butter, sugar, and eggs (adding one egg at a time). Add the vanilla. In a separate bowl, mix together the flour, baking soda, baking powder, and salt. Add the dry ingredients alternately with the sour cream to the butter-egg mixture.

To make the nut mixture, in a small bowl combine the nuts, cinnamon, cocoa, and brown sugar. Pour a third of the batter into a greased, lightly floured 12- cup Bundt pan. Sprinkle with half of the nut mixture. Spoon a third of the batter into the pan. Sprinkle with the remaining nut mixture. Cover with the remaining batter. Bake for 55 minutes. Cool the cake in the pan on a rack for 10 minutes. Invert the cake, still in the pan, on a serving plate. Leave to cool for 30 minutes, and then remove the pan.

Serves 8 to 10

Miss Finney's Fresh Apple Cake

Mattie Finney came to the Northwest from Tennessee and taught cooking and sewing to her students on Vashon Island until she retired.

Apple Cake

    2 cups sugar

    3 eggs

    1 cup vegetable oil

    1 teaspoon vanilla extract

    ¼ cup orange juice

    3 cups all-purpose flour

    1 teaspoon baking soda

    1 teaspoon ground cinnamon

    1 cup peeled, chopped apples

    1 cup flaked coconut

    1 cup chopped pecans

Sauce

    1 cup sugar

    ¼ pound (1 stick) butter

    ½ teaspoon baking soda

    ½ cup buttermilk

Preheat the oven to 325°F. In a large bowl, combine the sugar, eggs, oil, vanilla, orange juice, flour, baking soda, and cinnamon. Stir in the apples, coconut, and pecans. Pour into a buttered and floured Bundt pan. Bake for 1½ hours.

Remove the cake from the oven. Leave it in the pan.

While the cake cools, prepare the sauce by combining the sugar, butter, baking soda, and buttermilk in a large saucepan. Bring to a boil. Remove from the heat. Using a skewer, poke holes in the warm cake while still in the pan. Slowly drizzle the sauce over the cake, letting it soak in. After 10 minutes, invert the cake onto a serving platter. Don't remove the pan. Let cool in the pan for another 10 minutes, then remove.

Note: Inverting a Bundt cake for 10 to 15 minutes after baking traps the steam and allows for the easy removal of the cake.

Serves 8 to 10

Finnish Coffee Bread

A good holiday bread.

1 package dry yeast

¼ cup warm water

2 cups warm milk

¾ cup sugar

2 eggs, beaten

2 teaspoons ground cardamom

1 teaspoon salt

8 cups all-purpose flour

¼ pound (1 stick) butter, melted

Topping

2 eggs, beaten

¼ cup chopped, slivered almonds

Coarsely crushed sugar cubes

In a large mixing bowl, dissolve the yeast in the water. Add the milk, sugar, eggs, cardamom, salt, and 5 cups of the flour. Mix well. Mix in the melted butter. Add enough of the remaining 3 cups flour to make a stiff dough. Turn out onto a floured board and knead for 15 minutes.

Divide the dough into thirds, then divide each third into 3 pieces. Roll each piece between your hands, forming a cord 12 to 14 inches long. Braid the 3 cords together, then repeat the process twice more. You should have 3 loaves. Place the braids on greased baking sheets. Let rise for 45 minutes.

Preheat the oven to 425°F. Gently brush the tops of the loaves with beaten egg. Sprinkle with chopped almonds and coarsely crushed sugar. Bake for 25 to 30 minutes, until golden brown.

Makes 3 braided loaves

Rosemary's Pear Claws

Rosemary Pflugrath owned Rosemary's Kitchen in Wenatchee, Washington. She produced applesauce, fruit butters, and other items right out of her orchard. This is her recipe using pear butter.

¾ cup milk

½ cup sugar

1 teaspoon salt

¼ pound (1 stick) butter

2 packages dry yeast

⅓ cup warm water

3 large eggs

6 cups all-purpose flour

2 cups Pear Butter (recipe follows)

Powdered Sugar Icing

1 cup powdered sugar

2 to 3 tablespoons heavy cream

———

Chopped walnuts

In a large saucepan, warm the milk. Stir in the sugar, salt, and butter. When the butter has melted, remove the mixture from the heat and cool to lukewarm.

In a small bowl, dissolve the yeast in the warm water, then add to the lukewarm milk mixture. Transfer to a large mixing bowl. Whisk in the eggs. Add enough of the flour to form a soft dough. Knead until smooth. Cover and let rise for 1 hour in a warm place.

Punch the dough down and divide in half. On a lightly floured board, roll each half into a rectangle 6 by 18 inches. Spread 1 cup of the pear butter in the center of each rectangle. Fold the rectangles in half lengthwise. Press the edges together to seal. Slice off individual rolls every 3 inches. With scissors, make 2 cuts halfway into each roll on the folded side, not the sealed edge.

Place the rolls on a greased baking sheet and let rise for 20 minutes. Preheat the oven to 350°F. Bake for 25 minutes, until golden brown.

To make the icing, combine the powdered sugar and cream. Drizzle over the rolls, and sprinkle with the chopped walnuts.

Makes 12 pastries

Pear Butter

2 pounds pears

4 tablespoons butter

¾ cup sugar

¼ teaspoon ground cinnamon

Peel, core, and dice the pears. Melt the butter in a heavy-bottomed, medium-sized saucepan. Add the diced pears, cover, and simmer until soft, about 10 minutes. Mash the pears. Add the sugar and cinnamon and simmer over low heat, partially covered, for 30 minutes, or until the extra liquid has evaporated and the pear butter has a shiny, glazed look.

Oatmeal Griddlecakes

The oatmeal gives these hotcakes great texture. They go well with fried ham, and nothing beats the flavor of maple syrup when it collides on a plate with ham.

1½ cups oatmeal

2 cups buttermilk

½ cup all-purpose flour

1 teaspoon sugar

1 teaspoon baking soda

1 teaspoon salt

2 eggs, beaten

In a large bowl, mix together the oatmeal and buttermilk and let sit for 15 minutes to soften the oatmeal. Then stir in the remaining ingredients. Bake on a hot griddle, turning once.

Makes 12 griddlecakes

Blueberry Buttermilk Pancakes

You will find these aren't caky pancakes—what we call sinkers—but are light and tender. The berries pop open and the juice mingles with the syrup on your plate.

1 ½ all-purpose cups flour

½ teaspoon salt

2 teaspoons baking powder

½ teaspoon baking soda

1 egg, beaten

1 ½ cups buttermilk

2 tablespoons butter, melted

2 cups blueberries

Maple syrup or powdered sugar and melted butter

In a large bowl, mix together the flour, salt, baking powder, and baking soda. Add the beaten egg, buttermilk, and melted butter. Mix well. Stir in the blueberries. Drop by spoonfuls onto a hot, lightly greased griddle. Turn only once and serve with maple syrup or powdered sugar and melted butter.

Makes 12 to 14 pancakes

Priest Lake Waffles

When I was growing up, my family spent the summers at Priest Lake, Idaho. The special breakfast was waffles and huckleberry syrup.

2 cups all-purpose flour

¼ teaspoon baking soda

½ teaspoon salt

1 tablespoon sugar

2 cups milk

3 extra-large eggs, separated

4 tablespoons butter, melted

In a large bowl, mix the flour with the baking soda, salt, and sugar. In another bowl, combine the milk, egg yolks, and melted butter, and stir until well mixed. Add to the dry ingredients, and mix just until well blended.

Beat the egg whites until stiff but not dry, and fold into the batter just before baking. Lightly brush a cold waffle iron with solid shortening, then heat (to prevent sticking). Cook the waffles until golden. Serve with fresh berry syrup.

Note: After making waffles, always leave your waffle iron open to cool to avoid having batter stick to the iron the next time you use it.

Makes 6 to 8 waffles

Ricotta Pancakes

These are tender and light. I like to serve them with fresh fruit that has been lightly sugared and allowed to sit for 30 minutes. Fresh strawberries or peaches are the best.

> *8 ounces ricotta cheese*
> *3 eggs, separated*
> *½ teaspoon salt*
> *⅔ cup milk*
> *½ cup all-purpose flour*

In a large bowl, mix together the ricotta, egg yolks, salt, milk, and flour. Beat the egg whites until stiff but not dry, and fold into the batter. Bake on a hot griddle, turning once. The pancakes should be small, 2 to 3 inches across.

Makes 12 to 14 pancakes

Sourdough Apple Pancakes

My good friend Larry Brown is a sourdough expert. This is his specialty. Serve these with nicely browned pork sausages. When cooking with sourdough starter, remember never to use metal bowls or spoons.

⅔ cup yellow cornmeal

1⅓ cups unbleached flour

¼ cup sugar

1 teaspoon baking powder

2 teaspoons baking soda

1 teaspoon salt

½ teaspoon freshly grated nutmeg

¼ teaspoon ground cinnamon

2 apples, preferably Golden Delicious, grated

3 eggs

4 tablespoons butter, melted

1 cup Basic Sourdough Starter (page 204)

½ cup buttermilk

Syrup

4 tablespoons butter

½ cup maple syrup

Grind the cornmeal in a blender or food processor for a few seconds. In a medium-sized bowl, stir together the cornmeal, flour, sugar, baking powder, baking soda, salt, nutmeg, and cinnamon. Stir in the grated apple.

In another bowl, blend together the eggs, melted butter, sourdough starter, and buttermilk. Combine with the apple mixture and set aside for 30 minutes.

At the end of 30 minutes, pour ⅓ cup of the batter onto a hot, lightly oiled griddle. Cook until small bubbles appear on the surface, then flip. Repeat until all of the batter is used.

To make the syrup, melt the butter over low heat and stir in the maple syrup. Pour over pancakes.

Makes 16 to 20 pancakes

Challah French Toast

I don't like the skin that forms on French toast when the egg mixtures cooks. I found that if I cream the eggs and sugar, the skin does not develop. Brioche, as well as any other good egg bread, also works well here.

2 large eggs

⅓ cup sugar

1 cup half-and-half

½ teaspoon ground cinnamon

6 pieces challah or other egg bread

Using a mixer, cream together the eggs and sugar until light and fluffy. Add the half-and-half and cinnamon, and mix well. Pour into a shallow dish. Coat the bread slices with the egg mixture and then cook on a hot griddle until lightly browned, turning once.

Serves 4

Buttermilk Scones with Currants and Orange Zest

Crusty on the outside and soft on the inside, these scones are wonderful split open and filled with soft butter and raspberry jam. Close them up after buttering so that the butter can melt.

3 cups all-purpose flour

⅓ cup sugar

2½ teaspoons baking powder

½ teaspoon baking soda

¾ teaspoon salt

¼ pound plus 4 tablespoons (1½ sticks) chilled butter, cut into 6 to 8 pieces

¾ cup currants

1 teaspoon grated orange zest

1 cup buttermilk

Topping

1 tablespoon heavy cream

¼ teaspoon ground cinnamon

2 tablespoons sugar

Preheat the oven to 400°F. Using a mixer, combine the flour, sugar, baking powder, baking soda, and salt. Add the butter and cut into the flour mixture until well blended. Add the currants and orange zest. Pour in the buttermilk and mix only until blended.

Gather the dough into a ball and divide it in half. On a well-floured surface, roll out into two circles, ½ to ¾ inch thick, then cut each circle into 8 wedges. Place scones on a lightly buttered baking sheet and bake for 12 to 15 minutes. Mix together the cream, cinnamon, and sugar, and brush over the tops of the hot scones.

Makes 16 scones

Cloud Biscuits

A moist biscuit. The key to having them rise nicely is not rolling them too thin.

> *2 cups all-purpose flour*
> *1 tablespoon sugar*
> *1 tablespoon baking powder*
> *½ teaspoon salt*
> *⅓ cup shortening*
> *1 extra-large egg*
> *⅔ cup heavy cream*

Preheat the oven to 450°F. In a bowl, mix together the flour, sugar, baking powder, and salt. Blend in the shortening with your fingers until the mixture resembles coarse crumbs.

In a small bowl, beat the egg and cream together and add all at once to the flour mixture, stirring gently with a fork just until blended.

Turn out onto a well-floured board, then pat into a circle ¾ inch thick. Cut into 2-inch rounds and place on an ungreased baking sheet. Bake for 12 to 14 minutes, until the tops are golden brown.

Serve with melted butter and honey.

Serves 6

Dutch Babies

This puffed pancake was made famous at a restaurant in Seattle called Manca's. It's no longer open, but say "Dutch baby" in Seattle and everyone says, "Manca's." I like to serve it on Saturday mornings with the traditional toppings of melted clarified butter, lemon juice, and powdered sugar.

> *4 tablespoons butter*
> *3 extra-large eggs*
> *½ cup all-purpose flour*
> *½ cup milk*

Topping

> *¼ pound (½ cup) clarified butter*
> *Juice of 1 lemon*
> *½ cup powdered sugar*

Preheat the oven to 425°F. Melt the butter in a 10- or 11-inch cast-iron skillet over low heat (here a cast-iron skillet works better than any other kind of pan). Mix the eggs, flour, and milk in a blender. Pour the batter into the skillet with the melted butter. Bake for 25 minutes. To serve, top first with the butter, then the lemon juice, and finally, the powdered sugar.

Serves 2

Blueberry Blintzes

These are worth the effort for special-occasion brunches. You can make them ahead, except for the final sautéing, and refrigerate for 2 days.

Blintz Batter

4 eggs

¼ teaspoon salt

1½ cups all-purpose flour

2 tablespoons butter, melted

2 cups milk

Filling

½ pound cottage cheese

½ pound cream cheese

1 egg, beaten

2 tablespoons butter, melted

2 tablespoons sugar

1 teaspoon vanilla

———

Butter for frying

Blueberry Sauce (page 188)

Sour cream

To make the batter, beat the eggs until lemon-colored. Add the salt, flour, melted butter, and milk. Let rest for 30 minutes while preparing the filling.

To make the filling, combine the cottage cheese, cream cheese, egg, melted butter, sugar, and vanilla in a food processor and blend just until smooth.

For each blintz, ladle ⅓ cup batter into a lightly buttered 6-inch crêpe pan. Cook until lightly browned on one side (you don't have to turn it) and slip it out of the pan onto paper towels. To fill the blintzes, place 2 tablespoons filling on the brown side of each crêpe. Fold up envelope fashion. Sauté each blintz in butter, and serve warm with Blueberry Sauce and sour cream.

To prepare ahead, refrigerate the blintzes before sautéing. To serve, sauté in butter, cover with foil and heat in a 350°F oven for 20 to 25 minutes to warm the filling.

Makes 12 blintzes

Swedish Pancakes

Another treasure and tradition from our Scandinavian community.

> *3 extra-large eggs, separated*
>
> *2 cups milk*
>
> *⅛ teaspoon salt*
>
> *1 cup all-purpose flour*
>
> *2 tablespoons butter, melted, plus additional melted butter for serving over pancakes*

In a large bowl, beat the egg yolks, milk, salt, flour, and melted butter together. Using a mixer, beat the egg whites until stiff and fold into the batter. Bake on a hot griddle, turning once. The pancakes should be small, 2 to 3 inches across. Serve with melted butter and lingonberry jam.

Serves 4

Pastry for a Two-Crust Pie

My mother bakes the most wonderful pies. This is her technique for a tender, flaky pie crust.

> *½ cup Crisco shortening*
>
> *4 tablespoons butter*
>
> *2 cups all-purpose flour*
>
> *½ teaspoon salt*
>
> *½ cup ice water*

Drop the shortening and butter by spoonfuls into the well-mixed flour and salt. Cut the shortening and butter into the flour with a table knife, then blend well, picking up the flour with your fingers and rubbing your thumbs across your fingers, letting the flour fall back into the bowl. This is a picking and lifting motion, the fingers and thumbs working gently and smoothly. With this process you achieve a thorough blend and cornmeal consistency. Pick up handfuls of dough, squeeze, then let them crumble apart back into the bowl.

Add the water, a little at a time, mixing in lightly with a fork. Divide the dough in half, form into 2 balls, flatten slightly, wrap in plastic wrap, and chill for 30 minutes.

Roll half of the dough into a circle on a well-floured board. Once you start to roll, keep sprinkling flour underneath the pastry to prevent sticking.

Roll from the center of the dough circle to the edge. Keep flour on the rolling pin.

Note: I like the Foley ball-bearing rolling pin with a stocking cover and a pastry cloth as a rolling surface. The pastry cloth and well-chilled dough make the task of rolling out your crust much easier and eliminate the problem of adding too much flour.

Keep dough floured underneath.

Be patient. Take all the time in the world. Roll a thin crust!

Fold the dough in half and lift it into a pie plate (up to 10 inches). (Aluminum pie pans are the ones I like best.) Fill the crust with fruit or berries according to the recipe. Roll out the remaining dough and place it loosely over the pie. Trim the edges and seal with your finger-tips. Cut several slits in the top.

Makes 1 double-crust shell

Alice Stroh's Never-Fail Extra-Flaky Pie Crust

This is an easy dough to handle and makes a delicious, flaky crust. I especially like it for pumpkin pies.

> *3 cups all-purpose flour*
> *1 ½ teaspoons salt*
> *1 ½ cups shortening*
> *1 egg, beaten*
> *5 tablespoons carbonated soda water (club soda)*
> *1 tablespoon vinegar*

Using an electric mixer, mix together the flour, salt, and shortening until the dough resembles cornmeal. Stir in the egg, soda water, and vinegar all at once. Divide the dough into 3 pieces, cover with plastic wrap, and chill.

Roll out as described in the previous recipe.

Makes 3 single 9-inch crusts

Shoo-Fly Pastry Snacks

Uncooked pastry scraps

4 tablespoons brown sugar

4 tablespoons butter

¼ cup chopped nuts

Preheat the oven to 425°F. Gather up pastry scraps left over from making pie crusts. Roll out ¼ inch thick. Cream equal parts brown sugar and butter until fluffy and spread on top of the pastry. Sprinkle with chopped nuts. Cut in strips. Place on a baking sheet. Bake for 12 to 15 minutes.

Variation: Spread the rolled-out scraps with raspberry jam, roll up like a cigar, and bake. Let cool before eating or you will burn your tongue.

Chocolate Chip Walnut Pie

The Gallery restaurant in Sisters, Oregon, served this pie. It's very rich. Serve with a scoop of vanilla ice cream.

2 extra-large eggs

½ cup all-purpose flour

½ cup granulated sugar

½ cup brown sugar

½ pound (2 sticks) butter, melted

6 ounces chocolate chips

1 cup chopped walnuts

Pastry for a single-crust pie (use half of the recipe for Alice Stroh's Never-Fail Extra-Flaky Pie Crust on page 232)

Vanilla ice cream

Preheat the oven to 325°F. Beat the eggs. Add the flour and sugars. Mix well. Stir in the melted butter. Fold in the chocolate chips and walnuts. Roll out the pastry and fit it into a 9-inch pie pan. Pour the batter into the pie shell. Bake for 50 minutes.

Serve warm with vanilla ice cream.

Makes one 9-inch pie

Fresh Rhubarb Pie

Of all pies, this is my favorite. The tart rhubarb tastes so fresh at the beginning of spring.

Pastry for a two-crust pie (page 231)
1¼ cups plus 1 tablespoon sugar
5 tablespoons all-purpose flour
½ teaspoon ground cinnamon
4 cups diced rhubarb
2 tablespoons butter
2 tablespoons milk

Preheat the oven to 425°F. Roll out half of the pastry and fit it into a 9-inch pie pan. Combine 1¼ cups of the sugar, the flour, and cinnamon. Spread half of this mixture over the bottom of the pastry-lined pan. Add the rhubarb and sprinkle the remainder of the flour mixture over it. Dot with the butter. Roll out the remaining pastry and place on tope of the pie, sealing the edges carefully. Brush with the milk and sprinkle with the remaining 1 tablespoon sugar.

Bake on the lower rack of the oven for 30 to 40 minutes.

Makes one 9-inch pie

Rhubarb Custard Pie

Aunt Marje Kramis had a lovely garden in her backyard in Missoula, Montana. This is her recipe for rhubarb pie. I like the way the custard seals in the juices from the rhubarb.

3 cups thinly sliced rhubarb
1½ cups sugar
3 eggs, beaten
½ teaspoon ground nutmeg
Pastry for a single-crust pie (use half of the recipe on page 231)

Preheat the oven to 425°F. Stir together the rhubarb, sugar, eggs, and nutmeg. Roll out the pastry and fit into a 9-inch pie pan. Pour the rhubarb mixture into the pie shell. Bake for 15 minutes, then turn the heat down to 350°F and bake for 45 minutes, until the custard is set and light golden.

Makes one 9-inch pie

Anita's Swedish Lemon Tart

The crust is a crisp shortbread—a little difficult to roll out but worth it. Halfway through the baking time, put foil around the edges of the crust to prevent excess browning.

Shortbread Crust

> *1 ½ cups all-purpose flour*
> *½ pound (2 sticks) butter*
> *2 large eggs*
> *¼ cup sugar*
> *1 teaspoon salt*

Filling

> *1 cup heavy cream*
> *2 large eggs*
> *Juice and grated zest of 1 large lemon*
> *⅓ cup sugar*

Preheat the oven to 375°F. To make the crust, mix together the flour, butter, eggs, sugar, and salt in a food processor or mixer. Chill for 30 minutes. Roll out on a well-floured board and fit into a 10-inch tart pan.

To make the filling, beat together the cream, eggs, lemon zest and juice, and sugar. Pour into the unbaked tart shell and bake for 35 minutes. Serve at room temperature.

Makes one 10-inch tart

Lemon Butter Tart Filling

My neighbor Eve Currie used to have a Christmas tea every year, when she would serve the most wonderful lemon tarts. She would make the lemon butter in advance, keep it in the refrigerator in a glass jar, and the day of the tea would fill small tart shells with it and offer the finished tarts with hot tea to her guests. I have never seen a recipe like this for lemon filling and think it is a real treasure. It also makes a wonderful filling for coconut cake.

> *4 egg yolks*
> *2 cups (1 pound) sugar*
> *¼ pound (1 stick) butter*
> *4 egg whites, well beaten*
> *Juice and grated zest of 2 large lemons*

Using a mixer, cream the egg yolks, sugar, and butter together until very light and fluffy. Fold in the beaten egg whites and cook in a double boiler until the mixture thickens (about 15 minutes). Add the lemon juice and zest. Turn into a glass dish to cool. Use to fill small tart shells or as a filling for a cake.

Makes 1 pint

Adams's Graham Cracker Birthday Cake

Sydney Adams Moe is a very special friend. This is her birthday cake that she shares with family and friends. The graham cracker crumbs make this cake moist and coarse textured.

Graham Cracker Cake

> *¾ cup shortening*
> *¾ teaspoon salt*
> *1½ teaspoons vanilla extract*
> *1 cup sugar*
> *3 eggs, separated*
> *1 cup sifted all-purpose flour*
> *1 tablespoon baking powder*
> *1⅔ cups graham cracker crumbs (21 graham crackers, crushed)*
> *1 cup milk*

Chocolate Frosting

2 cups heavy cream

¾ cup cocoa

4 cups powdered sugar

2 teaspoons vanilla extract

Preheat the oven to 350°F. Using a mixer, combine the shortening, salt, vanilla, and sugar. Add the egg yolks and beat well.

In a separate bowl, sift together the flour and baking powder and stir in the graham cracker crumbs. Add alternately with the milk to the creamed mixture.

Beat the egg whites until stiff, then carefully fold in. Pour into 2 greased 9-inch cake pans (lined with waxed paper). Bake for 25 to 30 minutes. Cool for 5 minutes, then remove from the pans.

To make the frosting, blend together the cream, cocoa, powdered sugar, and vanilla. Let stand for 1 hour in the refrigerator. Whip. Frost the cake between the layers and on the top and sides. Refrigerate.

Serves 10

Warm Gingerbread Cake

This moist, sweet cake has a pronounced ginger and molasses flavor.

½ pound (2 sticks) butter

1 cup sugar

1 cup molasses

2 extra-large eggs

3 cups all-purpose flour

½ teaspoon salt

1 teaspoon baking soda

1 teaspoon ground cinnamon

1½ teaspoons ground ginger

1 teaspoon ground allspice

1¼ cups buttermilk

Lightly sweetened whipped cream

Preheat the oven to 350°F. Using a mixer, cream together the butter and sugar, then add the molasses and eggs.

In a separate bowl, mix together the flour, salt, baking soda, and spices and alternately add them and the buttermilk to the creamed butter and sugar. Mix well and pour into a greased and floured 9- by 13-inch cake pan. Bake for 35 to 45 minutes. Serve warm, topped with lightly sweetened whipped cream.

Makes 1 sheet cake

Buttermilk Chocolate Cake

You need a large sheet pan for this cake, which is thinner than a standard cake.

2 cups all-purpose flour

2 cups sugar

¼ pound (1 stick) butter

½ cup shortening

3 tablespoons cocoa

1 cup water

2 eggs, beaten

½ cup buttermilk

1 teaspoon baking soda

½ teaspoon ground cinnamon

1 teaspoon vanilla extract

½ teaspoon salt

Glaze

¼ pound (1 stick) butter

6 tablespoons milk

3 tablespoons cocoa

1 pound powdered sugar

Preheat the oven to 350°F. Put the flour and sugar in a large mixing bowl and mix well.

Combine the butter, shortening, cocoa, and water in a medium-sized saucepan and bring to a boil. Pour over the flour-sugar mixture. Mix lightly and add the eggs, buttermilk, baking soda, cinnamon, vanilla, and salt. Mix well and pour into a greased and floured 11- by 14- by 1½ - inch baking pan. Bake for 20 to 25 minutes.

To make the glaze, place the butter, milk, and cocoa in a medium-sized saucepan and bring to a boil. Let cool a bit and then pour into a mixing bowl with the powdered sugar and beat until the mixture thickens. Spread the glaze over the cake while still warm.

Makes 1 sheet cake

Cream Cheese Pound Cake

Pound cake is a good dessert when topped with sugared fresh berries and lightly whipped extra-thick cream poured over. The cream cheese makes this pound cake particularly moist.

¾ pound (3 sticks) butter, softened

8 ounces cream cheese, softened

3 cups sugar

6 extra-large eggs

1 teaspoon vanilla extract

1 teaspoon almond extract

3 cups all-purpose flour

Preheat the oven to 325°F. Using a mixer, cream together the butter and cream cheese. Add the sugar. Beat in the eggs, one at a time. Add the vanilla and almond extracts. Stir in the flour. Pour into a greased and floured tube pan and bake for 1 hour and 15 minutes. Let cool in the pan on a cake rack for 10 minutes. Then invert the pan onto a serving dish. After 15 minutes, remove the pan. This helps prevent sticking.

Makes 10 to 12 servings

Kitty's Applesauce Cake

A moist summertime square-pan cake.

½ cup shortening

1½ cups sugar

2 extra-large eggs, beaten

1 cup thick, unsweetened applesauce

2 cups all-purpose flour

¼ teaspoon salt

1 teaspoon baking powder

½ teaspoon baking soda

1 teaspoon ground cinnamon

½ teaspoon ground cloves

1 cup raisins

Frosting

2 cups brown sugar

1 cup granulated sugar

2 tablespoons white corn syrup

⅔ cup heavy cream

Preheat the oven to 350°F. Using a mixer, cream the shortening and sugar together, add the eggs, and beat well. Fold in the applesauce, flour, salt, baking powder, baking soda, and spices. Mix well. Stir in the raisins. Line an 8-inch square pan with waxed paper, pour the batter into the pan, and bake for 45 to 50 minutes. Let cool to room temperature before frosting.

To make the frosting, combine the sugars, corn syrup, and cream in a saucepan; place over low heat, and cook until the sugar dissolves. Cover the saucepan for 2 to 3 minutes to dissolve the sugar crystals. Uncover and cook to the soft ball stage (238°F). Cool to lukewarm, then beat to a spreading consistency and spread over the cake.

Makes one 8-inch cake

Christmas Lemon Pecan Pound Cake

This is good to make ahead and keep in your freezer.

> 1 pound (4 sticks) butter
>
> 2⅓ cups sugar
>
> 6 extra-large eggs
>
> 2 ounces lemon extract (that's right, 2 ounces!)
>
> 4 cups all-purpose flour
>
> 1½ teaspoons baking powder
>
> ½ teaspoon salt
>
> 1½ cups chopped pecans
>
> 1 tablespoon grated lemon zest

Preheat the oven to 300°F. Using a mixer, cream together the butter and sugar until light and fluffy. Add the eggs, one at a time, beating well after each addition. Add the lemon extract. Fold in the flour, baking powder, salt, pecans, and lemon zest, being careful not to overmix.

Line the bottoms of three 9- by 5-inch loaf pans with brown paper. Lightly butter the sides of the pans and the paper. Bake for 1 to 1½ hours, until firm in center.

Makes 3 loaf cakes

Coconut Cake with Lemon Cream Filling

James Beard served this in his home in New York, and I could have eaten the whole thing. The lightness of the whipped cream frosting with the lemon filling is a classic combination. It's a wonderful Easter cake.

Coconut Cake

> 1 cup flaked coconut
>
> 1 cup warm milk
>
> ¼ pound plus 4 tablespoons (1½ sticks) butter
>
> 1½ cups sugar
>
> 1 teaspoon vanilla extract
>
> 3 cups sifted cake flour
>
> 4 teaspoons baking powder
>
> ¾ teaspoon salt
>
> 4 egg whites

Lemon Cream Filling

¼ pound (1 stick) butter

Grated zest of 1 lemon

Juice of 3 large lemons

¼ teaspoon salt

1½ cups sugar

3 egg yolks

3 eggs

1 teaspoon vanilla extract

Frosting

2 cups heavy cream, whipped

½ cup powdered sugar

1½ teaspoons vanilla extract

1½ cups flaked coconut

Preheat the oven to 350°F. To make the cake, put the coconut in a small mixing bowl and pour in the warm milk. Let cool. Drain through a strainer, pressing the coconut with the back of a wooden spoon. Reserve the milk.

Using a mixer, cream the butter. Add the sugar and beat until very light and fluffy. Add the vanilla.

Sift the flour with the baking powder and salt, and add alternately with the milk from the coconut (1 cup). Fold in the coconut.

Beat the egg whites until stiff and fold into the cake mixture. Turn into two 9-inch cake pans that have been buttered, floured, and lined with waxed paper. Bake for 30 minutes. Cool on a rack.

Meanwhile, prepare the filling. Melt the butter in a double boiler. Add the grated zest, lemon juice, salt, and sugar. Beat together the egg yolks, eggs, and vanilla and add to the butter mixture, whisking continuously until it thickens. Cool. You can cover with plastic wrap and refrigerate until ready to frost and serve the cake.

Split the two cake layers in half horizontally. Place one half-layer on a cake plate and spread with a thin layer of lemon filling. Place another half-layer on top and spread with filling. Continue with the remaining split layers.

To make the frosting, whip the cream. Add the sugar and vanilla and continue whipping until stiff peaks form. Frost the cake and sprinkle with the coconut.

Serves 8

Mary Alice's Rhubarb Crunch

It's hard to call rhubarb a vegetable once you add the sugar and bake as lovely a dessert as this one. It's the first sign of spring, and this is a dessert everyone looks forward to.

Crumb Mixture

  1 cup flour

  ¾ cup oatmeal

  ¼ pound (1 stick) butter, melted

  1 cup brown sugar

  1 teaspoon ground cinnamon

Syrup

  1 cup granulated sugar

  1 cup cold water

  1 teaspoon vanilla extract

  1 tablespoon cornstarch

  ———

  4 cups raw rhubarb, diced

  ———

  Vanilla ice cream

Preheat the oven to 350°F. In a bowl, blend the flour, oatmeal, butter, brown sugar, and cinnamon until crumbly.

To make the syrup, in a saucepan combine the sugar, water, vanilla, and cornstarch and cook over medium heat until clear.

Put the rhubarb into an 8- by 8- by 2-inch glass pan. Pour over the syrup. Top with the crumb mixture. Bake for 1 hour. Serve warm, topped with vanilla ice cream.

Serves 6

Marianne's Lemon Tea Cookies

These cookies are real showstoppers. The surprise of the fresh lemon taste makes it impossible to stop eating them.

1 ½ teaspoons vinegar

½ cup milk

¼ pound (1 stick) butter

¾ cup sugar

1 extra-large egg

1 teaspoon grated lemon zest

1 ¾ cups all-purpose flour

1 teaspoon baking powder

¼ teaspoon baking soda

¼ teaspoon salt

Lemon Glaze

¾ cup sugar

¼ cup lemon juice

Preheat the oven to 350°F. In a measuring cup, stir the vinegar into the milk. Using a mixer, cream together the butter and sugar until fluffy. Add the egg and lemon zest and beat well.

In a separate bowl, sift together the flour, baking powder, baking soda, and salt, and add alternately with the milk to the butter-sugar mixture. Beat smooth after each addition. Drop from a teaspoon 2 inches apart onto an ungreased baking sheet. Bake for 12 to 14 minutes.

To make the glaze, mix the sugar and lemon juice together. Brush the tops of the hot cookies immediately with the lemon glaze.

Makes 2½ dozen cookies

Grandma Ide's Ginger Snaps

Lilian Gray learned to bake these cookies from her mother, Kathrine Ide. Doubled, this recipe makes enough cookies to feed a wheat harvest crew.

½ cup shortening

½ cup sugar

½ cup molasses

¼ cup cold water

3½ to 5 cups all-purpose flour

1 teaspoon ground ginger

1 teaspoon ground cinnamon

½ teaspoon ground allspice

½ teaspoon freshly grated nutmeg

¼ teaspoon ground cloves

½ teaspoon baking soda

Preheat the oven to 375°F. Using a mixer, cream the shortening and sugar well, then add the molasses and cold water. Mix 1½ cups of the flour with the spices and baking soda, then add to the shortening mixture. Add more flour until the dough is no longer sticky, around 2 cups. Chill the dough for 1 hour. Roll out one portion at a time to the preferred thickness. Cut with cookie cutters. Place on a lightly greased baking sheet and bake for 10 to 15 minutes, depending on the thickness of the dough.

Makes 8 dozen cookies

Snickerdoodles

The classic cookie, crisp and crunchy. With a bowl of fresh berries and cream—the perfect Pacific Northwest picnic dessert.

1 cup shortening

1½ cups sugar

2 extra-large eggs

2½ cups all-purpose flour

2 teaspoons cream of tartar

1 teaspoon baking soda

¼ teaspoon salt

1 cup sugar mixed with 2 teaspoons ground cinnamon

Preheat the oven to 350°F. Using a mixer, cream the shortening and sugar until light and fluffy. Add the eggs, one at a time.

In a separate bowl, mix together the flour, cream of tartar, baking soda, and salt. Add to the creamed mixture. Form into golf ball–sized balls and roll in the cinnamon sugar. Place on a greased baking sheet. Flatten with the bottom of a glass. Bake for 15 minutes.

Makes 2 dozen cookies

Salted Peanut Cookies

Firm, crisp, and peanut-flavored. The salted peanuts contrast with the sweet cookie dough.

½ pound (2 sticks) butter

2 extra-large eggs

1 cup brown sugar

1 cup granulated sugar

1 teaspoon vanilla extract

2 cups all-purpose flour

2 teaspoons baking soda

3 cups corn flakes

2 cups salted peanuts

Preheat the oven to 350°F. Using a mixer, cream together the butter, eggs, sugars, and vanilla. Mix in the flour, baking soda, and corn flakes. Stir in the peanuts.

Drop onto a greased cookie sheet and bake for 12 to 15 minutes.

Makes 2½ to 3 dozen cookies

Pecan Tea Cookies

A rich butter cookie that's perfect to offer after dinner as an accompaniment to a special ice cream.

½ pound (2 sticks) butter

1 cup sugar

½ teaspoon salt

1 egg

1 teaspoon vanilla extract

2 cups all-purpose flour

1 teaspoon baking powder

24 to 36 pecan halves (one for each cookie)

Preheat the oven to 350°F. Using a mixer, cream together the butter, sugar, and salt. Add the egg and beat well. Add the vanilla. Stir in the flour and baking powder. Knead well. Shape into 1½- to 2-inch rolls and chill well. Cut into ½-inch slices and top each slice with one pecan half. Place on a greased baking sheet and bake for 8 to 10 minutes, until a small golden brown ring forms around the edge. Remove from the baking sheet while still warm.

Makes 2 to 3 dozen cookies

Brown Sugar–Hazelnut Shortbread Cookies

The perfect cookie to serve with a bowl of fresh berries and cream.

> 2 cups all-purpose flour
>
> 1 cup hazelnuts, toasted and skins removed
>
> ½ pound (2 sticks) butter, softened
>
> ¾ cup packed brown sugar

Preheat the oven to 300°F. Grind the flour and nuts together in a food processor until the mixture becomes a fine powder.

Using a mixer, cream together the butter and sugar until smooth and creamy. Add the flour-hazelnut mixture. Wrap and chill for 2 hours or more.

When ready to roll out cookies, remove from refrigerator and let sit at room temperature for 20 to 30 minutes to soften slightly. Roll out dough ¼ inch thick and cut into 1-inch squares. Bake on a nonstick baking sheet for 20 to 25 minutes, or until a light golden color.

Makes 4 dozen cookies

Laughing Horse Theater Chocolate Chip Cookies

A family favorite. Crisp on the outside and soft on the inside. Got milk?

> ½ pound (2 sticks) butter
>
> 1 teaspoon salt
>
> 1 teaspoon vanilla extract
>
> ¾ cup granulated sugar
>
> ¾ cup brown sugar
>
> 2 extra-large eggs, beaten
>
> 1 teaspoon baking soda dissolved in 1 teaspoon water
>
> 2¼ cups all-purpose flour
>
> 12 ounces chocolate chips
>
> 8 ounces walnuts

Preheat the oven to 375°F. Using a mixer, cream together the butter, salt, vanilla, and sugars until light and fluffy. Add the eggs and continue beating for several minutes. Stir in the dissolved baking soda. Add the flour. Fold in the chocolate chips and nuts.

Form the dough into 1¾-inch balls. Place on a nonstick baking sheet and flatten to ½ inch thick. Bake for 15 minutes. Remove from the baking sheet and let cool. Store in airtight tins.

Makes 3 dozen cookies

Eve's Shortbread Cookies

A crisp, buttery, light-colored cookie that's just right with a cup of tea. The cornstarch makes this a more delicate shortbread.

>   *1 pound (4 sticks) butter*
>   *1 cup granulated sugar*
>   *1 cup cornstarch*
>   *3 cups all-purpose flour*

Preheat the oven to 350°F. Using a mixer, cream together the butter and sugar for 5 minutes, until light and fluffy. Mix in the cornstarch and flour. Turn out onto a board that is lightly dusted with cornstarch. Divide the dough in half. Press into 2 ungreased 8-inch square pans. Flatten the dough with your hands to about ½ inch thick. Thoroughly prick the surface with a fork to prevent blistering during baking.

Bake for 30 minutes. Remove from the oven and cut into small squares while still hot. Let cool in the pan. Remove when cool.

Makes 3 dozen cookies

Sugar Cookies

Serve with homemade ice cream or lemonade; these are my favorite summer cookies.

>   *3 extra-large eggs*
>   *½ pound (2 sticks) butter, softened*
>   *1 cup sugar*
>   *1 teaspoon vanilla extract*
>   *4 cups all-purpose flour*

1 teaspoon baking soda

2 teaspoons cream of tartar

Sugar

Preheat the oven to 375°F. Using a mixer, beat the eggs for 5 minutes, until lemon-colored and creamy. Whip in the butter, sugar, and vanilla. When very light and fluffy, mix in the flour, baking soda, and cream of tartar.

Roll into walnut-sized balls and dip in sugar. Flatten with the bottom of a glass. Place on a greased baking sheet and bake for 10 to 12 minutes.

Makes 3 dozen cookies

Nina's Torchetti Cookies

One of the reasons to leave I-90 and enter Cle Elum when driving across Washington State is to buy these cookies at the Cle Elum Bakery. This is a cookie to enjoy while drinking a latte.

2 packages dry yeast

1¼ cups warm water

5½ cups all-purpose flour

½ cup sugar

2 teaspoons salt

1 pound (4 sticks) butter, softened

Preheat the oven to 375°F. In a large bowl, dissolve the yeast in the water. Let sit 10 minutes. Add 1 cup of the flour, then the sugar and salt. Mix well and let sit 15 minutes. Add the remaining 4½ cups flour and mix in the butter. Refrigerate for 4 to 6 hours.

Pinch off golf ball–sized pieces of dough and roll into pencil-shaped strips, 6 inches long, on a board lightly sprinkled with granulated sugar. Shape into horseshoes, with the ends barely touching. Place on a parchment-lined baking sheet, and bake for 8 to 10 minutes. Place briefly under the broiler to glaze.

Makes 18 to 24 cookies

Lunchbox Oatmeal Cookies

Big, chewy cookies with a snap.

  1 cup shortening

  1 cup brown sugar

  1 cup granulated sugar

  2 extra-large eggs

  1 teaspoon vanilla extract

  2 cups all-purpose flour

  1 teaspoon salt

  1 teaspoon baking soda

  3 cups quick oatmeal

Preheat the oven to 375°F. Using a mixer, cream well the shortening, sugars, eggs, and vanilla. Mix in the flour, salt, and baking soda. Add oatmeal.

Drop spoonfuls onto a greased baking sheet and bake for 12 minutes.

Makes 2 to 3 dozen cookies

Old-Fashioned Peanut Butter Cookies

A crisp, delicious cookie that's not too sweet.

  ½ pound (2 sticks) butter

  1 cup granulated sugar

  1 cup brown sugar

  1 cup peanut butter

  2 extra-large eggs

  3 cups all-purpose flour

  2 teaspoons baking soda

  1 teaspoon salt

Preheat the oven to 375°F. Using a mixer, cream together the butter and sugars until light and fluffy. Beat in the peanut butter and add the eggs, one at a time. In a separate bowl, mix together the flour, baking soda, and salt. Stir into the peanut butter mixture. Roll into walnut-sized balls, and place on a lightly greased and floured baking sheet. Flatten with a fork dipped in cold water, making a crisscross pattern. Bake for 20 to 25 minutes.

Makes 6 dozen cookies

Dark Chocolate Brownies

These are chocolaty and soft rather than cakelike. You can frost them or dust lightly with powdered sugar.

3 squares (1 ounce each) unsweetened chocolate

⅔ cup shortening

4 extra-large eggs, beaten

2 cups sugar

1½ cups all-purpose flour

1 teaspoon baking powder

1 teaspoon vanilla extract

Dover Judy Frosting (optional; recipe follows)

Preheat the oven to 375°F. In a small saucepan, melt the chocolate and shortening together over low heat. Let cool to room temperature.

In a large bowl, beat the eggs and sugar together until well blended and creamy. Stir in the melted chocolate. Mix in the flour, baking powder, and vanilla. Spread in a greased 9- by 13- by 2-inch baking pan. Bake for 30 minutes. Frost when cool, if desired.

Makes 24 squares

Dover Judy Frosting

My Aunt Louise always used this frosting on her cakes. A rich, shiny chocolate frosting, it also works well on brownies.

1 cup powdered sugar

1 tablespoon butter, softened

¼ cup milk

1 extra-large egg

2 squares (1 ounce each) unsweetened chocolate, melted

In a bowl, mix together the powdered sugar and butter. Add the milk and egg and beat well. Slowly add the melted chocolate, stirring continuously. Set the bowl in ice water and beat until the mixture thickens.

Makes enough frosting for 1 pan of brownies

Marta's Almond Roca Candy

In Tacoma, Washington, the Brown and Haley Company has become known for its Almond Roca candy. I like to make this for a Christmas sweet.

1 pound (4 sticks) butter

2 cups sugar

5 ounces blanched almonds, finely chopped

1 large package (12 ounces) milk chocolate chips

In a saucepan, cook the butter and sugar over moderate heat until a candy thermometer registers 300°F, stirring constantly. Remove from the heat. Add three-fourths of the chopped almonds. Spread on a buttered 12- by 18-inch baking sheet. Sprinkle with the chocolate chips and spread them as they melt. Sprinkle the remaining almonds on top. Cool. Break into pieces.

Store in an airtight container.

Makes about 2 pounds of candy

Christmas Peanut Brittle

I like to make candy at Christmastime for our sweet bar. Everyone looks forward to indulging in "one of these and two of those."

2 cups sugar

1 cup corn syrup

½ cup water

2 teaspoons baking soda

2 cups peanuts

1 teaspoon vanilla extract

1 teaspoon butter

Mix the sugar, corn syrup, and water in a large enameled saucepan and cook over moderate heat until candy thermometer registers 280°F, or until the syrup is a light golden brown. Stir in the baking soda and remove from the heat at once. (The soda causes the syrup to bubble and foam up, and produces the foamy appearance of the hardened candy.) Add the peanuts, vanilla, and butter.

Pour the candy onto a large buttered marble slab or into a buttered 12- by 18-inch shallow pan, and spread quickly in a thin layer. When cold, break into pieces.

Makes about 2 pounds of peanut brittle

SAUCES & CONDIMENTS

The HIGHER PURPOSE of TIBETAN HOT SAUCE

*D*achen Kyaping, forty-something mother of one and the manufacturer of Khatsa, a line of Tibetan hot and savory sauces and marinades available in upscale food emporia throughout this country and Canada, tends to set her own agenda. So in deference to Dachen, first things first:

Tibetans don't eat rice. This may come as a shock to those who think that all Asians are rice eaters. But the fact of the matter remains: Tibetans don't eat rice.

Despite everything written by Western climbers heading high into the Himalayas, the indigenous hill people of those parts do not stir yak butter into their tea. The same for Tibetans. They don't add yak butter to their tea, either. It's just another ludicrous rumor.

"Yaks" are male; "dzo" aren't. The thought of trying to milk a yak to make butter sends the average Tibetan into such paroxysms of laughter that ancient prayers must be chanted to break the spell.

It's a little surprising that Dachen Kyaping hasn't found a way to turn this obscure bit of information to her marketing advantage. This is, after all, the woman who has named one of her hot sauces "Kuptsa." That's Tibetan for "hot butt." Dachen Kyaping gives one of her easy smiles and explains, "It warms you twice, at both ends. It's a liberating feeling." Khatsa, the company name, is Tibetan for "hot mouth." One taste of Khatsa Hot Sauce, or Fire Sauce, or Dead Hot Sauce (which is packaged with a copy of the Tibetan Book of the Dead and the slogan "Soul food to die for . . . and the book to help bring you back") is all it takes to realize the appropriateness of this product name. Khatsa indeed. It's what Buddha would call right use of language.

Dachen did not come naturally to the specialty food business, though trading is central to her heritage. Her family tree extends back through the centuries deep into the history of eastern Tibet, always showing up in one aspect or another of business, be it trading or some government position. Kyaping isn't the family name. It's more of a government title, like "Mr. Secretary of State." Drukyaltsang is the family name. It means "House of the Eight Dragons" and celebrates the dragon-printed silk brocade that a progenitor first imported from China to Tibet.

If there is a Tibetan word for tomato, that name should be attached to one of Dachen's grandfathers, a Tibetan general who studied things military with the British in India, developed a fondness for tomatoes while there, and, avid gardener that he was, brought seeds back to the family estate in eastern Tibet.

Dachen was born in Lhasa and left Tibet in the back seat of a chaffeur-driven car headed for India. She was four years old and gravely ill. Her father had sent her and her mother south to seek the medical help that would save her life. In the intervening months, the Tibetans rose up against China, China invaded Tibet, and the fortunes of the Drukyaltsang family changed forever. Dachen and her mother became refugees in India. The Chinese imprisoned her father, for no real reason, for what would stretch to twenty-one years.

Dachen arrived in Seattle with some of the first Tibetan refugees. She had had the good fortune of attending a Western missionary school in India, so transferring to an American high school was not as big a shock as it might have been. She studied commercial graphic design at the University of Washington, and followed that career into the software industry. Though she keeps her hand in graphic design (and applies all those skills to her own marketing problems), these days Khatsa consumes her time and attention. "I didn't want to leave a design portfolio as a legacy," Dachen says. "I believe in doing a lot with a little."

What is emerging from her father's recipes for hot sauces and marinades that use nettles and ginger and garlic and the like is another business altogether, a bigger business that Dachen calls Urban Nomad. Khatsa is a flavorful part of it. Urban Nomad is dedicated to bringing to modern society the best ideas and tools of the nomadic cultures of the world, in an effort to help simplify life everywhere.

"You have to have a purpose," Dachen says. "Urban Nomad is part of mine. Using some of the profits to help Tibet is another. When you go there and see what has happened, no one can sit still. To help the next generation know about the past, that's important for me, too."

Dachen Kyaping's father learned to cook in prison. He brought his sauces with him to this country when he was finally reunited with his family. It's only fitting that they have become the heart and soul of the Khatsa/Urban Nomad line. You might think of Khatsa as the taste of freedom. Or, if you are more inclined toward Buddhism, of liberation.

Sauces & Condiments

Krueger Pepper Farm's Salsa

At Krueger Pepper Farm in Zillah, Washington, a wide variety of peppers is available. They are in season from mid-August through September, the same time we get ripe, red beefsteak tomatoes. As a result, salsa has become a mainstay of our late-summer meals; it's especially good with grilled fish and meats.

6 vine-ripened tomatoes

2 fresh tomatillos (or 1 green tomato)

2 cloves garlic

3 Anaheim peppers

3 tablespoons red wine vinegar

1 or 2 jalapeño peppers

1 small white onion

½ cup fresh cilantro leaves

1 to 2 tablespoons lime juice, to taste

Salt and pepper to taste

Cut the tomatoes in half and gently squeeze out and discard the seeds. Dice the tomatoes and place in a bowl. Finely chop the tomatillos and add to the tomatoes. Mince the garlic and add to the bowl.

Roast the Anaheim peppers under the broiler until the skins blister, and put them into a small brown paper bag while still warm. Let cool. Remove as much of the skin as possible. Dice and add to the tomatoes. Stir in the vinegar.

Cut the jalapeños in half. Remove the seeds. Finely dice and add to the bowl.

Chop the onion and add to the mixture. Just before serving, add the cilantro leaves and lime juice, and season to taste with salt and pepper.

Makes 2½ cups

Auntie Alma's Mustard Sauce for Vegetables

This sauce is delicious on cooked cauliflower, brussels sprouts, or sautéed cabbage.

> *¼ pound (1 stick) butter*
>
> *2 tablespoons dry mustard*
>
> *¾ teaspoon salt*
>
> *1 teaspoon Worcestershire sauce*

In a saucepan, melt the butter. Add the rest of the ingredients, and serve over hot vegetables.

Makes 2½ cups

Tartar Sauce

I like the taste of dill pickle in tartar sauce much better than the traditional sweet pickle. The tartness works well with fish.

> ½ medium white onion
>
> 1 cup chopped dill pickle
>
> 1 cup mayonnaise
>
> 2 tablespoons lemon juice
>
> 2 tablespoons minced parsley
>
> 1 tablespoon chopped fresh dill

Finely chop the white onion; you should have ½ cup. Rinse with cold water and pat dry. Mix with the dill pickle, mayonnaise, lemon juice, parsley, and dill. Refrigerate for several hours to let the flavors blend.

Makes 2½ cups

Butter Cream Sauce

A light, creamy sauce that you can flavor with brandy or rum and serve warm over apple cake, steamed pudding, or bread pudding.

> 1 cup brown sugar
>
> ½ pound (2 sticks) butter
>
> ½ cup half-and-half
>
> 1½ teaspoons vanilla extract
>
> Dash of nutmeg
>
> Brandy, rum, or orange juice

Put the brown sugar, butter, and half-and-half in a saucepan. Simmer gently for 15 minutes. Add the vanilla and nutmeg. Just before serving, stir in the brandy, rum, or juice.

Makes 1½ cups

Herb Sauce

This is a nice sauce to serve with the Stuffed Flank Steak (page 76).

2 tablespoons butter

2 tablespoons flour

½ cup white wine

1 cup rich beef stock

1 tablespoon chopped parsley

½ teaspoon grated orange zest

1 tablespoon capers

Melt the butter in a small pan. Stir in the flour and cook slowly for several minutes. Stir in the wine and blend well. Add the beef stock. Sprinkle in the parsley, orange zest, and capers. Simmer until thickened and the alcohol taste of the wine has evaporated.

Makes 1½ cups

Rhubarb-Chutney Sauce

In the early spring, the Puyallup Valley yields a large crop of rhubarb, a popular and easy plant to grow in the Northwest. The first asparagus from eastern Washington usually arrives just at the peak of the rhubarb season; together, they herald the arrival of spring. My mother made a rhubarb pie from the garden every March. Rhubarb is also known as the "pie plant." The rhubarb completely breaks down in this recipe, forming a delicious sauce to serve with spring lamb or roast pork.

1 cup white vinegar

2 cups sugar

½ cup dried currants

2 cloves garlic, finely chopped

3 tablespoons chopped crystallized ginger

1 teaspoon crushed coriander seed

½ teaspoon crushed red pepper flakes

6 cups finely chopped rhubarb (about 2 pounds)

In a heavy, enameled saucepan, bring the vinegar, sugar, currants, garlic, crystallized ginger, coriander, and red pepper flakes to a boil. Add the rhubarb and simmer gently for 30 minutes, stirring occasionally, until the mixture thickens to the desired consistency.

Makes 4 cups

Cranberry-Horseradish Sauce

In the Aberdeen-Hoquiam area of Washington State—near the Olympic Rainforest, a beautiful part of the state and very damp—there are many cranberry bogs. My best friend grew up in Aberdeen, and while traveling in New England one fall, someone suggested that she might enjoy touring the cranberry bogs. She quickly declined!

My sister-in-law serves this condiment for Christmas dinner with an old-fashioned bone-in baked ham, beautifully glazed, and a steaming hot dish of scalloped potatoes.

> 2 cups fresh cranberries
> 1 small white onion
> ½ cup sugar
> ¾ cup sour cream
> 2 tablespoons creamy-style horseradish

Chop the cranberries and onion in the food processor. Add the remaining ingredients and process until smooth. Refrigerate.

Makes 3 cups

Fresh Horseradish

Fresh horseradish is delicious with roast beef or baked tongue.

> 1 pound horseradish root
> White vinegar
> 3 tablespoons sugar

Wash the horseradish, remove the thick peel, and grate. Mix well with white vinegar to cover. Add the sugar, mix well, and refrigerate. This condiment keeps well.

Makes 2 cups

Sweet-and-Sour Plum Sauce for Pork and Duck

We have an Italian plum tree that we harvest late in the summer. We shake the tree, gather the plums, and then freeze them and use the frozen plums to make plum sauce later in the year.

Frozen Sweetened Plums

5 quarts plums

2 cups water

1 cup granulated sugar

Sweet-and-Sour Plum Sauce

3 cups frozen, sweetened plums (thaw and remove the pits)

¼ cup red wine vinegar

1 teaspoon minced fresh ginger

Pinch of ground cloves

To freeze the plums: Place the plums in a 5-quart enameled saucepan. Pour in the water. Cover and steam briefly, just until the skins begin to split. Remove from the heat. Sprinkle the sugar over the plums. Let cool. With a slotted spoon, place the plums in freezer bags (3 cups per bag) and freeze.

To make the sauce: Place the plums, vinegar, ginger, and cloves in a 1½ - to 2-quart saucepan. Cover and simmer over medium heat, stirring occasionally, for 15 minutes. Serve warm with roast pork or duck.

Makes 3 cups

John's Sweet-Hot Mustard

John Ludtka makes this mustard every Christmas and gives it as gifts. It has a tangy sweetness that complements smoked meats and corned beef.

1 cup Colman's dry mustard

1 cup white vinegar

2 eggs, beaten

1 cup brown sugar

Mix the dry mustard and white vinegar in a small bowl and let sit overnight.

The next day, mix the eggs and brown sugar together with the mustard-vinegar mixture in a small, heavy saucepan. Cook, stirring continuously, over low heat until the mixture thickens.

Remove from the heat immediately and transfer to a bowl. Continue stirring to cool the mixture so that it doesn't overcook the eggs. Store in the refrigerator. Keeps 2 to 3 weeks.

Makes four or five 6-ounce jars

Paul's Sour Dills

Fresh small pickling cucumbers

20 cloves garlic, peeled

10 sprigs fresh dill

10 hot red peppers (optional)

3 quarts water

1 cup pickling salt

2 quarts white vinegar (5-percent acidity)

6 tablespoons pickling spice

Sterilize 10 quart canning jars and their lids. Fill each jar with cucumbers, 2 garlic cloves, and 1 sprig of dill. (If you like hot dills, add 1 small hot red pepper to each jar.) In a large saucepan, bring the water, salt, vinegar, and pickling spice to a boil and boil for 3 minutes to make the hot brine. Immediately fill the jars with the hot brine and seal. Process in water bath for 20 minutes.

Makes 10 quarts

Pickled Asparagus Spears

Pickled asparagus spears are the perfect thing to serve with smoked salmon. They are tart and complement the richness of the fish.

8 to 10 cloves garlic, peeled

3 to 4 pounds asparagus (depending on the size of the spears)

½ cup plus 2 tablespoons pickling salt

3 quarts water

2 quarts white vinegar (5-percent acidity)

1 tablespoon pickling spice (cloves removed)

Sterilize 8 to 10 pint canning jars and their lids. Put 1 garlic clove in each jar. Cut the asparagus spears to fit into the jars. Pack the spears into the jars.

In a large saucepan, bring the salt, water, vinegar, and pickling spice to a boil to make the hot brine. Boil for 3 minutes. Immediately fill the jars with the hot brine and seal. Process in a water bath for 20 minutes.

Makes 8 to 10 pints

TOOLS

LIVING THROUGH
the BLADE

There's no reason why a good kitchen knife can't last a cook's lifetime. The kitchen knives Bob Kramer makes in his Seattle shop, Bladesmith's, Inc., are of heirloom quality. These are working knives that can and should last the lifetimes of several cooks, one generation leading to the next.

"I've spent years and years figuring out what makes a great knife," Kramer explains. His voice, while gentle, is direct and carries with it the weight of a man who is absolutely confident about and excited by the work he does. "I can put that time and experience into an art knife somebody'll hang on the wall. The collectors are out there and ready to pay, believe me. But a knife like that never gets used. What I strive to do is combine beautiful metal, handles, and function, knowing that what I have made is going to be used. That way the creative energy gets passed along. It keeps moving past me through the blade."

The recipe for a great knife is simple enough. You start with aircraft-quality ball bearing carbon steel, heat it to a forging temperature between 1700° and 2100°F, and shape the blade with a hydraulic hammer to slowly draw out the metal like taffy, squaring it into shape. A good bladesmith, according to Kramer, can finish 90 percent of the blade shaping between the forge and the hydraulic hammer. The rest is "hogging off" excess steel at the grinding wheel, then finishing the blade to the precise shape demanded by its function. In Kramer's case that means chef's knives in three sizes, as well as fillet, boning, paring, slicing, and bread knives. He's also working on a Japanese-style kitchen knife.

Shaping is followed by hardening and tempering, two all-but-magical processes that make a knife hard enough to take a keen edge yet remain flexible. Kramer can take one of his knives, put the blade in a vise, and bend it 90 degrees without snapping it in half. The hard carbon steel takes such a beautiful edge that Kramer can chop through a two-by-four and then shave the hair off his arm. What this means for the home cook is that once the edge has been set on the knife it simply takes a little maintenance to keep that edge for up to a year.

Kramer prefers carbon steel over the stainless steel favored by commercial knife companies because it is stronger, it's easier to sharpen, and it takes a keener edge. Carbon steel does demand a little extra attention, however. Leave water on the blade and it will rust. Wiping a blade off with a lightly oiled cloth or paper towel is all the protection the steel needs.

Once the blade has been hardened and tempered, Kramer attaches the hardwood handle and sharpens the blade to a perfect edge. To do this sharpening, he puts the blade through a seven-stage grinding and polishing process. The place where Kramer completes the making of a chef's knife—the sharpening process—is the place where he first penetrated the world of knives and steel and fire.

In his thirty-eight years Kramer has been a magician. He has been a Ringling Brothers clown. He has practiced three different martial arts. He dropped out of college to sail around the world and ended up waiting tables instead in Houston for a year and a half. He first came to Seattle as a clown, then returned as a student determined to be an oceanographer. To listen to him talk, the one steady element in Kramer's life has been a quest to learn something as well as he possibly can—to master something, be that waiting tables or clowning or improvisational theater or magic or cooking. But nothing ever quite panned out until he found his way into knives.

As an apprentice cook in Seattle, Kramer had invested in a set of kitchen knives, had learned how to use them, and had struggled to keep them sharp. A critical decision in his life was to leave the kitchen and set up his own cutlery business. He invested $500 in knives and carried his stock in a gym bag from kitchen door to kitchen door.

"What I discovered was that most chefs don't have enough money to buy a new knife if they feel they have one that does the job. What they really wanted me to do was sharpen the knives they already owned."

For advice on sharpening, Kramer wrote to and called every major manufacturer of professional cutlery with offices in the United States. Most company representatives had no advice at all—they just sold the stuff. A couple referred him to the manufacturer of a $600 sharpening machine. "Basically, the machine ruined knives," Kramer said. "Just ground them right up. And the edges never held up. The cooks complained a lot. At first I thought they were just trying to get me to sharpen their knives over again for nothing. But listen to your customer long enough, I soon learned, and you'll hear what you need to do."

In his search for mastery, Kramer bought a plane ticket that took him through six major cities around the country. He haunted every cutlery shop and sharpening service he could find, asking questions, looking for answers. Mostly he found a wasteland.

But finally, in San Francisco, he found his standard of excellence at Columbus Cutlery, run by Mr. and Mrs. Peter Malattia, an older Italian couple. "They start their day folding the paper hats they wear to keep their hair clean," Kramer said. "Sharpening's a dirty and noisy business. I had run into a lot of paranoid people who wouldn't talk to me as soon as I made myself clear and they realized I wasn't a customer. And I ran into a lot of guys who just grind away with one stone and ruin the knives. But this couple took me in and showed me everything. They were so nice, and their work is stunning."

Kramer returned to Seattle with new ideas about sharpening, a new enthusiasm, and then found his true teacher—an Austrian tool maker who repaired and sharpened reusable surgical instruments for hospitals. "He showed me what I needed to know," Kramer said, "repeating a lot of what I had learned in San Francisco. It took another two and a half years to get the technique down." That was twelve years ago.

Kramer bought an old bread truck, built a work bench into the back end, and drove from restaurant to restaurant, sharpening and selling knives. And studying knives. And finally, he heard about a hand-forging school in Arkansas where he could learn how to make his own knives. The first course lasted two weeks. Kramer came home an apprentice knife maker and a member of the American Bladesmith Society (established in the mid-1970s to preserve the American tradition of hand-forging knives). He also came home with the life-changing knowledge that with a little time and a little skill he could make a better kitchen knife than anything sold on the commercial market.

Two years later he passed his test as a journeyman bladesmith. And two years after that—in 1998—he passed his master bladesmith's test, becoming one of sixty-seven recognized master knife makers in the country. In other words, at age thirty-eight Kramer finally came into his own, finally achieved what it was he had set out to do so long ago: to master something, not just be good at it.

The result of all this? Some of the finest kitchen knives any cook would ever want to hold. Works of art, really. Yet functional. Kramer builds his knives with the kind of cook in mind who's going to be using the tool eight hours a day, every day. And every time a cook picks up one his knives, Kramer knows that a little piece of him flows on through the blade. He has mastered an art that continues, and he continues with it.

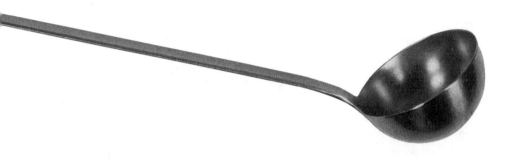

Tools

Tips for Buying and Maintaining Knives

WHAT TO AVOID: Cheap sets of knives sold in wooden blocks. The blades usually have some kind of serrated edge that will cut but won't slice in that classic rocking motion of a French chef's knife. To get that motion, the edge of the knife has to slide on the cutting board. With any kind of serration the edge will catch on the board. These knives simply won't do the job you want them to do.

WHAT TO BUY: Spend money on top-quality knives—any of the knives made commercially by the big companies. There's no reason a good knife that's well–cared for can't last fifty years.

SHARPENING: Have your knives professionally sharpened by someone who knows what he or she is doing. Sharpening devices made for the home too often take the profile out of a knife, and you are left with a chef's knife that won't rock.

MAINTENANCE: Steeling is the key to maintaining the edge on your knife. Invest in a ceramic stick (avoid the abrasive steels that come with carving sets). Hold it with the tip anchored on your cutting board, and stroke both sides of the edge of your knife on the stick, maintaining a shallow angle between blade and steel that approximates the angle of the edge. If the edge has become wavy, or has rolled over to one side, steeling stands it right back up. All it takes is a few strokes every time you use your knife. It's a habit thing.

A Few Good Tools

The same line that runs through Sharon Kramis's recipes runs through her kitchen, and mine as well. We're talking about simplicity here. What do you really need in order to cook and bake?

I have somehow managed to survive, for example, without benefit of a KitchenAid mixer (nor do I own a food processor or see much need for one). And yet I suffer KitchenAid-mixer envy every time I encounter this tool in some lucky soul's kitchen. If I could, I most certainly would spring for that machine. Sharon says she would take hers camping if she could.

Do you own a calibrated oven thermometer? No? Then how do you know what the temperature of your oven is at any given time? It may be all well and good to be off by twenty-five degrees when you are roasting a chicken, but you have to be spot on the right temperature if you plan on successfully baking anything. The same is true for instant-read meat thermometers. No kitchen should be without one. And where's the pepper mill? Sharon says a good pepper mill is one of the first things she looks for in a kitchen. It's kind of a tip-off to her that she's in the kitchen of someone who likes to cook.

Good metal measuring cups and spoons (and glass measuring cups for liquid) are essential unless you are so instinctual a cook that you *know* how much is just right. In fact, this is worth practicing: Measure a teaspoon of salt and dump it into your hand; then try to match the measure simply by sight. It takes practice, but you'll be surprised at how easy it is to know what a cup or a tablespoon looks like, be it liquid or solid.

Don't hesitate to buy good rubber spatulas and wooden spoons. But here's the deal: When your spatulas get raggedy and your spoons get nicked and nasty from poking around in a blender, throw them away and buy new ones. There's a piece of plastic out there with a curved edge and it's the perfect thing for scraping out a bowl. Nice tool.

Invest in good glass bread pans and baking dishes if you are inclined in that direction. Glass doesn't tend to over-brown. Aluminum pie tins yield the best pie crusts. Flimsy metal cookie sheets will burn cookies every time.

Nothing will brown a pork chop like cast iron. Nothing will brown hash browns and breakfast sausages like cast iron. So you need at least one cast-iron skillet (probably a ten-inch) and you need to follow the directions that come with it to season the metal. It's easy. And cleaning is easy, too: You simply avoid scouring. If you have to get something crusty out of a cast iron pan, use kosher salt and push it around with a piece of paper towel.

Heavy-bottomed cookware prevents headaches. I use All-Clad. In fact, I use the same All-Clad today that I used when this book was first published, and it was old then. I have sauté pans, sauce pans, pots, and stock pots. I love the ersatz wok and the steamer insert. In the intervening years, however, non-stick cookware has made stunning advances. At least one good piece is no doubt in order. Sharon loves her few pieces of Le Creuset enamelware. There's a small enamel pan with a pouring lip that she finds irreplaceable, and a steep-sided pan that's perfect for scrambled eggs—they tend to steam and fluff up. Sharon has also added a couple of terra-cotta baking dishes to her cookware. They work over direct heat as well as in the oven.

The point is, keep it simple. Select kitchen tools that will be effective and that will last.

If, on the other hand, you already own every tool ever designed for the advanced kitchen, maybe you need to have a garage sale and unload everything you haven't touched in the last couple of years. Of course, if I were to follow such advice I'd have to give up my hand-cranked Atlas pasta machine—and there's no way that's going to happen. That's what the darkest, hardest-to-reach corners of kitchen cupboards are for.

Index

a–b

abalone, about, 12

Acorn squash, baked, 114

Almond Roca candy, Marta's 252

Anchovies

    Anchovy Dressing, Dad's 152; Anchovy Dressing, for Great Greek Salad, 142; in Dad's Hot Slaw, 150–51

Appetizers

    Baked Oysters with Peppered Bacon, 13; Barbecued Pork Tenderloin, 84; Bon-Bon Chicken, 88–89; Fried Razor Clams, 31; Grilled Oysters in Herb-Butter Sauce, 17; Hood Canal Spot Prawns with Roe, 24; Italian Sausage–Stuffed Mushrooms, 104; Marinated Prawns, 23; Marinated Scallops with Salsa, 33; Oregon Blue Cheese Crumble, 137; Pickled Herring, 52; Razor Clam Fritters, 29; Smoked Salmon and Pecan Spread, 46; Steamed Clams with Parsley Butter, 27; Steamed Mussels, 31; Stir-Fried Geoduck with Vegetables, 30; Yelloweyed Rockfish, 53

Apples

    Apple Butter, 166–67; Apple Grunt, 168; Apple-Mincemeat Pie, 169; Applesauce Cake, Kitty's, 240; Apple Soup, Cloud Mountain, 166; Baked Apples with Walnuts and Vanilla Cream Sauce, 167; Blueberry-Apple Chutney, 186; Chicken and Apple Salad with Chutney-Lime Dressing, 148; Chutney-Spinach Salad with Red Delicious Apples, Marnie's, 145; Cranberry-Apple Relish, 185; Fresh Apple Cake, Miss Finney's, 220; Hot Spiced Cider, 176; Northwest "Waldorf" Salad, 136; Pork Loin Roast with Sautéed Apple Slices and Sauerkraut, 83–84; Sourdough Apple Pancakes, 226; varieties, 162–63

Applesauce cake, Kitty's, 240

Apricot varieties, 164

Asparagus

    One-Minute Asparagus, 113; Pickled Asparagus Spears, 262; Roasted Asparagus, 119–20

Avocado

    Avocados Stuffed with Crab Salad, 22–23; Broccoli, Mushroom, Avocado, and Tomato Salad, 143

Bacon

    Mushroom-Bacon Salad, 147; Smoked Bacon and Fresh Corn Chowder, 130

Bagna cauda, Nina's, 129

Baked beans, 128

Baked goods. See entries for individual varieties

Banana bread, 211

Barbecue. See Grilled dishes

Basil, tomato salad with, 144

Beans

Baked Beans, Mom's, 128; Dilly Green Beans, Ellie's, 109–10; Green Beans and Tomatoes, 105

Beef

    Beef Brisket with Chili-Beer Sauce, 78; Cabbage Rolls, Bernie Manofsky's, 80; Grilled Flank Steak, 74–75; Stuffed Flank Steak, 76; Swedish Meatballs, Anita's, 78–79; temperature guide, 66; Tenderloin of Beef with Red Wine, Walnuts, and Oregon Blue Cheese Butter, 76–77. See also Cattle; Liver; Veal

Beer

    Beef Brisket with Chili-Beer Sauce, 78; Beer Batter Fish and Chips, 56; Tillamook White Cheddar–Beer Soup, 132

Beets

    Beet and Sausage Soup, 116–17; Butter-Steamed Beets and Carrots, 115; Pickled Beets, 116; Roasted Beets, 119

Begonia

    Lemon Verbena and Tuberous Begonia Sauce, for salmon, 48–49

Bell peppers

    Stir-fried Baby Bok Choy, Shiitake Mushrooms, Sugar Snap Peas, and Yellow Peppers, 107; Tomato, Cucumber, and Green Pepper Salad, 141

Berries, 177–95

    freezing, 103; Forgotten Torte with Fresh Berries and Whipped Cream, 182; Hood River Cream Sauce with Berries, 180; varieties, 178–79. See also entries for individual berries

Biscuits, 228. See also Rolls

Black Cod in Swiss Chard with Lemon Butter Sauce, 58

Blackberries

    with Hood River Cream Sauce, 180; Tukwila Blackberry Jam, 180–81; Wild Blackberry Pie, 192; Willie's Blackberry Crisp, 192–93

Blintzes, blueberry, 230

Blueberries

    Blueberries and Cream Muffins, 182–83; Blueberry-Apple Chutney, 186; Blueberry Blintzes, 230; Blueberry Buttermilk Pancakes, 224; Blueberry-Orange Bread, 212; Blueberry Sauce, 188; Blueberry Sour Cream Coffee Cake, 218; Spiced Blueberry Jam, Overlake Farm's, 181

Blue cheese

    Oregon Blue Cheese Crumble, 137; Oregon Blue Cheese Dressing, 153; Oregon Blue Cheese, Bartlett Pear, and Hot Walnut Salad, 136–37; Romaine, Carrot, Blue Cheese, and Walnut Salad, 140

Bok choy, stir-fried, with shiitake mushrooms, sugar snap peas, and yellow peppers, 107

Breads, 203–209

    Banana Bread, 211; Blueberry-Orange Bread, 212; Graham Bread, Carpie's, 214; Finnish Coffee Bread, 221; Fresh Cranberry-

Orange Bread, 213–14; Honey–Whole Wheat Bread, 206–207; Oatmeal Bread, 203; Pumpernickel Bread with Orange Zest, 203–204; Rhubarb Nut Bread, 211–12; Sourdough Rye Bread, Alfred Schissel's, 205; Sourdough White Bread, 206; Squaw Bread, 208–209; Whole Wheat Nut-Raisin Yeast Bread, 207–208; yeast, baking, 202; Zucchini and Black Walnut Bread, 213. *See also* Buns; Rolls

Bread pudding, raspberry, 193–94

Bread salad, with tomatoes, 144

Breakfast/brunch dishes, 214–31. *See also* Blintzes; Coffee cake; Egg dishes; French toast; Muffins; Pancakes; Rolls; Scones; Waffles

Brittle, peanut, 252

Broccoli, Mushroom, Avocado, and Tomato Salad, 143

Broiler, oven, roasting with and without, 70–71

Brownies, dark chocolate, 251

Bundt cake, fresh apple, 220

Buns
Breakfast Sticky Buns, LaRene Morrison's, 217; Raised Whole Wheat Buns, 210. *See also* Rolls

Buttermilk
Blueberry Buttermilk Pancakes, 224; Buttermilk Chocolate Cake, 238–39; Buttermilk Scones with Currants and Orange Zest, 227–28

Butternut squash, baked, with nutmeg and maple syrup, 115

Butters and butter sauces
Butter Cream Sauce, with rum, brandy, or orange flavoring, 258; Butter Cream Sauce, for Steamed Cranberry Pudding, 186; Caper Butter, for pan-fried trout, 49–50; Chive-Tarragon Butter, for Parchment-Baked Lingcod, 57; Compound Butter for Lamb, 69; Oregon Blue Cheese Butter, for beef tenderloin, 76–77; Parsley Butter, for fried smelt, 52; Strawberry Butter, 188

c–d

Cabbage
Cabbage Rolls, Bernie Manofsky's, 80; Coleslaw, Lynnie's, 150; Coleslaw, Mother's, 149; Honey-Tamari-Sesame Dressing for Winter Salads, 154; Hot Slaw, Dad's, 150–51; Sauerkraut, Skagit Valley, 117; Sweet-and-Sour Cabbage, 118; Sweet-and-Sour Sauerkraut Slaw, 118; Shrimp and Shredded Cabbage Salad, Than's, 148–49

Cakes, 236–42
Applesauce Cake, Kitty's, 240; Buttermilk Chocolate Cake, 238–39; Coconut Cake with Lemon Cream Filling, 241–42; Cream Cheese Pound Cake, 239; Fresh Apple Cake, Miss Finney's, 220; Gingerbread Cake, Warm, 237–38; Graham Cracker Birthday Cake, Adams's, 236–37; Lemon Pecan Pound Cake, Christmas, 241; Pear Butter Cake, 172; Plum Sauce Cake, 175–76. *See also* Torte

Candy
Almond Roca Candy, Marta's, 252; Peanut Brittle, Christmas, 252

Cantaloupe, 179

Caper Butter, for pan-fried trout, 49–50

Carré d'Agneau à la Provençale (roasted rack of lamb), 69

Carrots
Butter-Steamed Beets and Carrots, 115; Golden Marinated Carrots, 111; Romaine, Carrot, Blue Cheese, and Walnut Salad, 140

Cast-iron skillets, 268

Cattle, raising, 64–66

Cauliflower with Tillamook Cheddar Cheese, 112

Challah French Toast, 227

Chanterelles. *See* Mushrooms

Cheddar cheese
Cougar Gold Cheddar and Potato Soup, 126–27; Tillamook White Cheddar–Beer Soup, 132; Walla Walla Sweet Onion and Cheddar Cheese Strata, 111

Cheese
Cougar Gold Cheddar and Potato Soup, 126–27; Oregon Blue Cheese Butter, for beef tenderloin, 76–77; Oregon Blue Cheese Crumble, 137; Oregon Blue Cheese Dressing, 153; Oregon Blue Cheese, Bartlett Pear, and Hot Walnut Salad, 136–37; Ricotta Pancakes, 225; Romaine, Carrot, Blue Cheese, and Walnut Salad, 140; Scalloped Potato and Cheese Casserole, 124; Tillamook White Cheddar–Beer Soup, 132; Walla Walla Sweet Onion and Cheddar Cheese Strata, 111

Cherries, varieties, 164

Chicken
Baked Chicken Dijon, Lynn's, 87–88; Bon-Bon Chicken, 88–89; Chicken and Apple Salad with Chutney-Lime Dressing, 148; Roast Chicken with Walla Walla Sweet Onions, Gretchen Mather's, 89

Chive-Tarragon Butter, for Parchment-Baked Lingcod, 57

Chocolate
Buttermilk Chocolate Cake, 238–39; Chocolate Chip Cookies, Laughing Horse Theater, 247–48; Chocolate Chip Walnut Pie, 233; Dark Chocolate Brownies, 251; frosting, for Adams's Graham Cracker Birthday Cake, 236–37; frosting, Dover Judy, 251

Chowders
Clam Chowder, Hap's, 26; Fresh Corn Chowder with Cheddar Cheese and Tomato Salsa, 130–31; Smoked Bacon and Fresh Corn Chowder, 130. *See also* Soups

Chutney
Blueberry-Apple Chutney, 186; Chutney-Lime Dressing, for Chicken and Apple Salad, 148; Chutney-Spinach Salad with Red Delicious Apples, Marnie's, 145; Rhubarb-Chutney Sauce, 259

Cider, hot spiced, 176

s–t

Sablefish, 38

Salad dressings, 152–55
> Anchovy Dressing, Dad's, 152; Anchovy Dressing, for Great Greek Salad, 142; Chutney-Lime Dressing, for Chicken and Apple Salad, 148; Honey-Lime Dressing for Fresh Fruit, 152; Honey-Tamari-Sesame Dressing for Winter Salads, 154; Kalamata Olive Vinaigrette, 91–92; Lemon Herb Dressing for Summer, 154; Malt Vinegar Dressing, for Yellow Finn Potato Salad, 138–39; Oil and Vinegar Dressing, My Favorite, 153; Oregon Blue Cheese Dressing, 153; Pear Vinegar, Walnut Oil, and Roasted Walnut Dressing for Fall, 155

Salads, 136–51
> Avocados Stuffed with Crab Salad, 22–23; Broccoli, Mushroom, Avocado, and Tomato Salad, 143; Chicken and Apple Salad with Chutney-Lime Dressing, 148; Chutney-Spinach Salad with Red Delicious Apples, Marnie's, 145; Couscous Salad with Fresh Corn, Sweet Red Pepper, and Cilantro, 146–47; Cucumber Salad, Japanese, 148; Dungeness Crab Louie, 151; fruit, Honey-Lime Dressing for Fresh Fruit, 152; Great Greek Salad with Anchovy Dressing, 142; Mushroom-Bacon Salad, 147; Northwest "Waldorf" Salad, 136; Orange, Red Onion, and Cilantro Salad with Pomegranate Seeds, 146; Oregon Blue Cheese, Bartlett Pear, and Hot Walnut Salad, 136–37; Potato Salad, Dad's, 138; Romaine, Carrot, Blue Cheese, and Walnut Salad, 140; Shrimp and Shredded Cabbage Salad, Than's, 148–49; Summer Tomato Rustic Bread Salad, 144; Sweet-and-Sour Cucumbers, 142–43; Tomato Salad with Fresh Basil, 144; Tomato, Cucumber, and Green Pepper Salad, 141; Wilted Lettuce Garden Salad, 140; Yellow Finn Potato Salad, 138–39. *See also* Coleslaw

Salad toppings
> Oregon Blue Cheese Crumble, 137

Salmon
> Alder-Planked Sockeye Salmon with Lemon Shallot Butter Sauce, 42; Barbecued King or Sockeye Salmon, 47; Creamy Scrambled Eggs with Smoked Salmon, 46–47; Gravlax, 45; Oven-Broiled King or Sockeye Salmon, 43; Salmon with Lemon Verbena and Tuberous Begonia Sauce, 48–49; Smoked Salmon and Pecan Spread, 46; varieties, 39; Whole Baked Salmon with Cucumber Sauce, 44

Salsa
> Krueger Pepper Farm's Salsa, 256–57; Marinated Scallops with Salsa, 33

Sand dabs, 40

Sandwiches
> Crab, Cheese, and Green Pepper Sandwich, 20; Grilled Crab and Cheddar Cheese Sandwich, 22; Oyster Loaf, 15

Saucepans, 269

Sauces
> Blueberry Sauce, 188; Butter Cream Sauce, with rum, brandy, or orange flavoring, 258; Butter Cream Sauce, for Steamed Cranberry Pudding, 186; Cranberry Sauce, Pasta & Co., 184; Cranberry-Horseradish Sauce, 260; Cranberry-Port-Cream Sauce, for grilled sturgeon, 54–55; cream sauce (gravy), for meatballs, 79; Cucumber Sauce, for Whole Baked Salmon, 44; Fresh Horseradish, 260; Gravlax Mustard Sauce, 45; Herb Sauce, 259; Hood River Cream Sauce with Berries, 180; Lemon Shallot Butter Sauce, for Alder-Planked Sockeye Salmon, 42; Lemon Verbena and Tuberous Begonia Sauce, for salmon, 48–49; Mustard Sauce for Vegetables, Auntie Alma's, 257; Oregon Blue Cheese Butter, for beef tenderloin, 76–77; Peanut Dipping Sauce, for Bon-Bon Chicken, 88–89; Plum Sauce, for Plum Sauce Cake, 175–76; Raspberry Sauce, Tamara's, 187; Rhubarb-Chutney Sauce, 259; Salmon Barbecue Sauce, for Barbecued King or Sockeye Salmon, 47; Sweet-and-Sour Plum Sauce for Pork and Duck, 260–61; Tartar Sauce, 258. *See also* Butters and butter sauces; Chutney; Relish; Salsa

Sauerkraut
> Skagit Valley Sauerkraut, 117; Sweet-and-Sour Sauerkraut Slaw, 118; with pork loin roast and sautéed apple slices, 83–84

Sausage
> Beet and Sausage Soup, 116–17; Homemade Italian Sausage, 85; Italian Sausage–Stuffed Mushrooms, 104; Oyster Sausage, 14; Potato-Sausage Soup, 20-Minute, 127; stuffing for flank steak, 76

Scallops
> Gingered Oregon Scallops with Lemon Zest and Fresh Cilantro, 33; Marinated Scallops with Salsa, 33; Singing Scallops Poached in Citrus, 34; varieties, 12

Scones
> Buttermilk Scones with Currants and Orange Zest, 227–28; Orange Scone Berry Cakes, 190

Shad, 39

Shellfish, 1–36

Shellfish dishes
> Cioppino, 36; Rockers Iko (seafood stew), 34–35. *See also* Clams; Crab; Crayfish; Mussels; Oysters; Prawns; Scallops; Shrimp

Shiitake mushrooms. *See* Mushrooms

Shortbread
> Brown Sugar–Hazelnut Shortbread Cookies, 247; crust, for Anita's Swedish Lemon Tart, 235; Shortbread Cookies, Eve's, 248

Shortcake, peach, 172–73

Shrimp
> Hood Canal Spot Prawns with Roe, 24; Marinated Prawns, 23; Shrimp and Shredded Cabbage Salad, Than's, 148–49; varieties, 11